Rutherford Mayne
Selected Plays

Dedicated to the memory of the men and women of the Ulster Literary Theatre, and to their successors.

Rutherford Mayne
Selected Plays

Edited by John Killen

Institute of Irish Studies
The Queen's University of Belfast

Published 1997
The Institute of Irish Studies
The Queen's University of Belfast

This book has received support from the Cultural Traditions Programme of the Community Relations Council which aims to encourage acceptance and understanding of cultural diversity.

British Library Cataloguing-In-Publication Data.
A catalogue record for this book is available from the British Library.

ISBN: 0 85389 667 4

Printed By W. & G. Baird Ltd, Antrim
Cover Illustration: 'A First Night At The Abbey'
by Grace Plunkett, reproduced by
by kind permission of Miss M. Donnelly.

ACKNOWLEDGEMENTS

The editor wishes to acknowledge the kindness and support he has received from the Governors of the Linen Hall Library, for their permission to make use of illustrations from the Rutherford Mayne archive, and for their encouragement in carrying out this research. He would also like to record his sincere thanks to Mary Campbell, and to her late husband, Flan, for saving the archive from dispersal or destruction on the death of Rutherford Mayne's daughter, Ginette Waddell and for enabling the Linen Hall Library to acquire the archive, and for their encouragement in this project.

Special thanks are also due to Constable and Co., London who gave kind permission to reprint *Bridge Head,* and to Miss M. Donnelly for her kind permission to reprint the illustrations by Grace Plunkett.

PLAYS BY RUTHERFORD MAYNE

The Turn Of The Road (1907)
The Drone (1909)
The Troth (1909)
Red Turf 1911)
The Captain Of The Hosts (1911)
If! (1913)
Evening (1914)
Neil Gallina (1916)
Industry (1917)
A Prologue (1925)
Peter (1936)
Bridge Head (1939)

CONTENTS

Portrait of Rutherford Mayne by John P. Campbell, 1909.

INTRODUCTION

Among the portraits that adorn the walls of the Abbey Theatre in Dublin, is that of a large, avuncular middle-aged man. The overall effect of this portrait is one of strength, but there is also gentleness and humour in the subject's demeanour. The face is lined – not handsome – the lived-in face of a man who has moved much in the world. The hair is grey and wiry, and suggestive of a huge vitality. The shoulders and hands are those of a man not unused to physical labour, but the shrewd clear eyes suggest the inner vision of the artist or writer. The portrait is of the Ulster actor and dramatist, Rutherford Mayne.

Today, the name Rutherford Mayne is known to a dwindling number of people as the author of Ulster farm kitchen comedies, such as *The Drone*, and for very little else. Hogan's *Dictionary of Irish Writers* (1979) lists the other plays he wrote and takes a page to assess his output; while *The Field Day Anthology of Irish Literature* (1991) devotes three lines to him. Rutherford Mayne, however, is a very important figure in the development of the theatrical tradition, not just in Ulster, but in Ireland.

Rutherford Mayne was the pen and stage name of Sam Waddell, the fourth son of the Rev Hugh Waddell, a Presbyterian missionary working in Japan. He was born in Tokyo in 1878, but because of family circumstances was brought up by relatives in the Banbridge area of Co. Down, and in Belfast. His mother died in 1892 and his father re-married.

In 1900 the Rev. Hugh Waddell settled in Belfast with his new wife and four youngest children, including Helen, the future classical scholar. A year later he was dead, and the elder brothers, including Sam, were left to support the family as best they could, taking jobs to pay for the education of their younger brothers and sisters.

Sam Waddell took employment with the Belfast building contractors McLaughlin and Harvey. At the behest of Spring Pyper, Vice Principal of Belfast Mercantile College, he put himself through night classes, graduating as an engineer in 1907, when he became resident engineer under the County Surveyor of Down, James Heron. In 1909 he joined the Irish Land Commission as a junior surveyor. In 1910 he married Josephine Campbell, sister of Joseph Campbell the poet and John Campbell the artist. In 1911 he was sent to supervise the redistribution of land on the great estates of the west of Ireland. From then until his death in 1967 he lived outside the north of Ireland; based in Dublin he travelled extensively in the south and west.

By the time he left Belfast, however, he had embarked on what was to be a lifetime involvement in the theatre: an involvement which was to see the birth of an Ulster (as opposed to Yeats's Leinster) theatrical tradition, innovative development of the play in Ireland in his maturity, and acting of the highest standard.

In 1902 Rutherford Mayne was introduced by his school-fellow and friend David Parkhill (who wrote under the name of Lewis Purcell) to a group of talented and enthusiastic actors and writers. This experience exposed Mayne not to a vague or conceptual acquaintance with theatre, but to living and breathing people with whom he had immediate empathy and rapport. In later life he reminisced:

> One night in digs Purcell suddenly appeared and induced me to buy tickets to go and see the society that he was interested in. They were performing, so far as my recollection goes, A.E.'s *Deirdre* and Yeats' *Cathleen Ni Houlihan* and I distinctly remember Padraig Gregory sitting like Peter at the receipt of custom when we went in.
>
> There was a sparse audience. But I was very interested by *Deirdre*, more than by *Cathleen*, because I had been a great admirer of what you might call rhetorical stuff such as actors love. I'm afraid I didn't quite catch what Yeats was at because the audience seemed to take it as a sort of rather funny peasant play. The beauty of the words was lost because the acting was so bad, to tell you the honest truth.

> But I was struck by *Deirdre* and particularly by two actors in it, John and Joseph Campbell. They had magnificent voices and they filled my idea of how a man should speak verse.

As well as the Campbells, Mayne met W.R. Gordon, Fred Hughes (the brother of the composer Herbert Hughes), Padraig Gregory, Jimmy Good, the actor, W.B. Reynolds, theatre critic of the *Belfast Telegraph*, and the prodigiously talented Morrow brothers.

Mayne was aware of the difficulty these performers had in acquiring permission to perform *Kathleen Ni Houlihan* in Belfast. Sam Hanna Bell, in his *Theatre in Ulster*, tells how Hobson and Parkhill travelled to Dublin to meet Maude Gonne's National Theatre Society. They sought permission to put on some of their plays, and help from some of their actors. Everyone was most cordial and helpful, except Yeats. Haughty

A First Night at the Abbey, by Grace Plunkett in her *Twelve Nights at the Abbey Theatre* (1929).

and aloof, Yeats refused permission for a performance of *Kathleen*. When Maude Gonne heard this, she told them: 'Don't mind Willie. He wrote that play for me and gave it to me. It is mine and you can put it on whenever you want to'. In spite of this, Yeats's antipathy to his Northern guests rankled, and on their way home in the train Hobson struck the arm of his seat and exclaimed 'Damn Yeats, we'll write our own play'. And so the Ulster Literary Theatre was born.

Among Mayne's personal theatre archive is a cartoon titled 'A Meeting of *Ulad* (Unlimited) at Loretto'. *Ulad* was the magazine of the Ulster Literary Theatre and Loretto was the Campbell family home. Attached to the cartoon and dated 12 December 1904 are the signatures of the founders of the theatre: Seosamh MacCathmhaoil (Joseph Campbell), John P. Campbell, John Cassell Morrow, Samuel Waddell, W.R. Gordon, David Parkhill, Wilfred Morrow, Jimmy Parkhill, Bulmer Hobson, Josephine Campbell and Frederick Cairns Hughes.

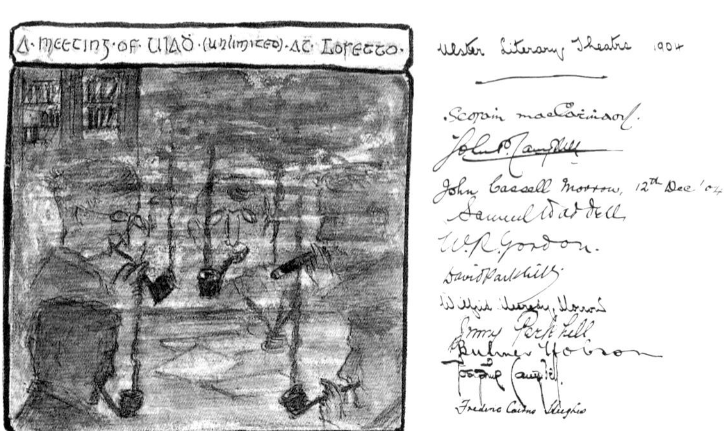

Satirical cartoon of a meeting of *Ulad* (Unlimited) at Loretto Cottage, the home of the Campbells.

The aims of the Ulster Literary Theatre were set out in the first issue of *Ulad*:

> We intend to strike our keynote through the Theatre where our own plays will be produced…We recognise at the outset that our art of the drama will be different from that other Irish art of drama which speaks from the stage of the Irish National Theatre in Dublin, where two men, W.B. Yeats and Douglas Hyde, have set a model in Anglo-Irish and Gaelic plays with a success that is surprising and exhilarating…We in Belfast and Ulster also wish to set up a school; but there will be a difference.
>
> At present we can only say that our talent is more satiric than poetic. That will probably remain the broad difference between the…schools. But when our genius arrives, as he must sooner or later, there is no accounting for what extraordinary tendency he may display…

Ulad – the magazine of the Ulster Literary Theatre, Vol. 1. No. 1. November, 1904. The intricate Celtic design is by John P. Campbell.

Arguably that genius was already amongst them in the form of Rutherford Mayne himself. First as actor, then as playwright and actor, Mayne was a mainstay of the Ulster Literary Theatre for the next decade and maintained contact with its participants throughout his life. In 1905 he played the part of Rab in Lewis Purcell's comedy *The Enthusiast*; John Campbell played Sam McKinstry and Jack Morrow played 'the enthusiast' James McKinstry. The theme of the play is the refusal of a traditional society to accept new ideas; unfortunately still true in Ireland 90 years after its first production. Writing in *Ulad*, Joseph de Paor had this to say of the character of *Rab*:

> ...The character in the little comedy, claiming almost more attention than The Enthusiast himself and certainly more appreciation is that of Rab, the farm servant. *Rab* is really a complete study, perfect in every detail; and if the author had never drawn another figure, he deserves much credit for having given us such a miniature.

That the acting of Rutherford Mayne had no little part to play in this appreciation of *The Enthusiast* will be borne out by later testimonies.

In 1906 Mayne saw his first play, *The Turn of the Road*, premiered by the Ulster Literary Theatre in the Ulster Minor Hall in Belfast. The play is set in the kitchen of a County Down farm and deals with the tensions inherent between labour (farming) and the arts (music). This play inspired the distinguished

Rab.

Ulster actor Whitford Kane, and awakened in him a pride in his northern roots. He records in *Are We All Met?*, his autobiography:

> Up to this time my entire theatrical experience had been English playhouses and I hardly knew anything about the Abbey or the Ulster theatres...
>
> It is for my introduction to the Ulster Literary Theatre, and to Rutherford Mayne in particular, that I am indebted for finding myself. One evening during one of my summer vacations, he took me to see his first play - *The Turn Of The Road*...This performance must have struck some national chord in me, for I went again next night; after that I was asked to join a gathering at the Arts Club. There I heard for the first time some of the beautiful folksongs and poems of my own country, and as I listened to them, I realised how Irish I really was, and also how intensely Irish Ulster was in spite of its many peculiar distinctions.

Kane's friendship with Mayne lasted for the rest of their lives. When the former had established himself in the American theatre and film world, he continued to correspond with his fellow Ulsterman.

In the spring of 1908, the company took *The Turn Of The Road* to the Abbey Theatre in Dublin. Joseph Holloway's comment on that occasion was:

> I have not enjoyed myself so much at a theatre for a very long time as at the Abbey tonight in witnessing the first performance in Dublin of the Ulster Literary Theatre...The players have talent and plenty to spare.

The Dublin production was attended by Yeats, Lady Gregory and Douglas Hyde and within the year *The Turn of the Road* had been brought out by Maunsel and Co., one of the first Ulster Literary Theatre plays to be published.

Cluiċeoiri·na·h-Eireann

The Theatre of Ireland.

Samhain Festival, 1908,

At The Abbey Theatre, on Monday and Tuesday, 23rd and 24th November,

Bi-lingual programme of the Abbey Theatre's Samhain Festival, 1908. The Celtic design is by John P. Campbell.

In 1908 Rutherford Mayne toured England with William Mollison's repertory company and amongst the company was Whitford Kane. On this tour Mayne's new play *The Troth* was premiered. Set in nineteenth-century Ireland it tells the story of two peasants faced with eviction, who pledge themselves to shoot the landlord – whoever escapes after the event is to take care of both families. On this tour Mayne played John Smith, the old man in his own play *The Troth*. So successful was it that Mollison used it as a curtain raiser throughout the tour.

The following year saw the publication of Rutherford Mayne's most instantly successful play – *The Drone*. Set in County Down it tells the story of a feckless old man who plays on the sympathy of his steady brother to avoid a lifetime of work. *The Drone* was first produced in the Abbey Theatre in April 1908 – in that production the author played Sam Brown – a servant man; his future wife Josephine Campbell played the heroine Mary Murray, and John Campbell played Alick McCready, her suitor. Revived many times, the play (and Mayne) toured England and

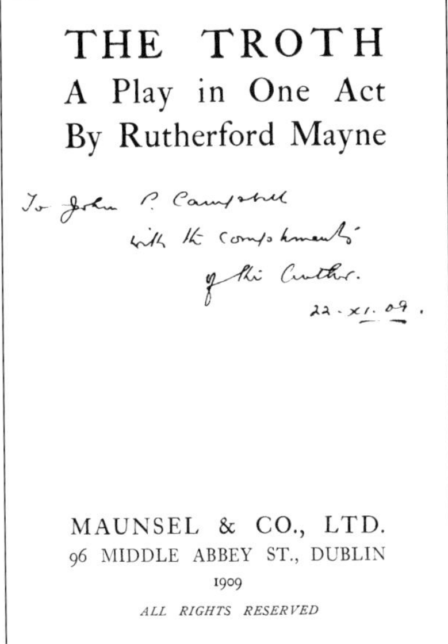
THE TROTH
A Play in One Act
By Rutherford Mayne

To John P. Campbell
with the compliments
of the author.
22.XI.09.

MAUNSEL & CO., LTD.
96 MIDDLE ABBEY ST., DUBLIN
1909
ALL RIGHTS RESERVED

This rare copy of Rutherford Mayne's one act play is dedicated to his brother-in-law, John P. Campbell.

Scotland with the Ulster Literary Theatre in 1923. In Glasgow the critics were kind:

> These players – Mr Rutherford Mayne, Mr Gerald MacNamara, Miss Muriel Wood and Miss Rose McQuillan – were easily the most competent amateurs I have ever seen...

In London they were even kinder:

> There has been nothing in London quite like *The Drone*, the comedy by Rutherford Mayne...since Lennox Robinson's *The White Headed Boy*...

Back in Belfast at the end of the tour local audiences continued to enjoy the play:

> No one can take Rutherford Mayne's place as John Murray, who manages to suggest an innate dignity and loveableness none of the others attempt.

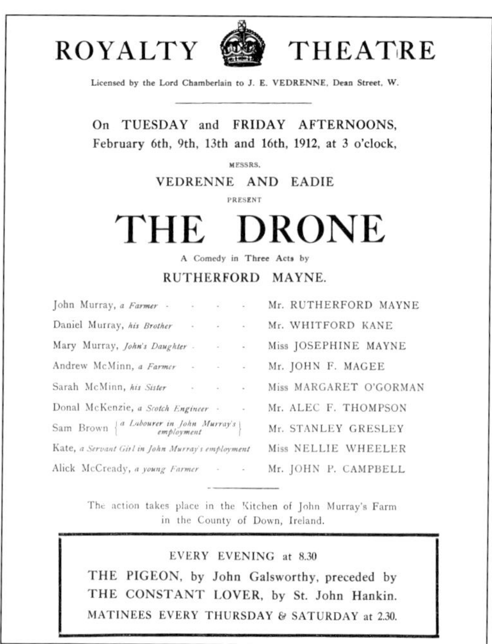
ROYALTY THEATRE

Licensed by the Lord Chamberlain to J. E. VEDRENNE, Dean Street, W.

On TUESDAY and FRIDAY AFTERNOONS,
February 6th, 9th, 13th and 16th, 1912, at 3 o'clock,

MESSRS.
VEDRENNE AND EADIE
PRESENT

THE DRONE

A Comedy in Three Acts by
RUTHERFORD MAYNE.

John Murray, *a Farmer*	Mr. RUTHERFORD MAYNE
Daniel Murray, *his Brother*	Mr. WHITFORD KANE
Mary Murray, *John's Daughter*	Miss JOSEPHINE MAYNE
Andrew McMinn, *a Farmer*	Mr. JOHN F. MAGEE
Sarah McMinn, *his Sister*	Miss MARGARET O'GORMAN
Donal McKenzie, *a Scotch Engineer*	Mr. ALEC F. THOMPSON
Sam Brown (*a Labourer in John Murray's employment*)	Mr. STANLEY GRESLEY
Kate, *a Servant Girl in John Murray's employment*	Miss NELLIE WHEELER
Alick McCready, *a young Farmer*	Mr. JOHN P. CAMPBELL

The action takes place in the Kitchen of John Murray's Farm
in the County of Down, Ireland.

EVERY EVENING at 8.30
THE PIGEON, by John Galsworthy, preceded by
THE CONSTANT LOVER, by St. John Hankin.
MATINEES EVERY THURSDAY & SATURDAY at 2.30.

First produced in the Abbey Theatre in 1908, *The Drone* was favourably received wherever it was performed. This programe is for a performance in the Royalty Theatre, London, in February 1912.

In the 1920s Rutherford Mayne acted both with the Ulster Literary Theatre and the Abbey. His Cetewayo in Shaw's *The Admirable Bashville* drew the following comment from the *Irish Times* critic:

> The great event of the evening was the appearance of Mr Rutherford Mayne as Cetewayo, so that he merely had to be himself to be amusing. His comments on English civilisation went right home, and his frenzied intervention in the fight was just what the audience eagerly anticipated...

In 1927 he scored his most notable acting success with his portrayal of Brutus Jones in Eugene O'Neill's *Emperor Jones*. This dark tragedy deals with the rise of a Negro to dominance over his fellows through trickery and brutality, only to suffer the

Scene from O'Neill's *Emperor Jones.* Rutherford Mayne played the lead to rapturous acclaim.

pangs of an uneasy conscience and to be overtaken by an irresistible fate. Mayne's performance prompted this from the theatre critic J.J. Hayes:

> Dear Mr Mayne,
>
> I use your pseudonym because it seems more natural – I do not know if you realise that you have made theatrical history by your portrayal of Brutus Jones.

> Nevertheless the fact remains that you have, and I have to offer you my sincerest and heartiest congratulations...

Seventeen years later Mayne was to play the part again at the Gaiety Theatre and to win this accolade from the critic of the *Irish Press*:

> The production was a personal triumph for Rutherford Mayne, veteran actor-playwright. His interpretation of the civilised Negro Emperor Jones was a model of restrained power, on which many of our younger players might find a basis for stage improvement.

By this time Rutherford Mayne had two further plays premiered at the Abbey. In 1930 the farce of student life, *Peter*, was staged to almost universal acclaim. Writing to Lennox Robinson about the play W.B. Yeats had this to say:

A scene from Mayne's 1930 farce, *Peter*, drawn by Grace Plunkett and published in her book *Doctors Recommend It*.

> The play shows great capacity for managing the stage, for keeping it vivid and amusing. I think it will be a great success at the Abbey.
>
> It is a godsend...of course we accept the play for the Abbey with the greatest possible satisfaction...

In 1934 he scored what may have been his most important theatrical success with his play *Bridge Head*. Based on his experiences in the Irish Land Commission, the play concerns the important and arduous task of land redistribution in the west of Ireland in the first half of this century.

Many years later, as his contribution to the Thomas Davis lecture series, Rutherford Mayne recalled with affection his work in the Land Commission:

> After some years' work with the contractors and county surveyors as a graduate of engineering in the old Royal University of Ireland, I got a notice from the Irish Land Commission. It was to the effect that I had been appointed as a junior surveyor in the survey branch and to report to that office to take up duty.
>
> The Land Act of 1903 was already six years in operation and an additional Land Act was passed in 1909. These two Acts between them swept into land purchase by state aid something like two thirds of the tenancy of Ireland. After the change of Government in Ireland...the Land Act of 1923 and subsequent Acts dealt with the remainder, and ended dual ownership of land.
>
> I was almost three years in the survey branch. I have no cause to regret it. The only regret was that the salary was small.
>
> Survey work is what its name at once indicates. Inspecting and checking the boundaries and areas of farms held by tenant purchasers, together with some other details as regards verifying particulars, as regards who was in occupation of the holding etc. This work

> took me into every County in Ireland, North, East, South and West. Fortunately for me, I was sent out with one of the best old hands of the survey staff. What I learned from him was of inestimable value afterwards, as the work I was at was gradually changed from examining old holdings to creating new ones.

And then came a career move which would provide him with the material for his most accomplished play.

> After a few periods of acting as a locum for resale inspectors on improvement works on new holdings, I was suddenly sent on short notice to assist a hard pressed senior inspector at work in the West – in County Galway… Here was a hard pressed senior inspector, not only engaged in valuing lands for purchase by the Land Commission, but also preparing schemes of division of these lands when purchased, for allotment as addition to existing congested holdings, and also in preparing new holdings for migrants.

His experiences in this precise and exacting task of re-distributing the land of Ireland, inspired the play *Bridge Head*. The title was suggested by his occupation: in Land Commission terms a bridge head was that piece of land necessary for entry from already acquired land into a tract of land newly acquired for distribution. A critic wrote of the play:

> It is the duty and the privilege of the National Theatre to present to us every aspect of Irish life fairly and sincerely…*Bridge Head* is a magnificent, if chilling, testimonial to the impartial unselfish service afforded us by the Civil Service…it is a grim picture of the sacrifice of the self…and it ends on a note of cynical disillusionment…

The *Bellman* of July 1942 said this of *Bridge Head*:

> When the history of the Irish Theatre comes to be written a century hence, *Bridge Head* may well occupy a place equal in importance to that of *The Playboy of the Western*

> *World*, since, like Synge's masterpiece, it is one of those plays which pointed the way...

Bridge Head was awarded the Casement Prize for the best Irish play of 1934-35. James Bridie, the adjudicator, commended it thus at the presentation:

> It is hard to find any fault in this good play. The theme is a strong one and the decorations with which it is enriched are completely relevant...The character work is brilliant, the situations are moving, and the dialogue is what dialogue ought to be. Indeed the play might serve as a model for a lecture course - not that one might wish it such an evil fate...

In his eighty-fifth year, and almost thirty years after writing *Bridge Head*, Rutherford Mayne was contacted by his agent to agree to the play's performance by BBC Northern Ireland, and to discuss television rights for a production on Italian television – proof if it were needed of the lasting quality of this fine play.

Photograph of a scene from *Bridge Head*. From *Cork Examiner*, 1 July 1939.

In his private life Rutherford Mayne was a most unusual man for his times, indeed for any times in Ireland. In 1909 he married Josephine Campbell, a Catholic; after she died in 1941 he married her sister Francis in 1943, not to be expected of the son of a Presbyterian minister and missionary. He was a most liberal man, who inspired love and loyalty in all he met. His letters to his family, especially to his only daughter Ginette are beautiful – and sometimes moving.

Writing to Ginette about the course of the Second World War, from Cruise's Royal Hotel in Limerick, on Monday 24 June 1940, he comforts her from afar:

> My own darling Ginette,
>
> I got your letter and a long one from mummy, and am writing this just before going into court. No wonder my darling child the news about the English convent and the dear poor nuns so upset you: and I [wish] I could have kissed your darling little head and tried to make the suffering you went through not quite so unbearably hard.
>
> The war must come to an end. Let us pray that it may not last one day longer than necessary and that the countless thousands of suffering may be released from their anguish.
>
> Be of good cheer, my darling child. The night will pass away, and then we can face the future with hearts up...
>
> Daddy

A description of the playwright/actor in *The Bell* of 1942 evokes the tenor of the man. Referring to his sister's play *The Spoiled Buddha*, the writer likens Mayne to the central character of the play:

> But the resemblance with the Buddha [is] a physical resemblance as well. It isn't however, the immobile, shiny chrysoprase Buddha of Mr Ernest Blythe, but a jolly ultra-human, heroic-sized Buddha, like the Buddha of Miss Waddell's play – a Buddha, of flesh and good red

blood, with a bright blue twinkle showing behind the almond eye-holes. And with it a six-foot frame and at least sixteen stone in weight. The straight, brush-like hair is still thick - in spite of the playwright's sixty-three years. The Etruscan-red complexion is the red of good earth heavily ploughed in deep, furrowed wrinkles in which

Photograph of Rutherford Mayne at work in the Irish Land Commission, *c.* 1950.

> you feel you could sink your fingers. There is a flaming sunset look about this immense man - a feeling of the heroic executed in burnished bronze that the early Epstein or the late Rodin could have cast superbly – even to the massive, grasped hands. With a great, brazen voice like a gong, and a laugh like a typhoon, to complete the impression of something somewhat larger than ordinary nature.

The importance of Rutherford Mayne in theatrical terms is that he wrote and acted in plays that put ordinary Ulster people in everyday Ulster dress, speaking contemporary Ulster dialect, before theatre audiences throughout these islands for the first time. He went on to experiment in theatrical stagecraft and to address one of the most potent forces in the Irish psyche – the hunger for land. Although his work may now be considered passé, he broke new ground and opened the way for successive generations of Ulster writers.

Rutherford Mayne died in 1967.

THE DRONE

A Play in Three Acts

TO SEVEEN

This Play was first produced at the Abbey Theatre, Dublin, by the Ulster Literary Theatre, in April, 1908, with the following cast:-

JOHN MURRAY	G. A. Charters
DANIEL MURRAY	Arthur Malcolm
MARY MURRAY	Seveen Canmer
KATE	Maire Crothers
SAM BROWN	Rutherford Mayne
ANDREW McMINN	John Field
SARAH McMINN	Bridget O'Gorman
ALICK McCREADY	Ross Canmer
DONAL MACKENZIE	Robert Henry

CHARACTERS

JOHN MURRAY	*A farmer*
DANIEL MURRAY	*His brother*
MARY MURRAY	*John's daughter*
ANDREW McMINN	*A farmer*
SARAH McMINN	*His sister*
DONAL MACKENZIE	*A Scotch engineer*
SAM BROWN	*A Labourer in John Murray's employment*
KATE	*A servant girl in John Murray's employment*
ALICK McCREADY	*A young farmer*

The action takes place throughout in the kitchen of John Murray in the County of Down.

TIME: *The present day*

ACT ONE

SCENE: *The farm kitchen of John Murray. It is large and spacious, with a wide open fireplace to the right. At the back is one door leading to the parlour and other rooms in the house, also a large window overlooking the yard outside. To the left of this window is the door leading into the yard. Opposite to the fireplace on the left side is another door leading into Daniel Murray's workshop, and beside this door is a large dresser with crockery. At the back beneath the window is a table near which* KATE, *the servant, a slatternly-dressed girl of some thirty years of age or more, is seated. She is carefully examining some cakes of soda bread, and has a bucket beside her into which she throws the rejected pieces.*

KATE: That one's stale. It would break your teeth to eat it. (*She throws the cake into the bucket.*) And the mice have nibbled that one. And there's another as bad. (*She throws both pieces into the bucket.*)

(BROWN, *the servant man, opens the door from the yard and enters. He is elderly, and with a pessimistic expression of face, relieved somewhat by the sly humour that is in his eyes. He walks slowly to the centre of the kitchen, looks at* KATE, *and then turns his eyes, with a disgusted shake of the head, towards the dresser as if searching for something.*)

BROWN: Well! Well! Pigs get fat and men get lean in this house.

KATE: It's you again, is it? And what are you looking now?

BROWN: I'm looking a spanner for the boss. The feedboard to the threshing machine got jammed just when halfway through the first stack, and he is in a lamentable temper.

KATE: (*Uneasily*) Is he?

BROWN: (*Watching her slyly to see what effect his words have*) And he's been grumbling all morning about the way things is going on in this house. Bread and things wasted and destroyed altogether.

KATE: Well, it's all Miss Mary's fault. I told her about this bread yesterday forenoon, and she never took any heed to me.

BROWN: Miss Mary? (*With a deprecatory shake of his head*) What does a slip of a girl like that know about housekeeping and her not home a year from the school in the big town, and no mother or anybody to train her. (*He stares in a puzzled way at the dresser.*) I don't see that spanner at all. Did you see it, Kate?

KATE: No. I've more to do than look for spanners.

BROWN: (*Gazing reproachfully at her and then shaking his head*) It's a nice house, right enough. (*Lowering his voice*) And I suppose old Mr Dan is never up yet. I was told by Johnny McAndless, he was terrible full last night at McArn's and talking — ach — the greatest blethers about this new invention of his.

KATE: Do you say so?

BROWN: Aye. No wonder he's taking a lie this morning. (*He peeps into the door of the workshop.*) He's not in his wee workshop?

KATE: No. Miss Mary is just after taking up his breakfast to him.

BROWN: Some people get living easy in this world. (*He gives a last look at the dresser.*) Well divil a spanner can I see. I'll tell the master that. (*He goes out again through the yard door, and as he does so,* MARY MURRAY *comes through the door from the inner rooms, carrying a tray with teacups, on it. She is a pretty, vivacious girl about eighteen years of age.*)

MARY: Who was that?

KATE: It's the servant man looking for a spanner for your father, Miss Mary. There's something gone wrong with the threshing machine.

MARY: (*Taking the tray to the table and starting to get ready to wash up the cups.*) I do believe sometimes that Uncle Dan's a lazy man.

KATE: (*Assisting her at the washing and stopping as if astonished at the statement*) And is it only now you're after finding that out! Sure the whole countryside knowed it this years and years.

MARY: (*Sharply*) The whole countryside has no business to talk about what doesn't concern it.

KATE: Oh, well, people are bound to talk, Miss. But then Uncle Dan is awfully clever. He's got the whole brains of the Murrays, so father says, and then, besides that, he is a grand talker.

KATE: Aye. He can talk plenty. Sure Sarah McMinn, that lives up the Cut, says its a shame the way he's going on this twenty years and more, never doing a hand's turn from morning to night, and she says she wonders your poor father stands him and his nonsense.

MARY: Who said that?

KATE: Sarah McMinn told Johnny McAndless that yesterday.

MARY: Sarah McMinn? Pooh! That hard, mean, old thing. No. I believe in Uncle Dan and so does father. He'll make a name for himself yet.

KATE: Well, it's getting near time he done it.

MARY: They say that Sarah McMinn just keeps her brother in starvation, and she just says nasty things like that about Uncle Dan because he doesn't like her.

KATE: Aye. He never did like people as seen through him, not but she is a mean old skin-a-louse. (*The voice of* DANIEL MURRAY *is heard calling from within.*) He's up, Miss.

MARY: Are you up, uncle?

(DAN MURRAY *opens the door from the inner apartments and comes into the kitchen. He is carelessly dressed and sleepy-looking as if just out of bed, wears a muffler and glasses, and appears to be some fifty years of age.*)

DANIEL: Yes. Did the *Whig* come yet?

MARY: Yes. I put it in your workshop.

DANIEL: (*Glancing at the clock*) Bless my heart, it's half-past one!

MARY: (*Reproachfully*) It is, indeed, uncle.

DANIEL: Well! Well! Time goes round, Mary. Time goes round. (KATE *picks up the bucket and goes out by the yard door.*) Where's your father? (*He crosses over to the workshop door.*)

MARY: He's out working with Sam Brown at the threshing all morning since seven o'clock.

DANIEL: Well! Well! A very industrious man is John Murray. Very. But lacking in brains, my dear — lacking in brains. Kind, good-hearted, easy-going, but — ah! well, one can't help these things. (*He goes into the workshop and brings out the paper and crosses back to sit down at the fireplace.*)

MARY: You were very late coming in last night, uncle.

DANIEL: (*Uneasily*) Eh? (*He settles down in an armchair and opens out the paper.*)

MARY: I heard you coming in, and the clock was just after striking two.

DANIEL: Well — I met a few friends last night. Appreciative friends I could talk to, and I was explaining that new idea of mine that I've been working at so long — that new idea for a fan-bellows. It's a great thing. Oh yes. It should be. I sat up quite a while last night, thinking it over, and I believe I've got more ideas about it — better ones.

MARY: Do you think you'll make money off it, uncle?

DANIEL: Mary — if it comes off — if I can get someone to take it up, I believe 'twill make our fortune, I do.

MARY: Oh, uncle, it would be lovely if you did, and I would just die to see that nasty McMinn woman's face when she hears about you making such a hit.

DANIEL: McMinn? Has that woman been sneering about me again? That's one woman, Mary, I can't stand. I can never do myself justice explaining ideas in company when that woman is present.

MARY: Never mind her, uncle. (*Coming close beside him*) Do you mind this time last year, uncle, when you went up to Belfast for a week to see about that patent for — what's this the patent was, uncle?

DANIEL: (*Uncomfortably*) Last year? This time?

MARY: Yes. Don't you remember you said you knew of an awfully nice boy that you met, and you were going to bring him down here.

DANIEL: Upon my soul, I had clean forgotten. Yes, yes. I think I did say something about a young fellow I met.

MARY: Was he nice, uncle?

DANIEL: (*Becoming absorbed in the newspaper*) Eh? I think so. Oh. He was — very nice chap.

MARY: Well, you said he was coming here to see me, and he never turned up yet.

DANIEL: Did I? Very possibly. I suppose he must have forgotten.

MARY: (*Walking away to the left and then back again pouting*) I'm sick of the boys here. There's only Alick McCready that's anyway passable. When will you see him again, uncle?

DANIEL: Well — possibly, when I go up to town again. Very soon, perhaps. That is if your father, Mary, can spare the money.

MARY: (*Thoughtfully*) I don't know, uncle. You see that would be five times now, and somehow you never seem to get anything done. That's what he said, mind you, uncle.

DANIEL: (*Mournfully*) Well! Well! To think of me toiling and moiling away in that workshop of mine, day after day, and week after week, and year after year — and there's all the thanks you get for it.

MARY: Uncle?

DANIEL: (*Somewhat irritably as he gets engrossed reading*) Well?

MARY: Look, if you went up to Belfast again soon, won't you see that boy? I wonder what he's like. (*She gets close beside her uncle and nestles beside him.*) Is he dark or fair?

DANIEL: Yes, yes. I think so.

MARY: Dark?

DANIEL: Yes. I believe he is dark.

MARY: And tall?

DANIEL: (*Trying vainly to read in spite of the interruptions*) Very tall.

MARY: Oh, how nice! And uncle, is he good-looking?

DANIEL: Very. Fine looking fellow.

MARY: That's grand; and uncle, is he well-to-do?

DANIEL: He has every appearance of it.

MARY: Oh you dear old uncle! (*She nestles closer to him.*) But maybe he wouldn't look at me when he has a whole lot of town girls to go with.

DANIEL: My dear niece, you don't know what a very good-looking young lady you are, and besides he saw your photograph.

MARY: Which photograph?

DANIEL: (*Perplexed*) Which photograph? Your own of course!

MARY: The one I got taken at Lurgan.

DANIEL: Yes. I think so.

MARY: Oh uncle! That horrid thing! Why didn't you show him the one I got taken at Newcastle?

DANIEL: My mistake. Very sorry, indeed, Mary, I assure you. But I tell you, I'll take the album with me next time. Will that do?

MARY: (*Laughing*) There. Now you're joking. (*Suddenly*) What do you do all the time you stay in Belfast, uncle?

DANIEL: (*Uneasily*) Um — um — business, my dear girl, business. See engineers and all that sort of thing, and talk things over. It takes time, you know, Mary, time.

MARY: You've been an awful long time inventing, uncle, haven't you?

DANIEL: Well, you know, Mary dear — time — it takes time. You can't rush an inventor.

MARY: Well look, uncle. You know I can just wheedle father round my wee finger, can't I?

DANIEL: You can indeed.

MARY: Well, look: if you promise to bring down this boy you are talking about, I'll get father to give you enough to have two weeks in Belfast. There. It's a bargain.

DANIEL: Um — well — he may not be there you know.

MARY: (*Disappointed*) O uncle!

DANIEL: You see he travels a lot and he may be away. He may be in London. In fact I think — yes. He said he would be going to London.

MARY: Then why not go to London?

DANIEL: (*Starting up and speaking as if struck with delight at the possibility*) Eh? I never thought of that! (*He collapses again.*) But no. Your father, Mary. He would never give me the money. No.

MARY: But you're more likely to meet people there who'd take it up, aren't you, uncle?

DANIEL: It's the place for an inventor to go, Mary. The place. (*Pauses.*) But I'm afraid when John hears about it — (*He becomes very dubious and shakes his head.*)

MARY: Well, look here, uncle. Do you mind the last time when he would not give you money to go up to Belfast about your patent?

DANIEL: (*Sadly*) I do.

MARY: You remember you got a letter a few days after asking you to come up at once and you had to go then. Hadn't you?

DANIEL: I had.

MARY: Well, couldn't we do the same this time?

DANIEL: (*Looking at her uneasily*) Eh?

MARY: Couldn't we get someone to send a letter? (*Pausing and thinking, then suddenly*) Oh, the very thing! You know that silly Alick McCready that comes running after me. Well, look, I'll get him to send a letter.

DANIEL: No good, my dear. I did it before — I mean letters on plain notepaper don't carry much weight. No.

MARY: What about — oh, I know! Uncle, a telegram!

DANIEL: Great idea! It is in soul!

MARY: And we'll put something on it like 'come to London at once to see about the patent,' or something like that. And he'd have to let you go then.

DANIEL: Mary, you're really a cleverer girl than your father thinks. (*Musingly*) Two weeks in London.

MARY: And don't forget the nice boy, uncle, when you go.

DANIEL: I'll do my best to get hold of him.

MARY: No. I want a good definite promise. Promise, uncle.

DANIEL: Well, really you know, my dear, he —

MARY: Uncle, promise.

DANIEL: Um — well, I promise.

MARY: You're a dear old thing. You see, uncle, I don't want to marry Alick McCready or Jim McDowell or any of those boys, unless there's nobody else.

DANIEL: Quite right, my dear, quite right. Two weeks in London. Splendid! But it's time I was going into my workshop. (*He rises and takes the paper with him.*) I must really try and do something this morning. (*Exit by workshop door.*)

MARY: (*Calling after him*) You won't forget, uncle? Will you?

DANIEL: No, certainly not.

MARY: I do hope uncle brings that nice boy. Dark — tall — well set-up — well-to-do.

(KATE *comes in again through the yard door, and looks at* MARY, *who is gazing vacantly into space.*)

KATE: Well? What notion have you got now?

MARY: Oh! just think, Kate! How would you like a boy who was dark and tall, and well set-up and well-to-do?

KATE: I'd just leap at him.

MARY: (*Laughing*) I think I will — if he comes.

KATE: I think you've plenty on hand to manage. (BROWN *opens the yard door and resumes his old position from which he stares at the dresser.*) You're back again, are you?

BROWN: Aye.

KATE: What ails you now?

BROWN: I'm looking the spanner.

MARY: The spanner?

BROWN: The spanner, Miss Mary. It's for turning the nuts like.

KATE: Have you never got it yet?

BROWN: Do you think I've got eyes in the back of my head? Underneath the seat, beside the salt-box, on the right near the wee crock in the left hand corner. (*He makes a movement to open one of the drawers of the dresser.*)

KATE: Will you get out of that, ignorance. It's not there.

BROWN: (*With an appealing look at* MARY) Maybe it's in the parlour?

MARY: Well, I'll take a look round. (*She goes through the door to living the rooms.*)

BROWN: (*Mysteriously*) Did you hear the news?

KATE: No. (*Very much interested*) What?

BROWN: Ach! You women never know anything.

KATE: What's the news? Somebody killed?

BROWN: No. More serious.

KATE: (*Alarmed*) God bless me! What is it?

BROWN: Andy McMinn has a sister.

KATE: (*Disappointed*) Ach! Sure I knowed that years ago.

BROWN: And she's trying to get a man.

KATE: Well. I knowed that this years.

BROWN: And Mr John Murray is a widow man.

KATE: You mean to be telling me that Mr John has a notion of that old thing? Go long with you!

BROWN: Did you ever hear tell of a widow man that never got married again.

KATE: Plenty. Don't come in here talking blethers.

BROWN: Whist. There's more in what I'm telling you than you think. And I'll hold you to a shilling that Sarah McMinn will be Mrs John Murray before one month.

KATE: Who told you?

BROWN: Ach! You've no more head than a yellow yorling. Where has Mr John been going to these wheen of nights?

KATE: (*Thinking*) Andy McMinn's!

BROWN: Aye. Do you think it is to see old Andy? And sure he's been talking to me all morning about the way the house is being kept. No hand to save the waste; bread and things destroyed; hens laying away; eggs ate up by the dozen and chickens lost and one thing and another. And hinting about what money a good saving woman would bring him. And Mr Daniel —

KATE: Sh — he's in there working.

BROWN: Working? Ah, God save us! Him working! The last man that seen Mr Dan working is in his grave this twenty years. (*He goes over next workshop door.*) I'll just peep in at him through the keyhole. (*He goes over and does so, and then beckons* KATE *over. She peeps in and grins. As they are thus occupied* ALICK MCCREADY *opens the door and stands gazing at them. He is a type of the young well-to-do farmer, respectably dressed and good-looking.*)

ALICK: Well! Well! Some people earn their money easy!

BROWN: Aye. In soul. Just look in there to see it. (MCCREADY *looks in and bursts into a loud hearty laugh.* BROWN *hurriedly goes out by the yard door and* KATE *by door to inner rooms.*)

DANIEL: (*Opening the door and standing there, perplexed-looking.*) What's the matter?

ALICK: Ah. I was just laughing at a wee joke, Mr Murray.

DANIEL: It must have been very funny.

ALICK: Aye. It was. (*Coming close to* DANIEL, *who walks slowly to the middle of the kitchen*) I say. Were you at McArn's public house last night?

DANIEL: (*Looking round cautiously to see that no one else can hear him*) Well, just a minute or two. Why?

ALICK: There was someone there told Andy McMinn this morning, I believe, that you'd been talking of a great invention altogether, and he was that much curious to see it that him and his sister Sarah are coming over this day to have a look at it.

DANIEL: Who? Sarah McMinn?

ALICK: Aye. She's very anxious to see it, I believe.

DANIEL: Um. Rather awkward this. She's not a woman that, plainly speaking, I care very much to talk about my ideas to.

ALICK: But have you got something struck out?

DANIEL: McCready, come here. (ALICK *goes closer to him.*) It is really a great idea. Splendid. But I've a great deal of trouble over it. In fact I've been thinking out details of a particular gear all morning.

ALICK: Aye. (*He looks at* DANIEL *and then endeavours to restrain unsuccessfully a burst of laughter.*)

DANIEL: (*Angrily*) You were always an ignorant fellow anyway and be d—d to you. (*He turns to go towards his workshop.*)

ALICK: Ah, Mr Murray, I beg your pardon. It's another thing altogether I'm thinking about. I just wanted a talk with you this morning. You have a nice wee girl for a niece, Mr Murray.

DANIEL: (*Somewhat mollified*) Well?

ALICK: (*Bashfully*) And I was wondering if you could put in a good word for me now and again with her.

DANIEL: Now, look here, Alick. We can all work nice and comfortably together, can't we?

ALICK: Aye.

DANIEL: Well, if you behave yourself like a man with some manners, and not like an ignorant clodhopper, I can do a great deal for you.

ALICK: Thank you, sir. You know, Mr Murray, I have as nice a wee farm, and as good stock on it as well, as any man in the county, and if I'm lucky enough to get that niece of yours, you'll always be welcome to come and pass a day or two and have a chat.

DANIEL: I think you and I will get along all right, Alick. There's one or two little things I need badly sometimes in this house. I mean I want help often, you know, Alick, to carry my points with John; points about going to see people and that sort of thing, and it's really very hard to manage John on points like that, unless we resort to certain means to convince him they are absolutely necessary.

ALICK: (*Uneasily*) Yes. I sort of follow you.

DANIEL: You know what I mean. John's a little dense, you know. He can't see the point of an argument very well unless you sort of knock him down with it. Now, if a thing is fair and reasonable, and a man is so dense that he can't see it, you are quite justified — at least, I take it so — to manufacture a way — it doesn't matter how — so long as you make that dense man accept the thing, whatever it is, as right. Do you follow me?

ALICK: I'm just beginning to see a kind of way.

MARY: (*Appearing at the door from the inner rooms*) I can't see that thing anywhere. (*She suddenly sees* ALICK.) Oh Alick! You here!

ALICK: Yes. It's a nice morning, and you're looking beautiful!

MARY: Oh, bother. (*She seems to suddenly recollect something.*) Oh, I say! Uncle! You remember? Uncle!

DANIEL: (*Somewhat perplexed*) Eh?

MARY: (*Motioning towards* ALICK) Telegram to come to London.

DANIEL: Ah — Oh, yes, yes.

MARY: Let's go into your workshop and tell Alick what we want. Come on.

ALICK: I'll do anything in the world you want.

(*They all go into the workshop. As they disappear,* JOHN MURRAY, *sweating and angry-looking, comes through from the yard followed by* BROWN. JOHN *is a tall, stout man, with a rather dour countenance and somewhat stolid expression. He is a year or so the elder of Dan in age. He goes to the dresser, puts his hand on the top shelf, takes down a spanner and throws it down angrily on the table.*)

JOHN: There. There you are, you stupid-looking, good-for-nothing, dunder-headed, Italian idiot you.

BROWN: You're something terrible cross this morning.

JOHN: (*Heatedly*) Is it any wonder? Away out at once now and put her to rights and quick about it. (BROWN *meekly goes out.*) The like of servant men nowadays, I never seen in my mortal days. A concern of ignorant bauchles, every one of them.

DANIEL: (*Opening the door of the workshop and peeping out. He sees* JOHN *and goes over to him with a genial air.*) Good morning John.

JOHN: (*Snappishly*) Good afternoon.

DANIEL: John, what do you think, I believe I have just come on to a great idea about —

JOHN: Ach! You and your great ideas! Here you've been blundering and blethering and talking these fifteen years and more, and I've never seen anything come of them yet.

DANIEL: (*Soothingly*) I know, John, I know. But I'm handicapped you know. Bad place to work in and all the rest of it: but you've been kind to me, John. Keeping a brother and helping him after he has lost all his money isn't a common thing with many men, but John a day will come sometime, and you'll get it all back. (*Impressively*) Every penny. Aye, and twice over.

JOHN: (*Softening*) Thank you, Daniel.

DANIEL: You will, John, you will. But don't cast up things like that about the time I've been. It hurts me. A thing like this takes time to mature, you know, John. The great and chief thing for an inventor is time. Look at Palissy, the great French potter, who found out how to make porcelain glaze. Why he worked for years and years at his invention. And there was the man who found out how to make steam drive engines. Look at the years those men spent — and no-one begrudged them.

JOHN: I suppose that now.

DANIEL: Certainly, John, nothing surer. And look at the fortunes those men made. But the great difficulty is trying to get someone to take up your patent. You see these men had the eyes of the world fixed on them. People knew all about them, and had their hands stretched out ready to grab what they invented. (*Pathetically*) I'm just a poor unknown man struggling in a wee dark corner.

JOHN: (*Touched*) Never mind, Danny. You'll make the name of the Murrays known yet, maybe.

DANIEL: I'll do my best, John. But mind you it would take me to be pushing on this thing that I have found out and bringing it before people to notice. You see I've got it all ready now except for a few small details.

JOHN: (*Much interested*) Have you now? I would like you sometime to explain it to me, Daniel. I didn't quite get on to it the last time you were telling me about it.

DANIEL: Some time again. Oh yes. But John I'll have to go to some of the towns soon to see people about it. The bigger the town the better the chance, and John – (*Impressively*) London's the place.

JOHN: (*Aghast*) London! In all the name of the world, yon place! Would Belfast not do you?

DANIEL: No. I don't like Belfast. They're a mangy, stick-in-the-mud, follow-in-the-old-ruts crowd. Never strike out anything new. It's a case of London or nothing.

JOHN: (*Dubiously*) It will be a terrible expense this London visiting.

DANIEL: It'll be worth it.

JOHN: Now, Danny, I would like to oblige you, but what do you think it would cost me?

DANIEL: Well, I could live cheap you know, John, and do without meals an odd day, and go steerage and third class, and that sort of thing. I would say about fifteen pounds roughly. That would let me stay more than a week.

JOHN: Fifteen pounds! God bless me, Daniel, would you break me? No, no, I couldn't afford to give you that much.

DANIEL: Maybe ten would do it. I could sleep out under the arches an odd night or two, and —

JOHN: No, no. I'll not have that. A Murray aye had a bed to go to and a sup to eat. (*After a contemplative pause.*) Here, I'll give you three pounds and you can go to Belfast.

DANIEL: I don't care much about Belfast. You know I have been there five times now, and I have never got anyone to look into the thing at all proper.

JOHN: You're too backward, Daniel, when it comes to the like of that. But ten pounds! No, I would like you to get on in the world right enough, Daniel, but I couldn't afford it. You know the way this house is being kept; it's lamentable. Tea and sugar and flour and things. Man, I'm just after paying off ten pounds to the McAfees for one thing and another, and it only a running account for two months. If I had a good housekeeper now, maybe things would alter for the better.

MARY: (*Coming out from the workshop followed by* ALICK) Oh, Uncle Dan! He says he'll go at once and get it — (*She stops short in confusion on seeing her father.*)

ALICK: How are you, Mr Murray?

JOHN: Oh! bravely. What's the news with you?

ALICK: I was just looking over some of them ideas of Daniel's about the new fan bellows.

JOHN: Aye. Now what do you think of it?

ALICK: (*Warned by* DANIEL *who nudges him.*) They're great altogether.

JOHN: Do you think there will be any sale for it at all?

ALICK: I think so. (*He perceives* DANIEL *motioning assent.*) I believe there would be indeed.

JOHN: Man, I wish I had the head of some of you young fellows to understand the working of them machinery and things. (DANIEL *goes back into the workshop.*) I've the worst head in the world for understanding about them sort of things. There's Daniel, a great head on him, Daniel.

ALICK: (*Slyly*) He has, right enough!

JOHN: (*Proudly*) One of the best. When he was a wee fellow, dang the one could beat him at making boats or drawing pictures, or explaining extraordinary things to you. None. Not one. A great head on him, Daniel. He'll do something yet.

ALICK: Did you know Andy McMinn's for coming over to see you this day, Mr Murray?

JOHN: (*Eagerly*) This day? When? Are you sure?

ALICK: Aye, so he said. About two o'clock or so. Someone told him about Daniel's great new idea, and he's very curious to hear about it.

MARY: He's always poking his nose into people's business.

JOHN: Whist. Andy McMinn's a very decent man. Tell me (*Rather bashfully*), was Sarah to come with him?

MARY: (*Alarmed*) Oh holy prophets! I hope not.

ALICK: Aye. She's coming too. She wanted to see it as well as Andy.

JOHN: Aye. Certainly, and she's welcome too. Mary, you can get the house ready, and the table set, and a nice tea for them when they come, and I can go and get tidied up a wee bit. (*He goes off through the door into the inner rooms.*)

ALICK: (*Leaning against the table and looking across at* MARY, *who is sitting at the opposite end*) You're as nice a wee girl as ever I —

MARY: You're an awful fool. Hurry, Alick, like a decent man and get that telegram sent.

ALICK: That uncle of yours, Mary, heth he's as canny a keoghboy as I've seen. It's the queer tears he'll be taking to himself in London if I know anything.

MARY: Hold your tongue. You've no business to talk about Uncle Dan that way. He could give you tons as far as brains go anyway.

ALICK: I believe that. (*He goes to the yard door, then turns back.*) I say, Mary. What name will I put on that telegram? 'Come to London at once about patent. Intend purchasing.' Hadn't we better have a name?

MARY: Yes. I'll just ask uncle. (*She knocks at door of workshop.*) Uncle!

DANIEL: (*Without*) Yes.

MARY: What name will we put to that telegram?

DANIEL: (*Without*) Oh, it's not particular. Wilson, or Smith, or Brown, or Gregg.

ALICK: I'll put Gregg on it.

DANIEL: Do well.

ALICK: Did you see the fluster that your father got into, Mary, when he heard that Sarah McMinn was coming over?

MARY: (*Alarmed*) What?

ALICK: Did you not see how he rushed off to tidy himself up when he heard Sarah McMinn was coming over?

MARY: (*Seating herself on chair to right of table*) Nonsense. Father wouldn't think of that woman.

ALICK: All right. But I think I know something more than you.

MARY: (*Anxiously*) What? Tell me.

ALICK: Come on and leave me down the loaning a pace, and I'll tell you.

MARY: (*Glancing at him, and then coquettishly turning her back to him as he leans against the table*) Oh, I can't. Those people are coming over, and that McMinn woman will be looking at everything and telling you how to do things in front of father, and all the rest of it.

ALICK: (*Entreatingly*) Leave me down the loaning a pace till I tell you the news.

MARY: (*Teasingly*) No.

ALICK: Come on.

MARY: No. (ALICK *moves sadly towards the door.* MARY *looks round, and then laughingly skips past him out through the yard door, and he follows her.*)

JOHN: (*Coming through the door from the inner rooms partly dressed, with a towel in his hands, evidently making much preparation to clean himself.*) Daniel! (*Loudly and crossly*) Daniel!

DANIEL: (*Peeping out from the workshop door*) Well!

JOHN: Tidy yourself up a wee bit, man, Andy McMinn and Sarah's coming over to see you.

DANIEL: (*Somewhat taken back*) Me?

JOHN: Aye. They want to see about the new invention. You can have the collar I wore last Sunday, and put on your new coat that you got in Belfast. (DANIEL *goes back into the workshop.*) I wonder what tie would be the better one? Yon green or the red one that Mary gave me last Christmas. Aye. (*Seeing no sign of* DANIEL.) D—n! Is he making no shapes to dress himself. Daniel!

DANIEL: (*Without*) Aye.

JOHN: (*Loudly*). Daniel!

DANIEL: (*Again appearing at the door*) Well!

JOHN: (*Impatiently*) Come on and get on you.

DANIEL: Ach. This is always the way. Just when a man has got the whole thing worked out and the plans of the apparatus just on the point of completion he has to stop.

JOHN: Never mind, Danny. You can do it again the night or the morrow morning. I want you to look decent. Come on and get on you.

DANIEL: (*Beginning to regard his brother with a sudden interest and suspicion*) Who did you say was coming?

JOHN: (*At the door to the rooms*) Andy and Sarah McMinn. (*He goes out.*)

DANIEL: (*Suddenly realising the import of the preparations going on*) McMinn. Mc — (*He stops short, and then in a horrified voice*) Surely to God he hasn't a notion of that woman? (*Calling tremulously*) John! John!

JOHN: (*At door.*) Hurry up, man.

DANIEL: (*Appealingly*) John. Tell me, John. You haven't — you're not going to — you haven't a notion of that woman?

JOHN: (*Hesitatingly*) Well, Daniel, you see the house needs some one to look after it proper, and I thought — well — maybe — that Sarah would be just as nice and saving a woman as I could get, but I thought I would keep it a bit secret, don't you know, because I don't know yet if she'd have me or not. And she could talk to you better nor I could about machinery and things that would interest you, for she has an agency for sewing machines, and knows something about that sort of thing, and you'd get on great with each other. Now, hurry and get on you. (*He goes out by the door into the rooms.*)

DANIEL: (*Looking after him in a helpless manner, and sinking into a chair.*) If — if she'd have him! O great God! If that woman comes to this house, I — I'm a ruined man.

(CURTAIN)

ACT TWO

The same scene some hours later. The curtain rises to discover Kate seated near the table at the back enjoying a cup of tea which she has made, and is drinking with relish.

KATE: I suppose they'll be wanting jam and sugar for the tea — aye — and some of them scones Miss Mary cooked yesterday, not but you couldn't eat them, and a pat or two of butter. (*She finishes off the remains of the tea.*) Now, that's a nice girl for you! Here's company coming till the house and tea and things a wanting and she goes and leaves all to go strolling down the loaning with that fool of a McCready.

(BROWN *opens the yard door and comes in. He replaces the spanner on the top shelf and then turns and looks at* KATE.)

KATE: Well?

BROWN: Well, yourself?

KATE: Do you see any sign of them McMinns yet?

BROWN: Aye. I see the trap coming over the Cattle Hill. There was three in it, as far as I could make out.

KATE: Who be to be the third party I wonder? Is it their servant man?

BROWN: Do you think old Andy McMinn's servant man gets leave to drive them about of an afternoon like the clergy's? Talk sense, woman.

KATE: Maybe it's yon Scotch body I heard was stopping with them.

BROWN: Aye. Yon Mackenzie. Ach, man, but yon creature would scunder you.

KATE: Aye.

BROWN: Ach! Cracking jokes and laughing that hearty at them, and I'm danged if a bat with one eye shut could make out what he was laughing at. (*Listening*) Here they are. I hear the wheels coming up the loaning. I'll have to go and put up the horse for them I suppose. (*He goes out by the yard door.*)

KATE: I wonder if the master seen them coming. (*She rapidly clears the table and then goes over to the door into the room.*) I better tell him. (*She knocks at the door.*)

JOHN: (*Without*) Aye. (*He comes and opens the door, dressed in his best suit of clothes.*) What's the matter?

KATE: They're just come, sir.

JOHN: (*Excitedly*) Are they? (*Comes into kitchen.*) Is my tie right, Kate? And my clothes — is there any dirt on the back of them?

KATE: (*Inspecting him critically*) You'll do grand. I never seen you looking better.

JOHN: Where's Mary? Why isn't she here?

KATE: She went out about something. She'll be back in a minute.

JOHN: Right enough, it would do her all the good in the world to have a sensible woman looking after her. She just gets her own way a deal too much in this house. (*He goes to window and looks out.*) Aye. Here they are! Tell Daniel to hurry. (KATE *goes off by the door to the rooms.*) Sarah's looking bravely. Man, that woman could save me thirty, aye forty, pounds a year if she was here. (*Suddenly*) Ach! Is Daniel never ready yet? (*Calls*) Daniel. (*Louder*) Daniel!

JOHN: (*Without*) Aye.

JOHN: Hurry, man. They've come. (JOHN *goes to the yard door and goes out.*)

DANIEL: (*In an exasperated voice*) Ach!

(JOHN *comes in followed by* ANDREW MCMINN, *an elderly nondescript sort of man, followed by* SARAH, *a sour-faced spinster of uncertain age. In the rear is* DONAL MACKENZIE. *He is wearing a tourist cos-*

tume of Norfolk jacket and knickers, and is a keen-faced, hard, angular-looking personage.)

JOHN: Yous are all welcome. Every one of you. You Andy and Sarah, and Mr Mackenzie. The Scotch is aye welcome, Mr Mackenzie.

MACKENZIE: Aye. That's what I said the last time I was in Ballyannis, and was verra thirsty, and went into a beer-shop to get a dram — Black and White it was. Verra guid. (*He laughs loudly at his own joke.*)

SARAH: We brought Mr Mackenzie along with us to see your brother, John. You see he's an engineer and knows a good deal about machinery and plans and things.

MACKENZIE: Aye. There's not much about machinery that I dinna ken, Mr Murray, from a forty thousand horse power quadruple expansion doon to a freewheel bicycle. (*Proudly*) I hae done spells work at all of them, you ken.

ANDY: I suppose Daniel's at home. Is he?

JOHN: Daniel? Oh aye, Daniel's at home. He's just tidying himself up a wee bit.

MACKENZIE: A wee bit paint and powder gangs a lang gait to make up defects, as you ken yourself, Miss McMinn. (*He laughs loudly.*) That's a guid one.

ANDY: (*Looking slyly at* SARAH) He's up out of bed then?

JOHN: (*Innocently*) Oh aye. He sits up late of nights working out things. (*He points to the door of the workshop.*) That's his workshop.

MACKENZIE: He works then?

JOHN: Aye. He works in there. (ANDY *goes over and goes into the workshop.*)

MACKENZIE: Because it doesna follow always, as I have discovered in my experience, that because a man has a workshop, he works. (*He laughs, evidently much pleased at his own humour.*)

ANDY: (*Looking out again through door*) There's nothing much to see in this place except a lot of dirty papers.

JOHN: That's the plans of the bellows he's working at.

MACKENZIE: (*Going over to workshop*) Come out, Mr McMinn, till I examine. (ANDY *comes out and he passes in.*) Eh. This is the plan of the great bellows. (*He laughs loudly.*)

ANDY: Is he making much headway with it, John?

JOHN: Indeed, now, I think he's doing bravely at it. He's keeping very close at it this day or two.

ANDY: There's a terrible amount of newspapers lying in there. Has he no other plans and drawings except what's there?

JOHN: Oh aye. He has plenty of plans and drawings somewhere, for I seen them once or twice.

MACKENZIE: (*Coming out*) I can't say much about that contrivance. (*He laughs.*) And, I say. Look here. He does more than draw bellows. He draws corks as well. (*He produces a bottle of whiskey almost empty.*)

JOHN: Ah, well. He's not a great transgressor either in the matter of a bottle. No, no.

ANDY: And the smell of smoke in the place!

SARAH: John, I think Daniel smokes far too much.

ANDY: He should be dressed by now.

JOHN: Aye. Oh, aye. He should right enough. He's a wee bit backward before women, you know, Sarah. (*Calls*) Daniel! (*He goes over and opens door into rooms.*) Daniel!

DANIEL: (*Without*) Yes. (*He appears at the door struggling vainly with his collar.*)

JOHN: Why didn't you come long ago. What kept you?

DANIEL: Your collar. (*He looks across at* ANDY *and* SARAH, *who have seated themselves at the back.*) How do you do, Andy and Sarah? You're very welcome. (*He looks at* MACKENZIE, *who stares curiously at him.*)

ANDY: This is a friend of ours, Daniel, that happened to be stopping with us last summer at Newcastle in the same house, and he came over for his holidays to us this time. We brought him over to see you. They calls him Mackenzie.

DANIEL: (*Crossing over to the left and taking a seat near the door of the workshop*) How do you do?

MACKENZIE: (*Patronisingly*) I'm glad to see you at last, Mr Murray, for I've heard a good deal about you.

SARAH: You see, Daniel, Mr Mackenzie is an engineer in one of the great Scotch engineering yards. (DANIEL'S *face expresses his dismay, which he hurriedly tries to hide.*) What place was it you were in, Mr Mackenzie?

MACKENZIE: I served six years in the engine and fitting shops with Messrs. Ferguson, Hartie and Macpherson, and was two years shop foreman afterwards to Dennison, McLachlan and Co., and now I'm senior partner with the firm of Stephenson and Mackenzie. If ever you're up in Greenock direction, and want to see how we do it, just ask for Donal Mackenzie, and they'll show you the place. (*Proudly*) We're the sole makers of the Mackenzie piston, if ever you heard of it.

DANIEL: (*Uneasily*) I'm sorry to say I haven't.

MACKENZIE: And you call yourself an engineer and you don't know about Donal Mackenzie's patent reciprocating piston.

JOHN: (*Apologetically*). You see we be a bit out of the world here, Mr Mackenzie.

DANIEL: Yes. Now that's one point. One great point that always tells against me. (*Getting courageous*) It really needs a man to be continually visiting the great engineering centres — Greenock, London —

MACKENZIE: (*Scornfully*) London's not an engineering centre — Glasgow, Hartlepool, Newcastle —

DANIEL: Well, all those places. He could keep himself posted up in all the newest ideas then, and inventions.

MACKENZIE: But a man can keep himself to the fore if he reads the technical journals and follows their articles. What technical papers do you get? Do you ever get the Scottish Engineers' Monthly Handbook, price sixpence monthly?

I'm the writer on the inventors' column. My articles are signed Fergus McLachlan. Perhaps you've read them?

DANIEL: I think — um — I'm not quite sure that I have.

MACKENZIE: You remember one I wrote on the new compressed air drills last July?

DANIEL: (*Looking across at* JOHN, *who is standing with his back to the fireplace*) I don't think I do.

JOHN: No. We don't get them sort of papers. I did buy one or two like them for Daniel, but he told me he would just as soon have the *Whig*, for there was just as much information in it.

MACKENZIE: (*Laughing*) O spirit of Burns! Just as much information — well, so much for that. Now, about this new patent, this new fan bellows that I hear you're working at, Mr Murray.

DANIEL: What about it?

ANDY: We both seen the drawings in there, Daniel, but I don't think either of us made much of it. Could you not explain it to him, Daniel. Give him an idea what you mean to do with it.

JOHN: Aye. Now's your chance, Daniel. You were talking of some difficulty or other. Maybe this gentleman could help you with it.

DANIEL: (*Shifting uneasily, and looking appealingly at* JOHN) Well. There's no great hurry. A little later on in the evening. (*He looks at* SARAH.) I'm thinking about Miss McMinn. I don't think this conversation would be very interesting to her.

SARAH: Oh, indeed now, Mr Murray, I just love to know about it. A good fan bellows would be the great thing for yon fireplace of ours, Andy.

ANDY: Aye. Soul, it would that.

DANIEL: (*Uncomfortably*) No. Not just yet, John. A bit later on. I'm shy, John, you know. A bit backward before company.

JOHN: You're a man to talk about going to see people in London.

SARAH: What? Was he going to London?

JOHN: Aye. He was talking about going to London, and I was half-minded to let him go.

ANDY: (*Who exchanges meaning glances with* SARAH.) Boys, that would cost a wheen of pounds!

MACKENZIE: Who wull you go to see in London?

DANIEL: (*Evasively*) Oh — engineers and patent agents and people that would take an interest in that sort of thing.

MACKENZIE: Have you anyone to go to in particular?

DANIEL: Oh, yes.

SARAH: It will cost a great deal of money, Daniel. Seven or eight pounds anyway. Won't it, Mr Mackenzie?

MACKENZIE: It would, and more.

JOHN: (*Looking at* SARAH *with evident admiration*) Man, that's a saving woman. She can count the pounds. (*Suddenly*) Daniel, away out and show Andy and Mr Mackenzie the thresher, and get used to the company, and then you can come in and explain the thing to them. I want Sarah to stay here and help me to make the tea. That fool of a Mary is away again somewhere.

ANDY: (*After a sly glance at* SARAH.) Aye. Come on, Daniel, and explain it to us. I hear there's a new kind of feedboard on her.

MACKENZIE: How is she driven, Mr Murray?

DANIEL: (*Uncomfortably*) How is she what?

MACKENZIE: How is she worked — steam, horse, or water power, which?

JOHN: (*Motioning* DANIEL *to go, which the latter does very unwillingly.*) Go on out and you can show them, Daniel. (DANIEL, ANDY, *and* MACKENZIE *go out through yard door.*) He's backward, you know, Sarah, oh, aye — backward; but a great head. A great head on him, Daniel.

SARAH: I suppose he is clever in his way.

JOHN: (*Seating himself close beside her and talking with innocent enthusiasm*) Ah, boys, Sarah, I mind when he went to serve his time with McArthurs, of Ballygrainey, he was as clever a boy as come out of the ten townlands. And then he set up for himself, you know, and lost all, and then he come here. He's doing his best, poor creature, till pay me for what kindness I showed him, by trying to invent things that he says would maybe pay off, some time or other, all he owes to me.

SARAH: (*Cynically*) Poor Daniel! And he lost all his money?

JOHN: Aye. Every ha'penny; and he took a hundred pounds off me as well. And now, poor soul, he hasn't a shilling, barring an odd pound or two I give him once or twice a month.

SARAH: Well! Well! And he's been a long time this way?

JOHN: Aye. (*Reflectively*) I suppose it's coming on now to twenty years.

SARAH: It's a wonder he wouldn't make some shapes to try and get a situation somewhere.

JOHN: Ach, well, you know, when Annie, the wife, died and left Mary a wee bit of a wain, I was lonesome, and Daniel was always a right heartsome fellow, and I never asked him about going when he came here.

SARAH: He must be rather an expense to you. Pocket money for tobacco, and whenever he goes out a night to McArn's, it's a treat all round to who is in at the time. And his clothes and boots, and let alone that, his going to see people about patents and things up to Belfast three or four times in the year. If he was in a situation and doing for himself, you could save a bit of money.

JOHN: (*Pensively*) Aye. Heth and I never thought much of that, Sarah. I could right enough. I'll think over that now. (*He looks at her, and then begins in a bashful manner.*) You weren't at Ballyannis School fête, Sarah?

SARAH: No. But I heard you were there. Why?

JOHN: (*Coming still closer*) I was expecting to see you.

SARAH: (*Contemptuously*) I don't believe in young girls going to them things.

JOHN: (*Gazing at her in astonishment*) But God bless me, they wouldn't call you young! (SARAH *turns up her nose disgustedly.*) I missed you. Man, I was looking for you all roads.

SARAH: I'm not a fool sort of young girl that you can just pass an idle hour or two with, John Murray, mind that.

JOHN: I never thought that of you, Sarah.

SARAH: Some people think that.

JOHN: (*Astonished*) No.

SARAH: They do. There's Andy just after warning me this morning about making a fool of myself.

JOHN: (*Puzzled*) But you never done that, Sarah.

SARAH: Well, he was just after giving me advice about going round flirting with Tom, Dick and Harry.

JOHN: Ah no. You never done that. Sure I knowed you this years and years, and you never had a boy to my knowing.

SARAH: (*Offended*) Well I had, plenty. Only I just wouldn't take them. I refused more than three offers in my time.

JOHN: (*Incredulously*) Well! Well! And you wouldn't have them!

SARAH: No.

JOHN: Why now?

SARAH: (*Looking at him meaningly*) Well — I liked somebody else better.

JOHN: (*Piqued*) Did he — the somebody — did he never ask you?

SARAH: He might yet, maybe.

JOHN: (*Hopelessly to himself*) I wonder would it be any use then me asking her.

SARAH: And I'm beginning to think he is a long time thinking about it.

(*Knocking at the door.*)

JOHN: (*Angrily*) Ach! Who's that?

BROWN: (*Opening yard door and looking in*) Me, sir. Mr Dan wants to know could you not come out a minute, and show the gentlemen what way you can stop the feedboard working.

JOHN: Don't you know yourself, you stupid-headed lump you. Away back at once. (BROWN *hurriedly closes the door after an inquiring glance at the pair.*) That's them servant men for you. He knowed rightly what way it worked, only he was just curious. (*Savagely*) He's a stupid creature, anyway.

SARAH: I think all men is stupid. They never see things at all.

JOHN: Now, Sarah, sure women are just as bad. There's Mary. She's bright enough someways, but others — ach —

SARAH: Mary needs someone — a woman — to look after her. Somebody that knows how to manage a house and save money. She's lost running about here. Now, I had a young girl with me once was a wild useless thing when she came, and when she left me six months after, there wasn't a better trained, nor as meek a child in the whole country.

JOHN: And you can manage a house, Sarah, and well, too. Can't you?

SARAH: I ran the house for Andy there twenty years and more, and I never once had to ask him for a pound. And what's more, I put some into the bank every quarter.

JOHN: Did you now? (*He looks at her in wondering admiration.*)

SARAH: Yes. And I cleared five pounds on butter last half year.

JOHN: (*With growing wonder*) Did you?

SARAH: And made a profit of ten pounds on eggs alone this year already.

JOHN: (*Unable to contain himself any longer*) Sarah, will you marry me?

SARAH: (*Coyly*) Oh, John, this is very sudden. (*Knocking at yard door.*) I will. I will. Will you tell them when they come in?

JOHN: (*Now that the ordeal has been passed, feeling somewhat uncomfortable*) Well, I would rather you waited a few days, and then we could let them know, canny, don't you know, Sarah. Break the news soft, so to speak. Eh?

SARAH: (*Disappointedly*) Well, if you want it particular that way I —

(*Knocking*)

JOHN: (*Going to door*) Aye, I'd rather you did. (*He goes to the door and opens it and* MARY *comes in.*)

MARY: I peeped through the window and I thought, perhaps, it would be better to knock first. It's a nice evening Miss McMinn. (*She takes off her hat and flings it carelessly on a chair.*) Where's Uncle Dan? I want to see him.

JOHN: He'll be in soon enough. He's out showing Andy and Mackenzie the thresher.

MARY: (*Laughing*) Uncle Dan! What does he know about — (*She stops short, remembering that* SARAH *is present.*) Mr Mackenzie?

SARAH: Yes. He's a gentleman, a friend of ours, engaged in the engineering business, who has a large place of his own in Scotland, and we brought him over here to see your Uncle Dan about the invention he's working at.

JOHN: You stop here, Mary, with Sarah, and get the tea ready. You should have been in the house when company was coming. Where were you?

MARY: Oh, just down the loaning.

JOHN: Who with?

MARY: Alick McCready.

JOHN: (*Sternly*) Aye. You're gay fond of tralloping about with the boys.

SARAH: He's not just the sort of young man I would like to see in your company, Mary.

MARY: (*Impertinently*) It's none of your business whose company I was in.

JOHN: (*Disapprovingly*) Now, Mary, remember your manners in front of your elders, and mind you must always show Miss McMinn particular respect. (*Impressively*) Particular respect. (*Going towards the yard door*) And you can show Sarah what you have in the house, and do what she bids you. Them's my orders. (*He goes out.*)

SARAH: (*Looking disapprovingly at* MARY) I wonder a girl like you has no more sense than to go gallivanting about at this time of day with boys, making talk for the whole countryside.

MARY: (*Sharply*) I don't have to run after them to other people's houses anyway.

SARAH: And that is no way to be leaving down your hat. (*She picks it up and looks at it.*) Is that your Sunday one?

MARY: (*Snatching it out of her hand*) Just find out for yourself.

SARAH: Now, you should take and put it away carefully. There's no need to waste money that way, wearing things out.

MARY: (*With rising temper*) Do you know it's my hat? Not yours. And I can do what I like with it. (*She throws it down and stamps on it.*) I can tramp on it if I want to.

SARAH: (*Smiling grimly*) Oh, well, tramp away. It's no wonder your father complained of waste and this sort of conduct going on.

(KATE *comes in through door from rooms.*)

MARY: Have you got the tea things ready, Kate?

KATE: Yes, Miss.

MARY: I suppose we better wet the tea.

SARAH: (*Looking at the fire*) Have you the kettle on?

MARY: Can't you see for yourself it's not on.

SARAH: Here, girl, (*to* KATE) fill the kettle and put it on. (KATE *looks at* MARY, *and with a shrug of her shoulders, obeys the orders.*) Where's the tea till I show you how to measure?

MARY: (*In a mocking voice*) Kate, get Miss McMinn the tea cannister till she shows you how to measure.

(KATE *goes to the dresser and brings the teapot and cannister over to* SARAH *at the table.*)

SARAH: But it's *you* I want to show. (MARY *pays no attention, but sits down idly drumming her fingers on the table.*) There now — pay particular attention to this. (*She takes the canister from* KATE, *opens it and ladles out the tea with a spoon into the teapot.*) One spoonful for your father and uncle, one for my brother and Mr Mackenzie, one for yourself and me, and half-a-one for Kate.

MARY: Do you see that, Kate?

KATE: Yes, Miss.

MARY: (*Mockingly*) Now the next thing, I suppose, is to weigh out the sugar.

SARAH: No. You always ask the company first do they take sugar before you pour out the tea.

MARY: No; not in good society. You put it on the saucers.

SARAH: Put some in the bowl, Kate, and never heed her.

MARY: (*Almost tearfully*) You've no business to say that; Kate! Who's your mistress here?

KATE: (*Very promptly*) You, Miss.

MARY: Then do what I tell you. Put on the tablecloth, and lay the cups and saucers, and make everything ready, and take no orders except from me.

SARAH: Very well. I'll learn her manners when I come to this house. (To MARY) I want to see the china.

MARY: Well, go into the next room and look for it.

SARAH: (*Going towards the door to the rooms*) You better mind what your father told you. (*She goes in.*)

MARY: (*Making a face after her*) You nasty old thing. (DANIEL *appears at the door from yard. He is nervous and worried-looking. He goes and sits down near the fireplace, wearily.*) Uncle Dan. (*She goes over close beside him.*) Wasn't it good of Alick? He went away to Ballyannis Post Office to get that telegram sent.

DANIEL: A very decent fellow, Alick. (*Gratefully*) Very obliging.

MARY: (*Confidingly*) Do you know, uncle, when he went off to send that telegram I was nearly calling him back. I don't care so very much now whether I see that boy you were telling me about or not. Is he — do you think, uncle — is he much nicer than Alick?

DANIEL: Nicer? (*He looks at his niece, and then begins to divine the way her feelings lie.*) Well, of course we have all our opinions on these things you know Mary, but Alick — well, after all there's many a worse fellow than Alick, isn't there? (MARY *does not answer, but puts her head close to her uncle.*) Ah, yes.

MARY: (*Suddenly*) Uncle! Do you know what has happened? I heard father proposing to Miss McMinn!

DANIEL: (*Groaning*) Oh my! I knew it would happen! I knew it would happen! When? Where?

MARY: In here. I wanted to slip in quietly after leaving Alick down the loaning when I overheard the voices. It was father and Miss McMinn. She was telling him how she had saved five pounds on butter last half year, and ten pounds on eggs this year, and then father asked her to marry him. I knocked at the door out of divilment, and she just pitched herself at him. I — I'm not going to stay in the house with that woman. I'd sooner marry Alick McCready.

DANIEL: (*Despairingly*) I would myself. I daren't — I couldn't face the look of that woman in the mornings.

MARY: It's all right for you to talk, uncle. You'll be working away at your inventions, and that sort of thing, and will have nothing much to do with her, but I'd be under her thumb all the time. And I hate her, and I know she hates me. (*Tearfully*) And then the way father talks about her being such a fine housekeeper, and about the waste that goes on in this house, it nearly makes me cry, just because I have been a bit careless maybe. But I could manage a house every bit as well as she could, and I'd show father that if I only got another chance. Couldn't I uncle?

DANIEL: (*Soothingly*) And far better, Mary. Far better.

MARY: And you could do far more at your invention if you only got a chance. Couldn't you, uncle?

DANIEL: No doubt about it, Mary. None. I never got much of a chance here.

MARY: I wonder could we both try to get another chance. (*Suddenly, with animation*) Uncle!

DANIEL: Well?

MARY: Aren't you going to explain that fan bellows thing you've been working at to them when they come in? (DANIEL *nods sadly.*) Well, look. That Scotchman — he understands things like that, and that's just the reason why that nasty woman brought him over. Just to trip you and show you up, and she thinks she'll make father see through you. But just you rise to the occasion and astonish them. Eh, uncle?

DANIEL: (*Uneasily*) Um — well, I don't know. That Scotchman's rather a dense sort of fellow. Very hard to get on with somehow.

MARY: Now, Uncle Dan, it's our last chance. Let us beat that woman somehow or other.

DANIEL: It's all very well, Mary, to talk that way. (*Suddenly*) I wonder is there a book on machinery in the house?

MARY: Machinery? Let me think. Yes, I do believe Kate was reading some book yesterday about things, and there was something about machinery in it.

DANIEL: For Heaven's sake, Mary, get it.

MARY: (*Calling*) Kate! Are you there, Kate? (KATE *comes in from the inner rooms.*) Where's that book you were reading last night, Kate?

KATE: (*Surprised*) For dear's sake, Miss! Yon dirty old thing! The one with the big talk between the old fellow and the son about everything in the world you could think of?

MARY: Yes, yes. Uncle Dan wants it. (KATE *fetches a tattered volume from the dresser and hands it to* DANIEL. DANIEL *opens it, and reads while the two girls peer over his shoulder.*)

DANIEL: (*Reading slowly*) 'The Child's Educator. A series of conversations between Charles and his father regarding the natural philosophy, as revealed to us, by the Very Reverend Ezekiel Johnston'.

KATE: (*Much interested*) Aye. Just go on till you see Mr Dan. It's the queerest conversation between an old lad and his son ever you heard tell of.

DANIEL: (*Reading*) Ah! 'The simple forms of machines. The lever, the wedge, the inclined plane — Father — and here we come to further consider the application of this principle, my dear Charles, to what is known as the differential wheel and axle. Um Charles — Father — Charles. Father.' (*He looks up despairingly at* MARY.) No good, my dear. Out of date. (*He, however, resumes reading the book carefully.*)

KATE: (*Nudging* MARY *and pointing to the door into the rooms*) She's going into all the cupboards and drawers, and looking at everything. (*She turns to go back and opens the door to pass through.*) I never seen such a woman.

MARY: (*Raising her voice so as to let* SARAH *hear her*) Just keep an eye on her, Kate, and see she doesn't take anything.

DANIEL: I might get something out of this. Atmosphere. Pressure.

MARY: Uncle Dan. (*He pays no attention, but is absorbed in the book.*) Uncle Dan, I'm going down the loaning a pace. Alick said he might be back, and I think — (*She sees he is not listening, and slips back to look over his shoulder.*)

DANIEL: (*Reading*) Charles. And now my dear father, after discussing in such clear and lucid terms the use of the barometer, and how it is constructed, could you tell me or explain the meaning of the word 'pneumatic'.

MARY: (*Going towards the yard door*) Good luck, Uncle Danny. I'm away. (*She goes out.*)

DANIEL: There's not much here about bellows. (*Hopelessly*) I wish I had made up this subject a little better. (KATE *comes in evidently much perturbed and angry.*)

KATE: The divil take her and them remarks of hers. Who gave her the right to go searching that way, I wonder? Where's the silver kept, and was it locked, and how many spoons was there, and why weren't they better polished; and part of the china broke.

SARAH: (*Comes to the door speaking. As soon as* DANIEL *hears her voice he hurriedly retreats across to the workshop.*) Where do you keep the knives and forks?

KATE: You don't want forks for the tea.

SARAH: I want to count them.

KATE: (*In amazement*) Oh, God save us! You'd think there was a pross on the house! (*She follows* SARAH *in through the door.* MACKENZIE *comes in, followed by* JOHN, *then* ANDY.)

MACKENZIE: And it was a great idea, you know. The steam passed through the condenser, and the exhaust was never open to the atmosphere.

JOHN: (*Evidently much impressed, and repeating the word in a wondering manner*) Aye. The exhaust!

MACKENZIE: Aye. The exhaust. But now I'm verra anxious to hear your brother explaining what he's made out about the bellows. It's the small things like that you ken that a man makes a fortune of, not the big ones.

JOHN: (*Impressed*) Do you think that now?

MACKENZIE: You know I take a particular interest in bellows myself. I tried my hand a good while working out a new kind of bellows, and I flatter myself that I know something about the subject.

JOHN: Aye. (*Looking round*) Where's Daniel? Daniel! Are you there, Daniel? (DANIEL *comes out and stands near the door.*) You could maybe bring them plans out you're working at and explain it to them now, Daniel. Eh? And wait, Sarah wants to hear it too. (*Calling*) Are you there, Sarah?

DANIEL: (*Seating himself sadly*) Aye. She's in there somewhere taking stock.

JOHN: (*Going next the door to the rooms*) Are you there, dear? (SARAH *comes out.*) Daniel's going to explain the thing to us, and you wanted to hear about it. Didn't you?

SARAH: I'm just dying to know all about it. (*She seats herself to the right at the back.* ANDY *sits on one side of the table and* MACKENZIE *at the other, expectantly, while* JOHN *goes over to the fireplace almost opposite his brother.*) You know, Mr Daniel, that's one thing we want very bad in our house — a good fan bellows.

DANIEL: They are very useful, very.

JOHN: Aye. They are that. (*To* SARAH) He has a good head on him, Daniel. Eh? (*To* DANIEL) Now go on and make it very plain so that every one can follow you. Bring out the plans and show us.

DANIEL: (*Uneasily*) I can explain it better without them. (*After a pause.*) Well, I suppose this subject of bellows would come under the heading of pneumatics in natural philosophy.

JOHN: Oh, now, don't be going off that way. Could you not make it plainer nor that?

DANIEL: (*Appealingly*) Well. Could I be much plainer, Mr Mackenzie?

MACKENZIE: (*Cynically*) I'm here to discuss fan bellows, not pneumatics.

DANIEL: (*Sotto voce*) D—n him. (*He pulls himself together.*) Well. Then I suppose the first thing is — well — to know what is a bellows.

ANDY: Aye. Man, Daniel, you start off just the same as the clergy. That's the way they always goes on expounding things to you.

SARAH: (*Severely*) Don't be interrupting, Andy.

MACKENZIE: (*Sneeringly*) Well, I think everyone here knows what a bellows is.

DANIEL: Everyone here? Do you, John?

JOHN: Aye. I would like, Daniel, to hear right what a bellows is. I mean I can see the thing blowing up a fire when you use it, any man could see that — but its the workings of it. What's the arrangements and internal works of the bellows now, Daniel?

DANIEL: Well, you push the handles together in an ordinary bellows and — and the air — blows out. (*Seeing that this statement is received coldly*) Now, why does it blow out?

JOHN: (*Disappointedly*) Because it's pushed out of course. There's no sense in asking that sort of a question.

DANIEL: Well, there's a flap on the bellows — a thing that moves up and down. Well, that flap has all to do with pushing the air.

JOHN: Maybe this scientifican business is uninteresting to you, Sarah, is it?

DANIEL: (*Brightening up at the suggestion*) I'm sure it is. Perhaps we better stop.

SARAH: (*Smiling grimly.*) Oh, not at all. I want to hear more.

MACKENZIE: You're wasting a lot of my time, Mr Murray. I came here to hear about a fan bellows.

DANIEL: (*Confusedly*) Oh, yes. Yes. Certainly. Fan bellows. There's a difference between a fan bellows and an ordinary bellows.

MARY: (*Opening door from yard and coming in*) Oh, Uncle Dan, are you explaining it to them. Did I miss much of it?

MACKENZIE: I don't think it matters much what time you come in during this.

JOHN: (*Impatiently*) Go on, Daniel.

DANIEL: It's very hard for me to go on with these constant interruptions. Well, I was just saying there was a difference between a fan bellows and an ordinary bellows.

MACKENZIE: Now, what is a fan bellows yourself, Mr Murray?

DANIEL: (*Hopelessly*) A fan bellows? Ah. Why now is it called a fan bellows?

MACKENZIE: (*Roughly*) Don't be asking me my own questions.

DANIEL: (*With a despairing effort*) Well, now we will take it for granted it is because there must be something of the nature of a fan about a fan bellows. It is because there are fans inside the casing. And the handle being turned causes these — eh — fans to turn round too. And then the air comes out with a rush.

JOHN: Aye. It must be the fans that pushes it out.

DANIEL: Exactly. Well, now, the difficulty we find here is — (*He pauses.*)

ANDY: Aye.

JOHN: Go on, Daniel.

DANIEL: You want a constant draught blowing. That's number

one. Then — well — the other. You see, if we took some of these fans.

MACKENZIE: Yes.

DANIEL: (*In a floundering way*) And put them in a tight-fitting case, and put more of them inside, and understood exactly what their size was, we could arrange for the way that —

JOHN: (*In a puzzled way to* SARAH) I can only follow Daniel a short way too. (*Repeating slowly*) Put them in a tight-fitting case —

BROWN: (*Appearing at the yard door with a telegram in his hand, and speaking with suppressed excitement*) A telegram for Mr Daniel.

DANIEL: (*With a gasp of relief.*) Ah! (*He tears it open and proudly reads it out aloud.*) 'Come to London at once to explain patent. Want to purchase. Gregg.'

(BROWN *goes out again.*)

MACKENZIE: Who? Gregg?

DANIEL: I suppose I better go, John?

JOHN: Let's see the telegram. (*He goes over to* DANIEL, *who hands it to him.*)

MACKENZIE: If you go to London, it'll take you to explain yourself a bit better, Mr Murray.

JOHN: (*Who has resumed his place at the fire, and is looking carefully at the telegram.*) That will mean how many pounds, Daniel, did you say?

DANIEL: (*Promptly*) Fifteen, John.

(MARY *goes out by the door to the rooms.*)

MACKENZIE: Who is Gregg?

DANIEL: Gregg? Ah. He's a man lives in London. Engineer.

JOHN: (*Dubiously*) Well, I suppose you — (*He pauses, then hands the telegram to* SARAH, *who stretches out her hand for it.*)

MARY: (*At the door.*) Tea's ready. (*She stands aside to let the company past.*)

SARAH: We didn't hear all about the bellows.

ANDY: (*Contemptuously*) No, nor you never will. (*He rises and goes through the door.*)

MACKENZIE: (*Rising and stretching himself wearily*) Any more, Mr Murray?

DANIEL: I refuse to discuss the matter any further in public. (*He goes off across to tea.*)

MACKENZIE: (*Going over to* JOHN *and looking at him knowingly*) Do you know what it is, Mr Murray? Your brother's nothing short of an impostor.

JOHN: (*Much offended*) Don't dare to say that of a Murray.

MACKENZIE: (*Shrugging his shoulders*) Well, I'm going for some tea. (*Exit.*)

SARAH: John, I've something to say to you again about Daniel, but the company's waiting. (*She goes out to the tea room.*)

JOHN: (*Sitting down moodily*) Aye.

MARY: Are you not coming, father?

JOHN: Aye.

MARY: Father! Surely you aren't going to marry that woman?

JOHN: Don't talk of Sarah that ways. I am!

MARY: Well, if you are, I'm going to say yes to Alick McCready. I don't want to yet awhile, but I'm not going to stay on here if that nasty woman comes. (*She kneels close beside her father and puts her arms round his neck.*) Oh, father, if you only give me another chance, I could show you I could keep house every bit as well as that woman. (DANIEL *appears at the door. He slips across to the workshop unobserved.*) Give me another chance, father. Don't marry her at all. Let me stay with you — won't you?

JOHN: You're too late. She's trothed to me now.

MARY: Pooh. I'd think nothing of that. (DANIEL *comes out of the workshop with a bag.*) Uncle Dan! What's the matter.

DANIEL: Mary, I can't eat and sit beside that Scotchman. (*He notices* JOHN *is absorbed in deep thought, and motions* MARY *to slip out. She does so, and he looks observingly at* JOHN, *and then goes to the table, and makes a noise with the bag on the table.* JOHN *watches him a moment or two in amazed silence.*)

JOHN: What are you doing, Daniel?

DANIEL: Just making a few preparations.

JOHN: Ah, but look here. I haven't settled about London yet, Daniel.

DANIEL: Oh, London, John. (*Deprecatingly*) Let that pass. I won't worry you about that. (*Broken-heartedly*) I'm leaving your house, John.

JOHN: (*Astonished*) What?

DANIEL: You've been kind, John. Very kind. We always pulled well together, and never had much cross words with one another, but — well, circumstances are altered now.

JOHN: You mean because I'm going to marry Sarah.

DANIEL: Exactly. That puts an end to our long and pleasant sojourn here together. I'll have to go.

JOHN: (*Affected*) Oh easy, Daniel. Ah, now, Sarah always liked you. She thinks a deal of you, and I'm sure she'd miss you out of the house as much as myself.

DANIEL: John, I know better. She wants me out of this, and I would only be a source of unhappiness. I wouldn't like to cause you sorrow. She doesn't believe in me. She brought that Scotchman over to try and show me up. You all think he did. You think I mugged the thing. You don't believe in me now yourself. (*He puts a few articles of clothing, etc., into the bag.*)

JOHN: (*Awkwardly*) Aye. Well — to tell you the truth, Daniel, you did not make much of a hand at explaining, you —

DANIEL: (*Pathetically*) I thought so. Look here. One word. (*He draws* JOHN *aside.*) Do you think Mackenzie invented that patent reciprocating piston that he's so proud of?

JOHN: (*Looking at him in amazement*) What?

DANIEL: (*Impressively*) Well. I know something about that. He stole it off another man, and took all the profits. I knew that. Do you think I'm going to give away the product of my brains explaining it to a man like that! No fear, John. (*He turns again to the bag.*) I'm taking details of my bellows, and my coat, and a few socks, and the pound you gave me yesterday, and I'm going to face the world alone.

JOHN: (*Moved*) No, no. You'll not leave me, Daniel. Ah, no. I never meant that.

DANIEL: If she's coming here I'll have to go, and may as well now.

SARAH: (*Without*) John Murray!

DANIEL: (*Retreating slowly to the workshop*) I'm going to get that other coat you gave me. It's better than this one for seeing people in. (*He goes into the workshop as* SARAH *comes out into the kitchen. She is evidently displeased.*)

SARAH: Hurry up, John. The company's waiting on you, and I don't know what's keeping you. Unless it was that brother of yours, more shame to him.

JOHN: Aye. Daniel kept me. (*Looking at her*) He's talking of leaving. You wouldn't have that, Sarah, would you?

SARAH: (*Sharply*) Leaving, is he? And a right good riddance say I. What has he done but ate up all your substance.

JOHN: (*Astonished*) You wouldn't put him out, Sarah?

SARAH: (*Snappishly*) I just wouldn't have him about the place. An idle, good-for-nothing, useless, old pull-a-cork.

JOHN: Do you not like him, Sarah? (*Somewhat disapprovingly*) You told me you thought a good deal of him before.

SARAH: Aye. Until I seen through him. Him and his letters and telegrams. Just look at that. (*She shows him the telegram.*) It comes from Ballyannis.

JOHN: (*Scratching his head in puzzled wonder*) I don't understand that.

SARAH: He just put up someone to send it. Young McCready or someone. You couldn't watch a man like that. No. If I come here, out he goes. You expects me to come and save you money and the like of that old bauchle eating up the profits. (*She goes towards the door into tea room.*) Come into your tea at once. (*Exit.*)

JOHN: By me sang he was right. (DANIEL *comes out and starts brushing his coat loudly to attract* JOHN'S *attention, and then goes across towards him and holds out his hand.*)

DANIEL: I'll say good-bye, John. Maybe I'll never see you again. (*He appears much affected.*)

JOHN: (*Touched*) Ach. Take your time. I don't see the sense of this hurrying. Stop a week or two, man. I'll be lonesome without you. We had many a good crack in the evenings, Daniel.

DANIEL: We had, John. And I suppose now that you'll be married I'll have to go, but many a time I'll be sitting lonely and thinking of them.

JOHN: Aye. You were always the best of company, and heartsome. You were, Daniel.

DANIEL: Well, I did my best, John, to keep — (*He half breaks down*) — to keep up a good heart.

JOHN: You did. I wouldn't like to lose you, Daniel. (*He looks at the telegram in his hand.*) But Daniel. This telegram. It comes from Ballyannis.

DANIEL: (*Taken aback, but recovering his self-possession*) Ballyannis? Ballyannis? Ah, of course. Sure Gregg, that London man, he was to go through Ballyannis to-day. He's on a visit, you know, somewhere this way. It's him I'm going to look for now.

JOHN: Was that the way of it? (*With rising anger at the thought of the way in which his brother has been treated*) And she was for making you out an impostor and for putting you out. I didn't like them talking of a Murray the way they done.

DANIEL: (*With sudden hope*) Are you engaged to that McMinn woman, John?

JOHN: Aye. I spoke the word the day.

DANIEL: Was there anybody there when you asked her?

JOHN: There was no-one.

DANIEL: Did you write her letters?

JOHN: No. Not a line.

DANIEL: And did you visit and court much at the home?

JOHN: No. I always seen Andy on business and stopped to have a word or two with her.

DANIEL: (*Appealingly*) Then, John, John, it's not too late yet. (*Desperately*) Give me — ah, give wee Mary another chance.

SARAH: (*At the door.*) Come in, John, at once. Your tea's cold waiting, and its no way to entertain company that.

JOHN: (*Angrily*) D—n her. Daniel! Out of this home you will not go. I'd rather have your crack of a winter night as two hundred pounds in the bank and yon woman. (*He reaches out his hand.*) I'll break the match. (*The two men shake hands.*)

(CURTAIN)

ACT THREE

The same scene two weeks later. The curtain rises to discover MARY *seated near table reading a cookery book to* KATE, *who, paying but little attention, is watching a pot boiling on the fire.*

MARY: Listen, Kate, to this. 'A most desirable addition to this most appetising dish from the point of view of a gourmet'

KATE: A what, Miss?

MARY: A gourmet.

KATE: Now what kind of a thing would that be.

MARY: It's French for a cook or something — I forget — 'a most desirable addition to this dish from the point of view of a —' (*The yard door opens, and* SAM BROWN *appears with letters in his hand.* MARY *immediately throws the book aside and rushes over to him.*)

MARY: Letters! Any for me, Sam?

BROWN: Aye. There's a post card for you, Miss Mary, and a registered letter for Mr John. The posty says he'll call on the road back for the account when you sign it. (*He hands the post card to* MARY *and looks carefully at the letter.*) It's like the McMinn writing that. (*He looks at* MARY, *who is reading and re-reading the postcard with a puzzled expression.*) Isn't Mr Dan to be home to-day from Belfast, Miss Mary?

MARY: Eh?

BROWN: Isn't Mr Dan expected home to-day from Belfast?

MARY: Yes.

BROWN: I wonder did he get the bellows sold? There was great talking about him last night in McArns. Some said he had sold it and made a fortune. (*He breaks off abruptly on seeing that* MARY *pays no attention to him, and then peers over to see what she is reading.*) Post cards is interesting things. Picture post cards is.

KATE: Go on out of this. We're tired hearing your gabble.

BROWN: (*Retreating to door and eyeing* KATE *meaningly*) The master was complaining again to me yesterday evening about the dinner he got. There's no mistake he likes his meat like myself, and right enough it was bad yesterday. I was chowing haws all evening to keep off the hunger.

KATE: And couldn't you have made it up with bread? There's plenty of soda bread.

BROWN: Bread? Soda bread? Aye. There's plenty of soda, God knows, but you couldn't call it bread.

MARY: (*Who has been listening to the latter part of the conversation, starts suddenly up, takes a piece of soda bread off the table and bites it hastily.*) Oh, Kate!

BROWN: Aye. It's soda bread, miss, and no mistake.

KATE: You would bake it yourself, you know, miss. I throwed the most of it out yesterday, and the hens wouldn't as much as look at it. (*Seeing* MARY *is almost on the point of tears*) Ach, never mind, Miss Mary. (*She looks at* BROWN, *who is listening.*) Go on you out of this.

BROWN: That's all the news this morning. (*He makes a grimace at* KATE *and goes out into the yard.*)

MARY: I can't understand this post card. (KATE *goes over and looks at it along with* MARY.)

'O wad that God the gift wad gie us,
To see oorselves as ithers see us.'

What does that mean? 'How's the uncle.' It's some cheeky person anyway — 'from D.M.' Who could that be?

KATE: It's not McCready, Miss, is it?

MARY: No. That's not his writing.

KATE: Och, Miss Mary! Do you see the picture of the Highland man dancing, and under it — 'A Mackenzie Clansman.' It's thon Scotch fellow sent it.

MARY: Just like the way he would do. I met him again one night we were over at the doctor's, and he was trying to make up to me all he was able.

KATE: Aye. You might do worse than take him.

MARY: I'll hand him over to you, Kate.

KATE: Ah, no, Miss. Thank you kindly all the same. Any word from Mr Dan about the boy he was to bring you?

MARY: No. I'm not going to bother any more about boys. I'm going to keep house from this on properly. But Uncle Dan said something in his last letter about a great surprise he had for all of us.

KATE: Surprise enough it will be, and he lands home with a ha'penny in his pocket. The last time he come home he borrowed a shilling of me and niver paid me back yet. Did he sell the plans of the bellows, Miss?

MARY: He didn't say. (JOHN MURRAY *comes through the yard door. He has evidently been working outside and has left his work in a hurry.*) Father, there's a letter for you. (*She hands it to him.*) A registered one too.

JOHN: Aye. So Brown was telling me. Maybe it's from thon McAlenan fellow that owes me two pound for the heifer. (*He tears it open.* MARY *and* KATE *watch him with interest. His face changes as he reads, and an expression of dismay comes over it.*)

MARY: (*Coming closer to him*) What's the matter, father?

JOHN: (*Fidgeting uneasily*) Nothing, child. Nothing. (*He looks at the letter again.*) Well I'm — (*He stops short on remembering* MARY *is there.*) She's a caution.

MARY: Father. Tell me. Is it from the McMinns?

JOHN: Aye. (*Pacing up and down*) I knowed she'd do it. I knowed she'd do it.

MARY: What?

JOHN: Sarah's taking an action against me.

MARY: An action?

JOHN: Aye. (*Consulting the letter*) For a thousand pounds.

MARY: (*Awestruck*) A thousand pounds!

JOHN: Aye. Now the fat's in the fire. She says I promised to marry her and broke it off. At least, it's Andy that writes the letter, but it's her that put him up to it. I know that too well. (*Reading*) 'To Mr John Murray. Dear Sir, You have acted to my sister in a most ungentlemanly way, and done her much wrong, and I have put the case intil the hands of Mr McAllen, the solicitor, who will bring it forward at the coming Assizes. If you wish, however, to avoid a scandal, we are open to settle the matter by private arrangement. Yours truly, Andrew McMinn.'

MARY: That's awful, father, isn't it? (*She sits down pensively.*)

JOHN: (*Going over to fireplace and standing there irresolutely*) Aye. It's a terrible mess, right enough.

MARY: (*Brightening up*) Sure she wouldn't get a thousand off you, father?

KATE: There's John McArdle up by Slaney Cross got a hundred pounds took off him by wee Miss Black, the school teacher.

JOHN: (*Uncomfortably*) Aye. Heth now, I just call that to mind. And he never got courting at all, I believe.

KATE: It just served him right. He was always a great man for having five or six girls running after him.

JOHN: And she hadn't much of a case against him.

KATE: The school children were standing by when he asked her in a joking sort of way would she marry him, and the court took their evidence!

JOHN: (*Hopelessly*) Aye. Men are always terrible hard on other men where women are concerned.

KATE: And a good job it is, or half the girls would be at the church waiting, and the groom lying at home ruing his bargain. (*She goes out by the yard door.*)

MARY: (*Going up to her father*) Father, has she a good case against you?

JOHN: (*After a moment of deep thought.*) No. I don't think it.

MARY: Don't worry so much then, father.

JOHN: It's the jury I'm so frightened of. They all come from the mountainy district at this Assizes, and there's not a man of them but wouldn't put a knife in me, the way I get beating them down in price at the fairs.

MARY: I don't think they'd give her fifty pounds when they see her. It's only good-looking girls would get big sums like a thousand pounds.

JOHN: It's all very well, Mary, but she could dress herself to look nice enough, the same Sarah, if she liked.

MARY: She could not, indeed.

JOHN: They say, at least Brown was hinting to me, that its yon Scotch fellow, Mackenzie, has put up the McMinns to this business. He and that connection are as thick as thieves.

MARY: He mightn't be so very fond of them. When a man sends post cards to a girl he doesn't know very well he's got a wee bit of a liking for her.

JOHN: What are you talking about? I never sent her any post cards.

MARY: Father, what are you going to do?

JOHN: (*Despairingly*) I'm d—d if I know.

MARY: Will you defend the case?

JOHN: I don't want to go near the court at all.

MARY: Father! (*Alarmed*) Father! Sure you wouldn't — you couldn't think of marrying her after all that row that happened? (JOHN *remains silent.*) Wouldn't you rather lose a thousand pounds and keep me, father? (JOHN *breaks a piece of soda bread morosely and eats it.*) Wouldn't you, father.

JOHN: Ah! (*He spits out the bread.*) Heaven save us, what kind of bread's that?

MARY: (*Taking away the bread and putting it behind her back*) Father! Ah please, please, don't marry her anyway. Sure you won't?

JOHN: (*Softening*) There, there, child. I'll think about it.

BROWN: (*Coming in hastily*) Here's Mr Dan coming up the loaning, sir, that grand looking you'd hardly know him, and a big cigar in his mouth.

JOHN: Daniel back?

MARY: Oh, I must go out and meet him. (*She goes out by the yard door quickly.*)

JOHN: Had he his luggage with him?

BROWN: Aye. He has yon big portmanteau of his, and a parcel of something or other.

JOHN: Away out and help him then, can't you? (BROWN *goes out.*) I wonder what kept him in Belfast all this time. I suppose he's spent most of the five pounds I gave him. Like enough. I never mind him coming back yet with a ha'penny on him. (*He sits down at the fireplace and looks again at the letter.*) A thousand pounds! And there never was a breach of promise case known where they didn't bring in a verdict for the woman. Never! (*He becomes absorbed in thought, and as he sits ruminating* MARY *opens the door, carrying a large brown paper parcel, followed by* DANIEL. DANIEL *is dressed fairly well, and seems to be in high spirits.* BROWN *follows him carrying a portmanteau.*)

DANIEL: (*Brightly*) Home again, John.

JOHN: (*Morosely*) Aye. It was near time, I think.

DANIEL: Saw quite a number of people this time, John. A great number. They were all very much interested. Fine town, Belfast. Growing very rapidly. Wonderful place.

MARY: Take me with you when you go again, Uncle Dan, won't you? What's in the parcel? (*She looks at it with great curiosity.*)

DANIEL: Ah, that — that's the great secret. Mum's the word. All in good time, Mary.

MARY: It's a secret? (*She looks at it again wonderingly.*)

DANIEL: Yes.

BROWN: Will I leave your bag here, Mr Dan?

DANIEL: Yes. Here's a sixpence for you. (*He hands it to* BROWN, *who salutes and goes out grinning.*)

JOHN: You're brave and free-handed with your money. Giving the like of that bauchle sixpence. The Lord knows but we will be wanting every ha'penny we can scrape together, and soon enough.

MARY: I didn't tell Uncle Dan yet, father.

DANIEL: (*Seating himself near the workshop door*) Has anything happened?

MARY: Yes. Sarah McMinn has —

JOHN: Read that letter, Daniel. (*He goes across and hands* DANIEL *the letter, and goes back to the fireplace to watch him.*)

DANIEL: (*Taking out his glasses and solemnly perusing the letter*) Um.

JOHN: Well? What do you think of that?

DANIEL: (*Endeavouring to appear cheerful*) Keep up a stout heart, John. You're safe enough.

JOHN: Oh, heth, I'm not so sure of that. Sure you never heard tell of a jury yet that didn't give damages against the defendant in a breach of promise case. Did you now?

DANIEL: Tuts, man. She has no case.

JOHN: Case or no case it doesn't seem to matter. What sort of case had Jennie Black against John McArdle, of Slaney Cross? None. What sort of case had Maggie McAndless against old William Boyd? None at all. I was at both of them trials, and says I to Pat McAleenan — 'the girl has no case at all!' But for all that they brought in a verdict for one hundred pounds against McArdle, and they put two hundred against old Boyd, and nearly broke the two of them.

DANIEL: It's very awkward this.

JOHN: Did you do anything, Daniel, about the bellows?

DANIEL: The bellows? Aye. (*He points at the parcel.*) A good deal, John. It's all there. But it's all not quite settled yet. A day or two more and you'll see. If all goes well I'll have a great surprise for you in a day or two.

JOHN: (*Disgustedly*) Ach! I suppose you spent every ha'penny of the money, too, that I gave you?

DANIEL: John. Another surprise for you! Those people I met and went to, put me up very cheap for the week. Very cheap. (*He produces some money.*) There's one pound ten and sixpence for you.

JOHN: What?

DANIEL: I'll keep the pound to do me to the end of the month and not ask you for any more, John, after that. That is if — well — (*He looks at the parcel.*) That thing there is all right.

JOHN: (*Pocketing the ten and sixpence after counting it carefully*) Daniel I'm sorry, but there's an account of some thirty shillings I owe the McArdles, and I want to pay it the night. So if you don't mind — (*He holds out his hand.*)

DANIEL: (*Unwillingly*) Well, I suppose it can't be helped, John. But it leaves me just with nothing. However, there you are. (*He hands the pound over to him.* SAM BROWN *opens the yard door and peeps in cautiously.*)

JOHN: (*Looking at him angrily*) What ails you anyway?

BROWN: If you please, sir, the posty wants the account signed for that letter.

MARY: Oh, I forgot all about it. (*She picks up the receipt for the letter from the table.*) I'll sign it for you, father. (*She goes over to* BROWN, *who whispers something. She nods.*) And I'll give it to him myself. (*She goes out following* BROWN.)

JOHN: It's a serious business, this, about the McMinns.

DANIEL: You're all right, man. Wait a day or two. Take my advice. Do nothing in a hurry. Sit down and think it over the way I do when I'm working out a new idea. Don't rush things. It will all come right in the end. Just you wait and see if it doesn't.

JOHN: Would it not be better to settle before going into the court? You know I couldn't stand being pointed out to of a Sunday morning and one and another talking — 'There's the man that Sarah McMinn took the breach of promise case against.' No, I couldn't stand that at all. It would be a disgrace to the Murrays for ever. I'm wondering now — (*He pauses lost in thought.*)

DANIEL: (*Alarmed*) John. Surely you wouldn't — you couldn't think of going back on what you said to me. Would you?

JOHN: I wonder, Daniel, would you mind so much after all if I married her?

DANIEL: (*In an agonised voice*) I couldn't stand it. No, John, I couldn't stay. Any other woman but that McMinn.

MARY: (*Appearing at the door followed by* ALICK MCCREADY) Come on in, Alick.

ALICK: Good morning, Mr Murray. How are you, Mr Dan? So you are back again? We're all glad to have you back.

DANIEL: Thank you, Alick.

MARY: Father. Alick says he heard Andy McMinn talking yesterday to some one at McArdle's shop, and he was telling them all about the whole business, and blaming it all on Uncle Dan.

JOHN: And so the people are talking of me already? Now that I come to think of it, it was your Uncle Dan, and a brave ha'penny it's going to cost me. One thousand pounds!

ALICK: Never mind, Mr Murray. Maybe Uncle Dan will do something yet. What about the bellows? (*Dan makes a horrified movement to stop Alick talking, but too late.*)

JOHN: Aye. Here, Daniel. I'll make a bargain with you. I'll leave you to the settling of the case, and you can find the money yourself to pay for it if you want to. And if you can't find the money, I'll marry her.

MARY: Father, surely —

JOHN: What? That's enough about it. I would as soon do without the marrying if I could. I don't want the woman at all, but I'll marry her before she gets a ha'penny off me. So you can settle it among yourselves. You can take charge of that letter, Dan, and make the best you can of it. (*He goes angrily out by the yard door.*)

DANIEL: This is a nice mess you put me in for, Alick. What the divil made you mention the bellows?

ALICK: I'm sorry, Mr Dan. I wasn't thinking.

DANIEL: The sooner you start and think a bit the better. If you don't help to settle the case — (*He looks angrily at* ALICK) — well — I've a good deal of influence with somebody. (*He looks significantly at* MARY, *who is again examining the parcel.*)

ALICK: I'll do my best, Mr Dan, to help you.

MARY: What will we do, Uncle Dan?

DANIEL: I suppose you've no money, Alick?

ALICK: Well, I haven't much ready money, Mr Dan, but I could lend you up to twenty pounds at a pinch.

MARY: Twenty pounds would hardly be enough. Would it, uncle?

ALICK: Better get hold of Andy and ask him.

DANIEL: I don't like going near that woman at all.

MARY: Alick! Could you not slip over and ask Andy to come across? You know what the McMinns are like. He'd come over for a shilling if he thought he'd get one. Ah, yes. You will, Alick. Won't you?

ALICK: I'll go straight across now if you — if you —

MARY: What?

ALICK: If you'd leave us along the road a bit.

MARY: Ach, you're a bother.

(DANIEL *goes over to the table, lifts the parcel, and then goes and sits down near the fireplace.*)

ALICK: Leave us a wee bit of the way, anyway. (*He goes towards the door and beckons her. She goes out after him.*)

DANIEL: (*Feeling the parcel*) I'm afraid, Dan Murray, it's all U. P. this time. I'm afraid it is. (*Then an idea seems to dawn on him, and he looks at the parcel.*) Unless — unless — well — I wonder now if I —

(KATE *and* BROWN *enter through yard door.* BROWN *is carrying a bucket filled with washed potatoes.*)

KATE: There. Put it down there. You didn't know we wanted that much, did you not? You're getting as big an old liar as Mr — (*She stops short on perceiving* DANIEL.)

BROWN: (*Looking up and then realising what had made her pause*) Aye. Go on. As who do you say, woman?

KATE: (*Recovering herself*) Just as big an old liar as Andy McMinn.

BROWN: Now, whist. The McMinns were aye decent folk. (*He glances across at* DANIEL, *who apparently is not listening.*) They're near people, and all that sort of thing, but once they say a thing they stick to it.

KATE: They're a lot of mean scrubs, the whole caboosh of them.

BROWN: (*Nudging* KATE *slyly*) I believe that once Sarah puts a price on a thing like a pig or a sow, or a hen, the divil himself couldn't beat her down in the price of it. She can beat the best dealer in the county from here to the Mourne. (DANIEL, *who has been listening uneasily, gets up and turns round to look at them.*) It's the fine cigar that you were smoking, Mr Daniel, this morning.

DANIEL: Cigar? Yes. Yes.

BROWN: Aye. A fine cigar, sir. There was a grand smell off it. I seen you coming up by the McMinns, sir, this morning on the road from the station.

DANIEL: Yes. On the road from the station.

BROWN: You didn't see them, but I noticed Andy and Sarah coming out to the gate when you had passed them and looking after you a long time.

DANIEL: Is that so?

BROWN: Aye. A long time, sir. I suppose, like myself, they smelled the cigar. Mr Andy, they say, is guy fond of a good cigar, and I understand that he'll be for getting a few boxes of them soon, for the sister, they say, is coming into a lot of money. It's well for the people can afford the like of them things.

KATE: Will you hold your tongue. There! I want no more of you now. You're only a nuisance in the house anyway. Go out and clatter to somebody else. I wonder the master didn't sack you long ago.

BROWN: The master? (*He retreats slowly to the yard door.*) The master knows to keep a good man when he gets one. He doesn't part soft with either good men or money. God bless him. (*He goes out.*)

KATE: Will I make you a drop of tea, Mr Dan? You'll be tired travelling.

DANIEL: It's hard to eat anything, Kate, when I'm worried. (*Despairingly*) I don't think there's another man living has the same worries as I have. Something awful! Where's the pen and ink, I wonder?

KATE: There's some here on the dresser, Miss Mary was using it today. (*She takes it over from the dresser to the table.* DANIEL *rises and goes over and sits down and begins slowly to write.*) Cheer up, Mr Daniel. Sure you sold the plans of the bellows anyway. Didn't you, sir? They had word up at the McAleenans the other night that you got two thousand for it.

DANIEL: (*Astonished*) Eh? They said that?

KATE: Aye. To be sure. McAndless told McArdle, and he told Smith the postman, and the postman told the McAleenans, and said he had seen letters about it. And McAleenan was up in McMinns the other night and told them, and I believe you never saw such an astonished crowd of people in all your lives.

DANIEL: He told the McMinns?

KATE: Aye, last night I think it was.

DANIEL: Last night? (*He looks at the letter.*) Yesterday was the 14th, wasn't it? Aye. It was. I wonder did they believe McAleenan?

KATE: I don't think they know right what to make of it. And yon Scotchman was there at the time, and mind you, Mr Dan, they say he looked quite serious when he heard it, and said such things as that happened many's a time.

DANIEL: (*Incredulously*) Mackenzie said that?

KATE: Aye. You know, I think its maybe because he has a wee notion of Miss Mary, sir.

DANIEL: It's quite possible. Quite possible. A nice wee girl is Mary. Far too good for the half of them about these parts. (*He takes up the parcel, pen, and ink, and paper, and goes across into the workshop.*)

KATE: (*Looking after him*) Poor creature. I'm feared he's for the road again if he doesn't worry out some way for himself. And God knows he's the one best fitted for it. (MARY *enters.*) Well, did you see him off comfortably?

MARY: Who?

KATE: Alick McCready.

MARY: Kate I wish you'd mind your own business.

KATE: It's a sore time I have in this house minding my own and every other body's business.

MARY: Kate. He said I couldn't bake a cake to save my life. I'll just show him that I can, and you're not to help me, mind you. I'm going to do it all myself.

KATE: Very well, Miss. Anything for a bit of peace say I.

MARY: Where's that recipe book? (KATE *hands it to her, and she begins to pour over the pages.*) 'Queen pudding.'

KATE: Ah, Miss Mary, don't be trying that again. Do you not mind how bad your poor old uncle was after it?

MARY: What's this Sarah McMinn was so good at? 'Plum cakes.' I'll try a plum cake.

KATE: (*Hopelessly and to herself*) She's clean daft.

MARY: (*Consulting the book*) I'll want eggs and flour and currants and suet and —

KATE: I think if I was you, I'd try something more easy.

MARY: But plum cakes are easy.

KATE: That's what I used to think till I tried one. I give it up, Miss. It's beyond me altogether.

MARY: I think that you believe I couldn't bake anything. Where's the flour?

KATE: There's none in the house, Miss Mary.

MARY: What?

KATE: You mind it was all used up this morning on account of them cakes you were doing that turned out bad.

MARY: Go down to McArdle's, Kate, and get a quarter stone on account.

KATE: Your da told me this morning, Miss Mary, that I wasn't to get any more from McArdles or any other place unless he gives me an order for it. Do you not mind?

MARY: (*Dejectedly*) So he did. I had forgotten.

KATE: Aye. Quite so, Miss. (*She sits down contentedly.*)

MARY: I wonder is Uncle Dan about?

KATE: Aye. He's in his workshop, Miss.

MARY: (*Going over and knocking at door of workshop*) Uncle Dan!

DANIEL: (*Without*) Yes.

MARY: Please, Uncle Dan.

DANIEL: (*Appearing at door*) Well, Mary?

MARY: Uncle Dan, could you give me sixpence?

DANIEL: (*Fumbling in his pockets*) Sixpence? Sixpence, Mary? Bless your wee heart. Here. Here's a two shilling bit. But Mary, mum's the word. Don't tell John I gave it to you.

MARY: No. Thank you, uncle. (DANIEL *goes in again.*) There, Kate, quick as you can and don't stop to talk to anybody. Sure you won't? (*She hands* KATE *the money and takes up the recipe book.*)

KATE: I'm not dirty-looking — am I, Miss Mary?

MARY: (*Absorbed in the book.*) No. You'll do grand. Flour, currants, raisins — we have all that — suet — I wonder —

KATE: Ach! You and your currants. Could you not tell a body was her face clean?

MARY: It's lovely. Hurry, Kate. (KATE *shrugs her shoulders disgustedly, and goes out by yard door.*) Flour, currants — (*She goes over to the workshop door and listens*) — raisins — (*A sound as of a blast blowing can be heard.* MARY *becomes intensely interested, and, throwing aside the book, kneels down and puts her head to the keyhole.*) He's actually got something to work. (*She peeps in.*) He has, indeed. (*She laughs, knocks loudly at the door, and then runs to the other side of the kitchen.* DANIEL *opens the door and cautiously peeps out.*) Uncle Danny! Ha! Ha! Uncle Danny! (*Dancing up and down in front of the fireplace*) Uncle Dan's a wonderful man! Uncle Dan's a wonderful man!

DANIEL: (*Amazed*) What's all this?

MARY: I'm a cleverer girl than you think, Uncle Dan! I know your great surprise. I've found it out. (*In a disappointed manner*) And you never told me! (*Pouting*) I think you might have told me anyway. It wasn't at all nice of you to keep it secret from me.

DANIEL: I just wanted to give you all a surprise, Mary.

MARY: And you've actually got it to work! That's splendid, uncle, isn't it? Father will be awful proud when he hears about it. And you did it all yourself, uncle?

DANIEL: Well, I took those plans, Mary, to a handy chap, an acquaintance of mine, and we talked a long time over it, and he made it out according to my design. I'm not sure — I think it works all right. Is there a screwdriver about, I wonder, Mary?

MARY: I don't know. And did you get it sold, uncle?

DANIEL: No, Mary, but I have hopes — great hopes.

MARY: Do you think you'd get more than a thousand pounds for it?

DANIEL: Don't know, Mary, don't know. Very hard to know these things. I must have a look for that screw driver. I think John had it last working at something in the parlour. (*He goes out by door to inner rooms.*)

MARY: I wonder would it really sell for a thousand pounds? (*Knocking at yard door.*) Come in.

(DONAL MACKENZIE *opens the door and comes in.*)

MACKENZIE: Fine afternoon, Miss Murray.

MARY: (*Coldly*) Good day to you.

MACKENZIE: I'm going off to Scotland verra soon, and I thought I would call over to see you before I went off. You're no angry, are you?

MARY: No. (MACKENZIE *seats himself at the table.*)

MACKENZIE: Did you get a post card?

MARY: I got some silly thing this morning that I tore up.

MACKENZIE: I'm sorry. I'm verra fond of you, Mary.

MARY: Miss Murray, please.

MACKENZIE: A girl like you is lost here, you know. Now, if you were a Scotch lassie you would have a great time enjoying yourself. In a place like Greenock we have a theatre, and we have a music hall and a cinematograph show on Saturdays and trains to Glasgow. You could have a grand time in Scotland.

MARY: Do you really like me, Mr Mackenzie?

MACKENZIE: Verra much. Indeed I —

MARY: Well. Look here. I would like you very, very much too, if you —

MACKENZIE: If I what, bonnie Mary?

MARY: I'd even let you call me Mary, and write to me if you wanted to, if you would do me a favour.

MACKENZIE: What's the favour?

MARY: Uncle Dan has brought home his fan bellows, and it works.

MACKENZIE: (*Laughs*) The fan bellows! I think he'll never make much of a fortune of his fan bellows.

MARY: Do you ever examine new inventions?

MACKENZIE: Aye. I'm a specialist on that, you know. I'm the writer of the inventions column in the Scottish —

MARY: Yes. Yes. That's all right. I know. Are all the inventions you write about good things?

MACKENZIE: Eh? Ninety-nine per cent rotten, lassie. Ninety-nine per cent perfectly rotten. People don't invent a reciprocating piston that works every day in the week, or a fan bellows either.

MARY: But if you liked the inventor you could do him a good turn all the same?

MACKENZIE: Aye. I did that often.

MARY: Then could you do a good turn for Uncle Dan? For me?

MACKENZIE: Eh?

MARY: Uncle Dan has a fan bellows in that workshop. Go in and look at it, and examine it, and if you like me even a wee bit, you — (DANIEL *re-enters. He stops short on seeing* MACKENZIE, *and seems to become very uncomfortable.*) Uncle Dan! Mr Mackenzie's going to examine your bellows.

DANIEL: I don't allow everybody to go and look at it. No. I refuse. It's my property and no one else's.

MARY: Uncle Dan. (*She looks at him meaningly.*) Mr Mackenzie has promised to give his opinion on it.

DANIEL: It's not protected yet by patent.

MACKENZIE: Andy McMinn is coming over, Mr Murray. He has got orders from his sister to settle the case for her. Are you going to pay the money?

DANIEL: That is a matter of my own deciding. (MARY *goes over to her uncle and whispers to him.*)

MACKENZIE: Verra well. I may go. (*To* MARY) I would have done you that good turn, Miss Murray; but there's no enmity between us. And — (*Lowering his voice*) — I hope you get the best of the McMinns in the bargain. Don't give in, Mr Murray, easy. Take my tip. I'm from the stables, you know. (*He laughs knowingly.*)

MARY: Here's Andy now — (*She looks out through the window*) and Alick's with him. (*She opens the door,* ANDY MCMINN *and* MCCREADY *enter.* MCCREADY *glances at* MARY *and* MACKENZIE, *and goes over sulkily to the fireplace.* ANDY *advances awkwardly towards* DANIEL.)

DANIEL: (*Genially*) Good afternoon, Andy.

ANDY: Good afternoon. (*He looks at* MACKENZIE, *who nods curtly.*) I suppose you know I've power to settle the case.

DANIEL: Well, you wrote the letter, and so, in point of law, I think it is you who should look after all this unfortunate business. Believe me, Andy, I sympathise with you. I do indeed. (MARY *and* MACKENZIE *become absorbed in conversation near the table.* ALICK McCREADY *stands at the fireplace looking at them and unable to conceal his jealousy, makes sundry odd noises to distract* MARY'S *attention. She pretends not to hear him.*) I have your letters here. (*He searches in his pocket and produces it.*) Yes. One thousand pounds. Do you not think that a trifle high?

ANDY: Well. You know we could have as easily claimed two thousand, but we didn't like to break you altogether; so we just said that a thousand would come pretty near it.

MACKENZIE: Mr Daniel, may I look at the bellows?

MARY: Uncle Dan, I'm sure you won't object. (*She makes a gesture as if asking him to assent.*)

DANIEL: (*Looking hard at her, and then seeming to understand what she is about*) Yes. Yes. I'll thrash out the matter here with Andy. (MACKENZIE *goes across into the workshop, followed by* MARY. McCREADY *sits down disconsolately at the fireplace and begins to smoke his pipe moodily.*) A thousand pounds is impossible. Absolutely out of the question.

McCREADY: (*To himself*) Ach. She only torments me.

DANIEL: (*Looking over wonderingly*) Eh? (McCREADY *makes no response, but sits with his back to the two of them.*) People behave strangely sometimes, Andy. Very strangely. Now to go on with our business. I don't think, in the first case, that this was an affair of the heart, as the Frenchmen say.

ANDY: Eh?

DANIEL: You don't understand French? Of course not. No. It wasn't a love affair, I mean. I don't think Sarah was in love with John, was she?

ANDY: (*Hesitatingly*) Well — indeed, now, I don't know that she was.

DANIEL: No. We're all aware of that. He was just what we'd call a likely man. That's all.

ANDY: Aye. He would have been a good match for her.

DANIEL: Yes. Quite so, Andy. (*He makes notes in a pocket book.*) Nothing like notes, Andy. Now, so much for the love part of the business. They never exchanged letters?

ANDY: No. No letters.

DANIEL: Of course in a breach of promise letters are a great help. A great help. I'm very glad, however, just for your sister's sake, that she never wrote any to John. Imagine them reading out the love letters in the open court, and all the servant boys gaping and laughing.

ANDY: It's not nice, right enough. It's one thing I wouldn't like.

DANIEL: Well. No love. No letters. Next thing. He never courted her?

ANDY: Well, he came over and sat in the house a few nights.

DANIEL: Yes. No doubt. But hadn't he always some message on business to transact with you? Loan of a plough or a horse, or something like that?

ANDY: (*Uneasily*) That's so, of course.

DANIEL: Ah, yes.

ANDY: But I seen him with his arm round her the night of the social at the schoolhouse.

DANIEL: Andy. That's a wee failing of John's. I often warned him about doing that sort of thing indiscriminately. A bit of a ladies' man, John, in his way. I saw him do the same nonsense four or five times that night with other girls. John likes to think himself a bit of a gay dog, you know. It's not right — I don't think myself it's a bit proper to put your arm round a girl's waist on every occasion, but sometimes it's quite allowable. A night like a social, for instance.

ANDY: Aye. Of course a social's different.

DANIEL: Certainly. Well, now. No love, no letters, no courting, no photographs exchanged? (*He looks at* ANDY *inquiringly.*) No photographs exchanged. (*He notes it down.*) No ring? In fact, Andy, no nothing.

ANDY: But he proposed to her right enough.

DANIEL: Who said so?

ANDY: (*Astonished*) What? Do you mean to deny he didn't?

DANIEL: My dear Andy, I don't know. There was no one there but the two, I suppose, when he asked her. There's only her word for it.

ANDY: He wouldn't deny it himself?

DANIEL: Well. That depends on whether he really asked her to marry him of course. And it's not likely that John would be inclined if his memory was at all bad — it is a bad memory he has, you know. He forgets often to return your ploughs and that sort of thing.

ANDY: (*Blankly*) Aye. He has a bad memory.

DANIEL: Yes. Just so. And the fact that a verdict of one thousand pounds would hang on it would hardly make it any better. Would it? You've a bad case against us, Andy. A rotten case! In fact, looking over the whole thing carefully, do you really believe you'd make even a ten pound note out of us?

ANDY: (*Despairingly*) I wish Sarah had come and settled the case herself.

DANIEL: Ah, no. You've a better head, Andy, for seeing the sensible side of a thing, far better. (MARY *comes out of the workshop smiling gaily.*) Well?

MARY: Uncle Dan, he's delighted with it.

ANDY: What with? The bellows?

MARY: Yes. Go in, Andy, till you see it.

ANDY: Is it true, Daniel, you were offered two thousand for it?

DANIEL: We'll just go in and have a look at it. (ANDY *and he go into workshop.*)

MARY: (*Looking across at* ALICK. What's the matter?

ALICK: Nothing. I'm going home. (*He goes across to the yard door.*)

MARY: Alick!

McCREADY: Goodbye.

MARY: And I was going to go to all the trouble of baking a big plum cake for you, you big ungrateful thing.

McCREADY: (*Stopping at the door.*) I know what your plum cakes would be like. (*He opens the door and stops again before going out.*)

MARY: Well, get that big, ugly Maggie Murphy to bake them for you then.

McCREADY: (*Looking out through door and then coming inside again.*) I say, here's Kate and your father coming and a load of flour.

MARY: (*In a frightened voice*) Kate and father?

McCREADY: He seems to be in a bit of a temper.

MARY: (*In a frightened voice*) He's caught her with the flour!

McCREADY: (*Laughing*) Flour? Aye, she's carrying about three stone of it! Boys, but that would make a powerful pudding!

MARY: It was to have been the nicest one I could have baked.

McCREADY: (*Coming in and going over to her.*) Mary!

MARY: What?

McCREADY: You wouldn't come to my house where there would be no stint of flour or raisins or anything else, and I'd eat all you cooked for me no matter if I was dying after it.

MARY: Go to your house!

ALICK: Aye. Look here, wee girl. I got this — (*He fumbles and produces a ring.*) Let me put that on your wee finger, won't you?

MARY: Oh, Alick, what a lovely wee ring. (*She allows him to put it on her finger, and is shyly kissing him when* JOHN *enters, followed by* KATE, *who is trying vainly to stop a leak in the bag of flour which she is carrying.* KATE *goes to the dresser and places the bag on it.*)

JOHN: (*Severely to* MARY) Mary. Did you send her for more flour?

MARY: (*Meekly*) Yes, father.

JOHN: And didn't I leave word there was no more to be got without my orders? (MARY *hangs her head.*) It's lamentable the waste in this house! I was just looking at the pass book last night, and you'd think this house was a bakery to see the amount of flour comes into it.

MARY: (*Submissively*) I'm sorry, father.

JOHN: When I was out on the road, I seen a trail of flour leading up our loaning, and says I to myself, Jeminy, father, are they getting some more! So I followed up the mark and just caught up on her coming through the gate.

MARY: (*A little defiantly*) It's paid for, Kate, anyway. Isn't it?

KATE: It is, Miss. (*She busies herself putting the flour into a box, and then slips out during the next speech.*)

JOHN: Eh? Who give you the money?

MARY: (*Going over to her father and whispering*) Uncle Dan is in there, father, with Andy McMinn and Mr Mackenzie, the Scotch engineer, looking at his bellows.

JOHN: (*Amazed*) Eh? Andy McMinn? Is Dan settling the case?

MARY: I believe he'll do it yet.

JOHN: (*Admiringly*) He has a great head on him, Daniel.

MACKENZIE: (*Coming out from workshop and going over to* MARY) MARY: I'm sorry. It's such a rotten thing that — (*He sees* JOHN.) How are you, Mr Murray.

JOHN: Fine day.

MARY: (*Appealingly*) Mr Mackenzie, what did you say to Andy about it?

MACKENZIE: What did I say? Oh, ma conscience — I said it was a grand thing. (DANIEL *and* ANDY MCMINN *come in from workshop.*)

ANDY: (*Nervously*). Brave day, John.

JOHN: Aye. It is.

ANDY: Sarah gave me power to settle the case.

JOHN: I'm glad to hear it.

MACKENZIE: I tell you what it is, Mr Daniel Murray. It's a good thing that — a right good thing, and I'll make you an offer for it.

ANDY: (*Eagerly*) What's it worth?

MACKENZIE: (*With a look at* MARY) It's worth — it's worth more than all the damages your sister will get from Mr Murray.

DANIEL: (*Suddenly*) I tell you what it is, Andy, and believe me when I tell you, I'm sacrificing a great deal. I'll make a deal with you. Instead of a lump sum cash down, I'll hand over all the rights and royalties of that same bellows to you to settle the case.

ANDY: (*Dubiously*) I — I don't know.

DANIEL: You will have all the expense of the law, the bad name that your sister will be having over the head of being in a breach of promise, and all the expense of solicitors and lawyers. Then, after that, trying to get the money out of us, and, mind you, we will fight you to the last ditch. Won't we, John?

JOHN: Aye.

DANIEL: There now. What do you say, Mr Mackenzie?

MACKENZIE: I tell you what it is, Mr Murray. I'll make you an offer for —

ANDY: (*Hastily*) I'll take your offer, Daniel.

DANIEL: One second. I drew up a wee agreement for you to sign, and I'll fetch the bellows. (*He goes into the workshop.*)

JOHN: Andy I think —

MARY: I think Uncle Dan's a fool to throw away the thing that way. I do indeed. (DANIEL *comes out with the parcel and the pen, ink and paper.*)

DANIEL: Just sign your name to that, Andy. It's a sort of agreement to settle the case — you can read it for yourself. (*He hands a sheet of paper to* ANDY *with the pen.*) It's to show that the whole thing is fixed up to the satisfaction of everybody. (ANDY *looks at it and then signs.*) Ah. Good! Now, Alick, and you, Mr Mackenzie, just witness it and the date. (*They both sign.*) And now, Andy, there's your bellows. (ANDY *looks at it, and then takes it under his arm.*) And may you have the best of luck with it. (ANDY *looks wonderingly at the parcel in his arm and moves slowly towards the door.*)

MACKENZIE: Noo, my reward, Miss Murray — Mary rather. (*He goes forward and she stretches out her hand for him to shake, when he notices the ring, and stops short.*)

JOHN: I hope you're satisfied, Andy.

ANDY: I'm just wondering, Mr Mackenzie, do you think —

MACKENZIE: I think nothing for a year. I'll — I'll — I'm for Scotland in the morning. (*He goes out morosely through the door.*)

DANIEL: There, Andy. There's company home for you, and good luck to you. It's a sad heart I'll have this night.

ANDY: I'm wondering what — (*He goes to the door.*) Ach! She couldn't do better herself. No ring nor nothing and a thousand pound bellows. (*He wanders out abstractedly.* DANIEL *closes the door after him and looks sadly but triumphantly across at* JOHN, ALICK *and* MARY *go to the window together and look out after* ANDY.)

DANIEL: Well, John?

JOHN: (*With a sigh of intense relief and gratitude.*) Dan, I've said it before, and I'll say it again, you've a great head on you, Daniel.

(CURTAIN)

PETER

A Comedy in Three Acts and a Prologue

Peter was first produced at the Abbey Theatre Dublin on the 28th January 1930 with the following cast.

PETER GRAHAME	Arthur Shields
CHARLEY PRENDERGAST	Denis O'Dea
BILLY STEPHENS	Fred Johnson
ROSIE	Gertrude Quinn
SAM PARTRIDGE	F. J. McCormick
MRS ANNE McCLEERY	Maureen Delaney
MR JOHN MCCLEERY	Eric Gorman
TOM	Barry Fitzgerard
MRS S. NELSON SCOTT	P. J. Carolan
COLONEL BLAKE	Michael Scott
MRS BLAKE	Meriel Moore
JOAN BLAKE	Eileen Crowe
GUESTS	Christine Hayden Frolie Mulhern U. Wright J. Linnane
THE BLUE ROOM GIRLS	Sara Patrick Cepta Cullen Doreen Cuthbert Chris Sheehan
BUTTONS	P. Farrell

The play was produced by LENNOX ROBINSON and was dedicated to LENNOX ROBINSON for all the generous aid he gave the author and to F. J. McCORMICK for his creation of 'Sam Partridge of Ballymena'.

CHARACTERS in order of their appearance.

BILLY STEPHENS CHARLEY PRENDERGAST	*Students along with* PETER *at an Irish University*
ROSIE	*The maid at* PETER'S *lodgings*
PETER GRAHAME	*An engineering student*
SAM PARTRIDGE	*Proprietor of the Excelsior Hotel, Portahoy*
TOM	*An old waiter*
MRS. ANNE McCLEERY JOHN McCLEERY	*A retired shopkeeper and his wife, guests at the Excelsior Hotel*
COLONEL BLAKE	*An old Indian Army Officer*
MRS BLAKE	*His wife*
JOAN BLAKE	*Their niece*
NELSON SCOTT	*Inspector for Tourist Agencies*
BUTTONS	*Page boy at the Excelsior Hotel*
MISS VAN DE MEIZER	*An American visitor, guest at the Excelsior Hotel*

PETER

PROLOGUE

SCENE: *The sitting-room of* PETER GRAHAME'S *dingy lodgings on the first floor. A door at back to landing, another to bedroom on the right. A large window to the left overlooking the street. Sideboard, bookshelf, table, piano, chairs; books and glasses, cigarette packets, etc. The time is about 1 a.m.*

PETER: (*Shutting door at back*) Goodnight, Stephens. Goodnight, Charley. Goodnight!

(*A pause. He makes his way wearily over to the armchair, sits down, slowly takes off his collar and tie, then his shoes. He stares moodily at his socks. One of them is badly holed and his toes are showing through it. He pulls it off with an effort and examines it, then throws it carelessly aside, rises and walks slowly towards his bedroom. He suddenly sees his hat lying on the floor in front of him, gives it an exasperated kick, opens his bedroom door and switches off the light.*)

(BLACKOUT)

ACT ONE

Same scene as Prologue. The darkness gradually gives way to the bright daylight of a summer morning. No-one is in the room. Loud pronounced knocking on door at back.

VOICES: Are you there, Peter? Peter? (*pause*) Peter!

(CHARLEY PRENDERGAST *and* BILLY STEPHENS *enter.*)

CHARLEY: H'm — not up yet. Lazy dog! (*Looks at table with bottles and glasses etc.*) Just as it was when we left him last night. Poor devil!

STEPHENS: Is there a tincture in the bottle? (*He examines it.*) There is. Have a nip?

CHARLEY: No. Important appointment with the guv'nor this morning at eleven.

STEPHENS: Further explanation of refusal unnecessary. Well. I'm not going home till Friday. So, here goes. (*He pours out a drink.*) Cheerio!

CHARLEY: Good luck!

STEPHENS: (*Looking at bottle*) I suppose Peter could do with some. (*Goes to bedroom door.*) I wonder is the rascal asleep? (*He suddenly sees the hat and picks it up.*) I say, Charley, was he wearing it like this yesterday ?

CHARLEY: Don't remember.

STEPHENS: Oh no, you wouldn't. You don't give a damn. You've got through of course, and are off, I suppose, to a nice little job. But poor Peter and I — it doesn't matter what sort of hats we wear — *(at door)* — poor fellow, does it?

CHARLEY: Is he awake?

STEPHENS: (*Listening*) Not a mouse stirring. Here, let's give him a bugle call.

BOTH (*Singing*) Hey, Peter! Wake up Peter!

Angels calling
Houses falling
Babies bawling
Hey Peter! Wake up!
If you ain't gonna wake up, we can't wait
One minute longer; the trains am whistling —

STEPHENS: (*Emits long piercing whistle.*) Wake up!

(*Simultaneously the two doors open,* ROSIE *the maid at one, with a breakfast tray on which is also a letter. At the other,* PETER, *in pyjamas. He does a few steps of jazz, suddenly observes* ROSIE *and flies back into his bedroom.*)

ROSIE: Mr Grahame's breakfast and a letter for him. (CHARLEY *makes room for the tray on the table.*) Thank you, sir. Will you tell him — his breakfast, sir?

CHARLEY: Yes. Looks a very good breakfast too. Very appetising.

STEPHENS: Worth about fourpence I should say! (*To* ROSIE) Come here Phyllis — Is that your name?

ROSIE: No, sir.

STEPHENS: And what do they call you then?

ROSIE: Rosie sir.

STEPHENS: Ah! Rosie, yes. A rose by any other name. Come here, Rosie.

ROSIE: (*Retreating*) Will you tell Mr. Grahame? (*She sees the damaged sock and quickly takes it up.*) His breakfast.

STEPHENS: 'Course we'll tell him, my sweet Rose of Tralee. Are you very fond of Mr Grahame?

ROSIE: I am. I only wished he kept better company. Excuse me. (*Exit.*)

CHARLEY: One for you Stephens.

STEPHENS: Must get him out before the tea's cold. (*Knocks.*)

PETER: (*Off*) Who's that?

STEPHENS: (*Falsetto*) It's your own wee Rosie with the breakfast, darling!

PETER: I'll be out in a second.

STEPHENS: Hurry. There's the devil's own breakfast waiting for you out here. Grapefruit, prunes, fillet of plaice, bacon and eggs, marmalade, jam, tea and coffee.

PETER: What? (*He appears at door in shirt and trousers, barefooted, carrying a collar.*) What's that you say?

CHARLEY: Never mind him Peter. Are you shaved yet?

PETER: Just found the razor. I can't find my socks anywhere.

STEPHENS: Letter for you there, Peter.

PETER: Excuse me boys. (*He opens and reads letter. Rereads it.*)

STEPHENS: The old folks at home — including Uncle Joe — broken-hearted, receive news that the prodigal son has not made good in his final engineering.

PETER: A very good guess, Stephens. It is from Uncle Joe.

STEPHENS: Well. What says our Uncle Joe?

PETER: Ach. (*He throws letter over to* CHARLEY.) Read it out to him, Charley.

CHARLEY: (*Reading*) 'Ballywilder House, Ballywilder, Co. Leitrim.'

'Dear Peter,

As I expected, your name is missing from the results list. Whatever possessed your unfortunate parents to think you had any vocation for engineering I don't know. As you have now expended all that was allowable out of their estate, and as what is left is just barely sufficient to house and keep your sister, go and look somewhere to clothe and feed yourself.

If you haven't *brains* enough to qualify for an engineer, you might have the brawn, though I doubt it, to be a navvy. You had better though return at once and make arrangements for the future.

Your Uncle Joe.'

STEPHENS: Nice soothing letter-writer, your Uncle Joe!

CHARLEY: Where's your sister staying?

PETER: At Ballywilder. Uncle Joe bought the place from us after father's death. Didn't give us much for it either. But she has a home there anyway. (*A pause*) Yes. I have been. No doubt about it.

STEPHENS: No doubt about what?

PETER: That I've been a bit of an ass. Dancing, singing, capering, play-acting. Fool, idiot. Making goms laugh while I was only wasting their time and my own. (*More cheerfully after a moment's thought.*) Still, I didn't waste too much time at it. Did I, Charley?

CHARLEY: (*Hesitates.*) N — no. Not too much. I suppose.

PETER: It was that old McMenemin stuck me. I know it was. (*He suddenly discovers one sock.*) Ah! here's one sock. Where's the other, I wonder! (*Pauses*) I know it was McMenemin, I got 50/50 in everything bar geology. I know I got 60 easy in Mat. Physics, 70 in Strains and Stresses, and this time I got near full marks in Docks, Harbour and Canals. But those fossils! Those damned trilobites! What they got to do with engineering anyway ? I hate that old brute. 'When you are old, Mr Grahame, you will realise the importance of time even in the formation of geological strata.'

CHARLEY: I say. That reminds me, Peter. May I borrow your geology?

PETER: Yes. Take it and welcome. It's somewhere on that bookcase.

(*Knocking.*) Come in.

ROSIE: (*Entering*) The mistress sent this up with her compliments sir. (*Hands him a letter.*) And she told me to tell you she's waiting below for an answer as she's going out shopping this morning.

STEPHENS: Judging from the breakfast, it won't take her long to buy grub for the dinner. Wait a minute, Rosie, till he gets his socks on.

PETER: (*After a cursory glance at the note*) Yes, Rosie, my socks. Tell Mrs Murphy I couldn't possibly answer my correspondence till I put on my socks. I've found one but I'm hanged if I can find the other.

ROSIE: (*Shyly*) I beg your pardon, I'm sorry sir, but — I — I've got the other one. There was a big hole in it, but I'll have it ready for you in a minute or two. I'm putting a stitch in it.

STEPHENS: Bless me, does she stitch your socks! Do you, Rosie?

PETER: She does. Thank you, Rosie. I'll wait for it.

CHARLEY: What's the note about, Rosie? Last month's bill?

ROSIE: Yes sir.

STEPHENS: Got the wherewithal on you to pay it, Peter?

PETER: I had yesterday.

CHARLEY: How much is it?

ROSIE: Six pound ten up to last Saturday night.

STEPHENS: Rosie!

ROSIE: Yes sir.

CHARLEY: Tell Mrs Murphy, he's dressing. That he hasn't taken his breakfast yet, and that in half-an-hour he'll see her and square up.

ROSIE: All right sir. But she said I was to wait.

STEPHENS: Wait? Wait where?

ROSIE: Wait here until he sent it down with me.

STEPHENS: Wait here! Arrah, have some sense about you, Rosie. Fond and all as we are of you Rosie, there's some times ladies are *de trop*. Go down and tell her what Charley said.

CHARLEY: Yes go down and finish off that sock.

ROSIE: (*Hesitating*) Very well sir. But you — you'll answer it, won't you sir? Soon. If you don't, she'll be up herself.

STEPHENS: God forbid such a calamity should happen! Yes, yes, he will. He certainly will. Won't you, Peter?

PETER: I — might. (*He looks mournfully at* ROSIE.)

ROSIE: Your breakfast sir. It's getting cold.

PETER: Yes, yes. Right. I'll have to think this thing out, Rosie.

(*Exit* ROSIE, PETER *seats himself at the table, pours out a cup of tea and rereads the letter.* STEPHENS *sits down opposite* PETER *at the table.)*

STEPHENS: Nice morning's correspondence, Peter.

PETER: Yes.

(CHARLEY *extracts a book from the case, and seats himself beside* STEPHENS.)

CHARLEY: (*Examining book*) Some funny marginal notes here, Peter. (PETER *makes no reply but looks glumly at the letter.*) Sorry I can't help you, but I just managed to scrape enough to get home with.

STEPHENS: Misfortunes never come singly. They come in squadrons and platoons. Reminds me of Partridge. Went out with him yesterday before I met you boys, got two punctures one after another. He was talking about you, Peter.

PETER: Who's Partridge?

STEPHENS: Sam Partridge of Ballymena.

PETER: I don't remember any such bird from Ballymena.

STEPHENS: (*Incredulously*) Do you mean to tell me that you don't remember Sam Partridge, the Dives from Ballymena who dined us all sumptuously last year, the night of the big match?

PETER: No.

CHARLEY: He remembered *you* all right.

STEPHENS: Well, Partridge took me for a spin yesterday on the Bray Road. A huge giant of a car and by jove she could shift. Cabinteely to Bray in four minutes, I thank you. And he talked a lot about you, Peter.

PETER: Did he?

(*The two students eye* PETER *curiously. Pause.*)

PETER: Well? (*He sips his tea.*) Cheerio!

STEPHENS: What's on you now, Peter?

PETER: Ach! Everything. Uncle Joe, exams, engineering, navvying, socks and stitches — well, yesterday was yesterday, no use thinking about it, still I can't help —

CHARLEY: (*Who has resumed examining the book.*) I say, Stephens, look!

STEPHENS: I say! Jolly fine. Did *you* draw this girl's face, Peter?

PETER: Where?

CHARLEY: Here. On the margin. Jolly nice girl, Peter.

STEPHENS: Yes. Who is she?

PETER: Oh — no-one in particular.

CHARLEY: I see something scrawled here underneath her portrait which might be a clue. Listen! (*Reads.*) 'Where in the world will you find anything like the beauty of a young girl? Exquisite, like a fragrant rose.'

STEPHENS: Hear hear! Good man Peter.

CHARLEY: (*Looking critically at drawing*) The chin is a bit — um — too big and her nose is — (*With a start*) — aha, now I've got you, Peter! She's that girl who passed us yesterday in a big blue Chrysler car and bowed to you, Peter!

STEPHENS: Well, sure we'll probably meet her again, won't we Peter? Cheer up! Your boat hasn't sunk yet, Peter.

PETER: It sure has now.

STEPHENS: Aren't we all of us little sailing boats tacking this way and that? Trying to dodge into harbour, trying to pass our finals.

CHARLEY: Hopeless for you.

STEPHENS: I agree. Some get in all at once. Here's Charley in for a snug berth, nice fair breeze behind, sunshine, guns saluting, bands playing, flags flying, mammas waving — all that sort of thing. But you and I Peter — well, cheer up old sort, we'll sail into port some day.

PETER: Some day, yes. When we're old men, I suppose.

CHARLEY: Well, I want to be fixed up before I'm old.

PETER: (*Angrily*) Old! Old! Damn the old! (*He rises and walks about, talking excitedly.*) All the examiners, they're old. All the people who give you jobs, who sack you from jobs, who make you swat for jobs, they're all old, old! And they use us, you, me; fetch and carry me this, bring and carry me that — they sit down and give us orders; kill us or spare us. (*Suddenly*) Well, there's one thing they can't have, they can't get; they can't take from us —

CHARLEY: Can't take — what, Peter?

STEPHENS: Shut up. His girl, of course. (*Snatching up and waving the book*) His girl. My girl, your girl, all the girls that we fall in love with. But he's wrong. Some old fellow's bound to nobble them.

PETER: (*Excitedly*) No, never! They belong to us, not to them. They're ours. We were born with them — they're our own age — (*Triumphantly*) Aha! That's where we have those old fellows. The beauty of youth belongs to us, not to them. Bah! They're too old. They don't count. They wouldn't look at them. They despise them.

CHARLEY: Who does what?

STEPHENS: Shut up! Don't interrupt him! Go on, Peter.

PETER: That's the one thing, I say, that they can't rob us of, they can't trick us out of. They'd like to, those old ones. Make it so difficult that we could never win. But they can't and they shan't. Never.

CHARLEY: (*Reading from book.*) 'Where in the world can you find anything like the beauty of a young girl? Exquisite — like a fragrant rose.'

STEPHENS: Rosie!

PETER: (*Angrily*) What do either of you know or care about beauty?

STEPHENS: No offence meant. Be a good child now and eat your breakfast, Peter. Here, I'll cut some bread for you. (*He does so* PETER *sits down again.*)

CHARLEY: Tell us, Peter, about that girl in the big blue Chrysler. Who is she, Peter?

PETER: None of your business.

(CHARLEY *wanders over to bookcase examining its contents*).

STEPHENS: 'The flower that sat in the car, tra-la, has nothing to do with the case.'

CHARLEY: (*Suddenly*) I say, Peter! Do you mind letting me have a loan of your 'Stoney'? You won't want it for a couple of months.

PETER: Take it and welcome.

(CHARLEY *is taking the book out of the case when he suddenly drops it, and seizes another one.*)

CHARLEY: Hello! Where did you pick this up?

PETER: What?

CHARLEY: Griffith's 'Harbours, Docks and Canals. New Edition Revised'. I say, where'd you scrape together two quid to nobble this? (*He looks inside*) 'To Peter from Joan.' Who's Joan?

PETER: She's a girl.

STEPHENS: Is that a fact? And did she give you that?

PETER: She did.

CHARLEY: Jove, I didn't know you had a 'Griffiths'. Lend it, too, Peter?

PETER: No, not that. You can have any of the others.

CHARLEY: Right-o! But I'd have liked to have the 'Griffiths'. Who's Joan?

PETER: Girl I once met.

CHARLEY: Must be a decent sort.

PETER: Why?

CHARLEY: Spending forty bob on a book like this for a fellow she met — (*He pauses and grins*) — once did you say, Peter?

PETER: Well, once or twice or maybe.

STEPHENS: Look here, Peter, I'm fed up waiting in this hole; a walk would do you good. We might see a few more beauties of your own generation — where's your shoes? *(He begins to search the room.)*

PETER: My shoes? Somewhere about. I suppose, Charley — (*He looks sadly at the note from* MRS MURPHY) — it's not much use — asking you to help with this?

CHARLEY: Six-ten? No Peter. (*Looking at the books*) Sorry, but I'd give you a quid for the 'Griffiths' if you'd part.

PETER: No.

STEPHENS: (*Finding a shoe and flinging it over*) Here's one shoe, anyway. And here's the other. But you can't go about with only one sock on. Has she never got it stitched yet? Cheer up, Peter! We might see that blue Chrysler girl again.

CHARLEY: Who was that blue Chrysler one, Peter?

PETER: That's Joan.

CHARLEY: What!

STEPHENS: Where did you meet her?

PETER: One day this winter I was swatting up Geology, looking for specimens up in the hills, and a girl drove past.

STEPHENS: Fast?

PETER: She was driving slowly. I was on the road looking at a lump of quartz and she nearly ran me down. She stopped, or the car stopped; she laughed and I laughed, and then I helped her to start it again: then she gave me a lift down — and — that's all.

STEPHENS: I see! (*Intones in a high pitched clerical voice*) And he thereupon told her *all* about himself and all about Docks, Harbours and Canals.

CHARLEY: (*Like some suave 'uncle' in a Children's Hour broadcast*) Yes and then, dear children, he met her in secret, and without the knowledge or consent of her parents or guardians, and told her the story of poor engineering Peter.

STEPHENS: (*Suddenly clutching* CHARLEY *in a frenzied embrace.*)

'And Joan — Oh Joan darling — honestly I'm afraid I'm going to fail in my final. Joan darling I really know nothing about the one great subject I'm specialising in — Docks, Harbours and Canals.' (*In his ordinary voice*) And so he got the book. (*Mischievously*) Sounds rather like the truth, Peter.

PETER: It is. Told by a pair of cynics.

CHARLEY: I see. That's how you got 90 in Docks and Harbours. Good man, Peter!

PETER: (*Angrily*) You two can go to hell. Get out! A fool I was to tell you.

STEPHENS: (*Who has crossed to the window.*) I say boys, here he is!

CHARLEY: Who?

STEPHENS: That fellow. He's at the door now, below. Gee, what a car the man has! Brass and silver and blue and gold! (*Knocking below.*) Yes, that's just the way he would knock.

PETER: Who is he?

STEPHENS: The chap I met yesterday. The football dinner man. The big pot, Partridge. I told him we'd be here, this morning.

PETER: What's he wanting with me anyway?

(*Loud knocking at the sitting room door.*)

PETER: Come in. (*Enter* SAM PARTRIDGE. *He is middle-aged, but quick and alert in manner, speaks with rather boisterous self-assurance in a pronounced accent and is very smartly dressed.*)

PART: Excuse me. *Pardonnez-moi*. Aye. You're here all right, Billy — what's this your name is? And this, I suppose, is Mr Grahame?

STEPHENS: No, that's Prendergast. This is Grahame here.

PART: Och aye, aye. How're ye, Mr Grahame. I suppose you remember me.

STEPHENS: Mr Partridge, Peter. (PETER *bows.*)

PART: (*Shakes hands, brusquely.*) Aye, I'm Sam Partridge of Ballymena. D'ye remember me? Och, go on with you! D'ye not remember the night of the football *conversazione*? Peter Grahame! Isn't that you?

PETER: Yes, I'm Peter Grahame.

PART: Of course you remember. And your pal here. Wasn't he there that night?

STEPHENS: Yes. Charley Prendergast — Mr Partridge.

PART: Prendergast, aye. He came over in Strongbow's time! Ha ha! Looking for Eva. Did you find her yet, Charley? Ha ha! How're you, Charley?

CHARLEY: Quite well, thank you.

PART: Aye. Indeed you look it. And how've you been doing since, Peter? Any coorting? Well, 'pon my soul, Peter, you were the great value that night. Great! Cripes, Peter, but you were the hell of a man at the Irish jig, and dancing the Billy John Ashcroft breakdown — let alone the jazz and the Rooshian dancing. It's a year ago now, but I never forget you. So when I seen the Billy artist here yesterday, the first thing I says to him, 'Where's that Grahame fellow?' (*A pause*) I hear you got stuck in the exam, Peter?

PETER: Yes.

PART: (*Interrupting*) Aye. Ah well, you can't do everything, can you? (*Looking at* CHARLEY) I remember Charley now. Wasn't it Charley played the accompaniment for you?

STEPHENS: (*Grinning*) Yes.

PART: Aye, oh aye. Charley, he done his part well, but man, Peter, you were the star turn that night! I'll never forget you. Says I to McLoughlin, the Chairman of the County Council — he was there that night — says I, that fellow would make his fortune, a regular fortune, man, on the stage. (*Looking delightedly at* PETER) You couldn't help but laugh at that fellow even if he done nothing but look at you. Ha ha! (PETER *looks reproachfully at him.*) That's it! That's it! The doleful Jester in the Yeoman of the Guard. Jack Point! The dead spit of him! But for the Lord's sake, Peter, buck up. You're not dead yet.

PETER: (*Maddened*) I'm damn near it.

PART: (*Delighted*) Ha ha ha! Well, soul, you do make me laugh. You're an artist. (*Looking at the tray*) Are you just after your breakfast? (*Examines it.*) Holy God, what a breakfast! Well, that's the last breakfast of the kind you're going to eat, my son. (*Suddenly*) D'ye know Portahoy?

PETER: Portahoy?

PART: Aye — on the sea-coast.

PETER: Yes. I was there once, I think, about ten years ago with my Uncle Joe and mother.

PART: (*Contemptuously*) Ach! Your mother and Uncle Joe! Spade and bucket, down for the day, eating cockles. I wish to God your Uncle Joe seen it now! It's booming, man, booming. None of your ordinary charabanc trippers' business, but real class like. Great! Kind of an Ulster lido like, if you could imagine the thing. Last year — great! This year — better! And who done it? One man and one man only. And who's that? Me! Sam Partridge of Ballymena. And how? Art and beauty. Nature supplied the beauty — it's a beautiful place, there's not the like of it in the United Kingdom — Blackpool and them places, bah! Nothing naturally beautiful about them. Portahoy and Killarney — Heaven's reflex — Portahoy! But it wanted art, and Sam Partridge, he supplied the art.

STEPHENS: Up the Partridges!

PART: I practically own the place, you know. I bought up all the leaseholders and have the biggest share in the big new hotel — Hotel Excelsior — just got it done up in the latest style; sofas and cushions and armchairs; late dinner at night — and choked off all them old commercials by charging them twenty shillings a night; bed and breakfast — none of your seven bob touches for me. And now I have a real nice place for the idle rich and them classes. Don't let me be stopping you eating your breakfast, Peter, but by the holy, you should see the breakfast I put up for them people. Six courses, man! Grapefruit and prunes and porridge, fish, bacon, ham and eggs, scrambled eggs and poached, and bacon and fish —

PETER: Any jam?

PART: Aye, and jam, and marmalade — and I've got the best *maitre d'hôtel* special over from Deauville, and the best chef out of the Savoy, and you could go on eating all day in the dining-room and never want to leave it. Simply gorgeous!

PETER: Look here, Mr Partridge, what's the good of coming here and telling me all about these things at your wonderful hotel? Is it a way you have of asking me to breakfast or dine there, or what is it?

PART: It is. (*Looks at* PETER *and laughs knowingly.*) It is. Ha, ha, ha! It certainly is!

PETER: Thanks very much. Today or tomorrow?

PART: For a fortnight — longer, maybe. I want you and Charley here — what d'you call him — Prendergast. *(Looking at* STEPHENS) This Billy fellow, he's no good for me, but I want the two of you boys to eat, dine, drink and sleep like that for a solid fourteen days, and longer —

CHARLEY: Sorry I can't possibly —

PART: Right. But I want Peter. I must have Peter. You'll come?

PETER: I don't quite get you, Mr Partridge.

PART: I told you about the breakfast; would you like to know what you'd have for lunch?

PETER: Woa! Wait a bit. All this eating business doesn't quite appeal to me. I don't want all that grub. I want something else. I don't suppose I'll ever see it.

PART: Ha, ha, ha! Good Lord! When you look like that you do put me into fits. Well, look here, you know the sort of danger a hotel like that gets into. Too many old fellows and women sitting in the drawing-room and the lounge doing nothing but playing patience and dozing and smoking and knitting and taking a turn round the esplanade and the cliff head and that sort of thing. Well, that's no use to me. I don't want the place turned into a sort of a high-class Turkish Baths for old crocks. I want a bit of life and jizz about it, you know. I want young ones as well. They're the ones that matter. Use them — always use the young ones for the benefit of the old ones. And if they like the place, they'll make the Pa's and Ma's and the Uncles and Aunts stick it. But you got to amuse them. Use them and amuse them. Now Peter, you're just the sort of young fellow I want.

STEPHENS: What he's trying to get you to see, Peter, is that he's offering you a job — the run of your teeth and a free bed.

PETER: Yes, that's plain enough. For a fortnight?

PART: Aye, and longer if it suits.

PETER: Yes, well. You do that. What do I do?

PART: Well, look here. Take the morning. You get breakfast — grapefruit and —

PETER: Yes, yes, I know. Consider we've had breakfast. What then?

PART: Well, after breakfast, some old fellow wants a game of golf.

PETER: Golf?

PART: Yes, 3 holes or 9 or 19. He tells us in the office and I gives you the tip and you goes off to him and fixes up a match. Or maybe an old lady wants a game of croquet.

STEPHENS: Croquet?

PART: Yes, croquet. Right! Peter gets the tip and offers to play. D'ye understand Peter? Then in the evenings you drop into the drawing-room and do a turn or two at the piano, not professional like but nicely and artistically as if it were the usual thing to do Paderewski or Chopin at the piano, and I buzz round the place and say that's a clever lad at the piano and nobody should miss hearing him, and they all come in like, then I gets Peter here to give them a bit of a song. And then my little orchestra plays, and there's dancing, and then comes along my young dancing quartette — kind of a cabaret business — but nice don't you know — all the latest foxtrots —

STEPHENS: What! Your young dancing quartette?

PART: Aye, or sextette or whatever you call it.

STEPHENS: Young, are they?

PART: Of course — I wouldn't have anything else. Now, Peter.

(*The latter gets up and walks moodily towards the bedroom door.*)

PETER: Just a moment. (*Enters room and closes door.*)

STEPHENS: Partridge! (*He hands him over* MRS MURPHY'S *note.*) Square this for him.

PART: (*Looking at it.*) Six-ten — Right! Look here, you two boys go down and square the old lady. (*He gives* STEPHENS *some notes.*) And wait for me in the car. I want to speak to PETER a minute or two alone. (*Exit* STEPHENS; CHARLEY PARTRIDGE *whistles.*) Peter!

PETER: (*Off*) Yes. Just a moment. (*Enters*) Sorry, I'd forgotten to brush my hair.

PART: You hard up, Peter?

PETER: Yes, broke.

PART: Ach! Don't you worry. Leave that to me. Free quarters, Peter, best of grub and a fiver a week. And have a *nom-de-plume* or whatever you call it. Call yourself say, Peter Gordon. (*He crosses and closes entrance door carefully.*) I don't want those two fellows to hear this, Peter. (*Bashfully*) The thing is, Peter, there's a very special girl coming to the Excelsior.

PETER: (*More interested*) Yes?

PART: And it's time Sammy Partridge was hooking on, you know?

PETER: Well?

PART: Well, from all the talk of Stephens and that lot, you seem to have a way with the weemin, Peter.

PETER: No I haven't. But I like them.

PART: Aye. Sure that's what has them reciprocating! Well, this special girl, Peter — she's a nice-class girl, you know — came last two summers and any amount of dough, not that I want that very much — I've got plenty of that all right — but Peter, I'm terrible gone on this particular one. I never done much in the coortin' line when I was — well — a bit younger like you, and I feel terrible awkward now with nice-class young girls, talking and laughing and gagging and doing the gay like, don't you know Peter, and if you and me and she and the cousin —

PETER: Cousin? What cousin?

PART: Her cousin or her aunt, or whatever other woman company she has, like if we all went for a stroll in the evening, and you did most of the talking.

PETER: That's impossible.

PART: Well, you done most of the arty sort of talk like, and amused them; you could then nose off with the cousin and give me a bit of scope like, with the —

(*Knocking at the door.*)

PETER: Come in.

ROSIE: (*With note on salver.*) Mistress said to give you this, Mr Grahame, and I'm sorry to have kept you waiting so long for this. (*Hands him a sock.*)

PETER: Thank you, Rosie. (*Exit* ROSIE.)

PART: Well, Peter?

PETER: Wait a moment. (*Putting on sock*) I can't answer till I've put on my sock and read my correspondence. (*Reads.*) Great Scott! 'Paid with thanks!' (*Looking at* PARTRIDGE) You did this?

PART: Aye, och yes. It's nothing, you know, Peter. Sure you'll do just as much for me and more. Pack up your troubles in your old kit bag! Will you come?

PETER: Six pounds ten down and the rest in weekly instalments! (*Suddenly, with delight*) When do I begin work?

PART: Day after tomorrow. I'll call for you and bring you down. Come with me now and I'll give you a spin in the car, and lunch with me at Jammets.

PETER: Go ahead. I'll follow you down.

PART: (*Pulls papers from his pocket.*) There's a couple of prospectuses and views of the hotel and the new grounds.

PETER: (*Reading*) The Excelsior Hotel, Portahoy. Very fine it looks. What's that beyond the hotel. Out to sea in the distance, below the mountains?

PART: Oh that! That's a big new harbour they're working at. Tremendous thing — worth seeing. Don't be long Peter. (*He goes out.*)

(QUICK CURTAIN)

ACT TWO

TIME: *A few days later.*

SCENE: *One of the lounges of the Excelsior Hotel, Portahoy. It commands a view of the hotel grounds, sea and mountains beyond. In the foreground can be seen a new harbour in course of construction. The lounge is empty.* PARTRIDGE *can be heard talking, then suddenly appears in immaculate morning dress. He is followed by* TOM *the waiter assisting a large stout gentleman who is rather unsteady on his feet.*

PART: All clear. In here, Tom. This way Mr Scott!

SCOTT: (*Insistent on stopping to look out to sea.*) Woa! Yes. That's an extraordinary fine view. Have you no telescope — for guests? Why haven't you — a telescope? What's that thing out there to sea in the distance? Just below the mountains?

PART: Oh that? That's a big new harbour they're working at. Tremendous thing. Worth seeing.

SCOTT: Yes. If you had — telescope. Should have telescope. Essential for first-class sea-coast hotel. Take a note of that, please, waiter. I insist on — on telescope. Most essential.

PART: Right. Take a note of that Tom.

TOM: Yes sir. We'll have one for you tomorrow.

SCOTT: (*Slightly mollified.*) Hm. S'nice view — all ri'.

PART: Great. (*Proudly*) To the right — (*He points.*) — South Foreland Rockery. Choicest of Alpine flowers and shrubs — to the left — the Rhodendrums — left centre — the Lovers' Walk.

SCOTT: Yes — (*Chuckles delightedly.*) I — I like that — 'The Lovers' Walk' — first class hotels — should always have —

'Lovers' Walk' — v' good — that is. Romance — romance, most important. You go one up on that.

PART: That's great. Right. Turn to starboard, Tom. (*They steer Scott towards a seat.*) Now. (*He is deposited carefully in it.*) Now isn't this a nice cosy kind of a place to pass the afternoons. The snooze parlour I calls it.

SCOTT: (*Annoyed*) No — no — no — no. Tut — tut — tut. Not snooze. Snooze — vulgar — common word. Use word like — eh — siesta. Yes, that's it. Siesta room — lounge.

PART: Right. Make a note of that, Tom. Put that cushion round a bit more. This way, Tom. (*He looks critically at* SCOTT.) Now. How d'ye like that for a snoo — for a — for siesting?

SCOTT: Excellent. Thanks v' much. (*He settles down.*) And a most excellent lunch. V'good indeed. Hm. V'comf'ble here. Very.

PART: Good. (*The sound of a loud talking merry party coming along the passage outside.*) Tom. Stop that crush coming in here. Can't have any disturbance of Mr Scott's siesting. Quick. (TOM *hurries off and can be heard shepherding the party elsewhere.*)

SCOTT: V'comf'ble here. Nice. M'yes. Good place for snooze — siesta — snooze — siesta — snoo — (*He falls asleep.*)

(PARTRIDGE *satisfied that all is well, goes off. An elderly couple drift slowly into the lounge and seat themselves. They are* MR AND MRS McCLEERY. *The latter carries a capacious work basket from which she extracts a large ball of wool. Her husband has a notebook in which he writes at odd moments.*)

MRS McC: (*After a long pause.*) Have you done much, John dear? (*She commences to knit.*)

MR McC: No. (*Irritably*) It's terrible hard work, this. My brain isn't as quick or alert as it used to be.

MRS McC: Well dear, sure your heart is in the work anyway. These few days down here and nothing to worry about, and them dinners and lunches, its doing you good, dear. Could I help you, dear?

MR McC: (*Testily*) One moment, Annie. (*To himself*) Bog — fog — bog —

MRS McC: I'm sure I could help you, dear. What's the word, darling?

MR McC: Bog.

MRS McC: Bog. Bog. Were your thoughts on the bog, darling? (*The ball of wool slips away.*)

(TOM *re-enters. He is rather taken aback to find the* MCCLEERYS *installed in the lounge, but says nothing.*)

MR McC: Yes. Bog — fog —

TOM: Yes sir. Excuse me, sir. (*He retrieves the wool and hands it to* MRS MCCLEERY.)

MRS McC: Oh, thank you, Tom.

MR McC: (*Meditatively*) Bog — bog —

TOM: (*Puzzled but interested*) Excuse me, sir. You want some — what sir?

MRS McC: Oh, it's all right, Tom. Mr McCleery only wants a little word to rhyme with bog. That's all.

TOM: Is that so, sir! (*He tries to peer into* MCCLEERY'S *notebook.*) Excuse me, sir. Bog, did you say sir? Well now, there's — bog — and there's fog — and there's log — and there's — ach! sure there's thousands of words that end in og. I never was much good at them sort of things, but wee Joe, the night boots, has a great head for that sort of thing. (*He produces a small notebook and stumpy pencil.*) That's it! That's it! I heard Joe at one a few nights ago. 'There was once a young man in a fog —' (SCOTT *stirs and grunts.*) Excuse me ma'am. Have to — you know. Very important gentleman over there ma'am. (*He crosses to* SCOTT *and stands waiting the latter's awakening.*) 'There was once a young man in a fog — '

PART: (*Entering briskly*) Tom! Tom!

TOM: Yes sir.

PART: Have you seen Mr Peter?

TOM: Mr Peter? Mr Gordon, sir? Yes sir. He was up very early this morning, sir, down at the new harbour, and he's been out golfing with Colonel Blake since breakfast.

PART: (*Looking over at the* MCCLEERYS) Who are the old couple?

TOM: McCleery, sir. (*Reassuringly*) It's all right, sir. Very quiet, sir. Wouldn't disturb a fly, sir.

PART: Right. Well, under no account have Mr Scott disturbed either. (*He crosses to the* MCCLEERYS.) Nice afternoon, Mrs McCleery.

MRS MCC: (*Gratified by the attention*) Very nice indeed. (*She hastily nudges her husband.*) John! This is Mr Partridge. (*Sotto voce*) The owner, darling, of the hotel. (MCCLEERY *looks up and bows.*)

PART: How d'ye do! I hope you're being well looked after. Would you not now prefer the main lounge to sit in? It's brighter and gayer than this place.

MRS MCC: Oh thank you so much, Mr Partridge but my husband likes rest and seclusion for his literary work, and I — well, what my husband likes I like too. So we just sit here in this nice quiet corner every afternoon.

MR MCC: I find I can write here better than anywhere else at this time of day.

PART: Right. (*Crosses to* TOM.) If Mr Scott wakes up and wants — well, you know — a little nourishment — the best in the house — see he gets it, Tom.

TOM: Yes sir.

PART: I don't mind that old couple, but anybody else that comes along — young chatty people or any noisy ones — shunt them along to the main lounge.

TOM: I will sir, certainly sir.

PART: I told you before what he is, Tom, and what he means to this hotel. So don't forget. (*Pauses.*) Aye. You said Mr. Peter was out golfing with the Colonel?

TOM: Yes sir.

PART: Aye. Well, here. (*Produces card.*) I want you to give him a note of these extra arrangements, and tell him that I want to see him. Urgent business. And he's to pay particular attention to Miss Van de Meizer. Lady up in No. 45.

TOM: (*Taking card*) I know the lady, sir. No. 45. Yes sir.

PART: And in case I miss seeing him, tell him privately that he wasn't just up to the whack last night at the singing. He'll have to put a bit more jizz in it than he done last night.

TOM: (*Marking card*) More jizz. Yes sir.

PART: Make Mr Scott a bit more comfortable with that cushion. (TOM *does so. Exit* PARTRIDGE.)

TOM: (*Going carefully over card, making notes on it.*) Do him well, the best in the house, Mr. Scott, No. 45, Miss Van de Meizer, extra attention. Singing, more jizz, Mr Peter. Right. (*He moves over to* MCCLEERY.) What's this we were at when we were interrupted? Poetry! Aye. 'There was once a young man in a fog —'

SCOTT: (*Drowsily*) Um. Um. Um. (*Blinks at* TOM.) Oh! Waiter.

TOM: (*At attention*) Yes, sir.

SCOTT: Another — um — um — another whiskey and soda.

TOM: Yes, sir. Certainly sir, Large or small, sir?

SCOTT: Um. Um. Large. (*Suspiciously alert on seeing* MCCLEERY.) No — Small. (*Nods to* MCCLEERY.) How do! Um. Small.

TOM: Yes sir. (*Exit.*)

SCOTT: Um. Yes. Very good. Nice here. Um. Comf'ble. (*Settles down again.*) Um.

MRS McC: (*After a scrutiny of* SCOTT.) Do you know the gentleman, darling?

MR McC: (*Looking over his glasses at* SCOTT) Don't think so. (*Suddenly*) Oh! I've got it! I've got it? Dog!

MRS McC: Of course, so it is. Isn't that splendid, love! I just knew you'd do it. How many lines have you got now, darling? And would you let me hear them, love? There's no-one listening.

MR McC: (*Reassured on this point after a glance around.*)

'Away where the curlews cry on the bog,
There sounds the faint wild bark of the dog,
And Oh! to be there
When the —'

TOM: (*Entering, up L, with glasses*) Excuse me, sir. Your drink, sir.

SCOTT: Um. Very good. Um. Yes. Put in all the soda. Um. V'nice here. Comf'ble. (*As* TOM *pours out a drink, there is the long prolonged sound of a siren as from a great distance away.*) What's that?

TOM: Siren sir. The new harbour works, sir. They generally give two blasts sir.

SCOTT: What they blow twice for? Um?

TOM: First one is warning — tide has turned enough to get up steam — get ready for work, sir. Second one means commence work, sir. It won't go for a long time yet, the second one, sir.

SCOTT: Um. Second one what?

TOM: Second one means — commence work, sir. If you were inclined to bathe, sir, them sirens is very useful.

SCOTT: Um. Bathe? No. no, not just now. Later. Um. V' comf'ble here. Bathe? (*Decisively*) No!

TOM: No sir.

(SCOTT *sips his drink, then closes his eyes.* TOM *looks at him admiringly. Once more the ball of wool slips from* MRS. MCCLEERY'S *lap.* TOM *retrieves it.*)

MRS MCC: Oh, thank you so much.

TOM: (*To* MR MCCLEERY) Excuse me, sir, but we were talking about — aye — bog, sir. Bog — fog —

SCOTT: (*Sleepily*) Um. V'nice here. Comf'ble. (*Stares in a stupified way at the whiskey and soda then closes his eyes in slumber again.*)

MRS MCC: (*After a critical survey of* SCOTT) Who's the gentleman?

TOM: Mum's the word, ma'am. (*Impressively*) I wish I was him. What a job! (*Confidentially*) He's the Astronomer Royal ma'am.

MRS MCC. (*To her husband*) Darling? Tom says the gentleman over there is the Royal Astronomer.

MR MCC: (*After a sharp look at* SCOTT.) Nonsense!

TOM: 'Tis a fact ma'am. He marks places like this with stars, d'ye understand. He's the Chief Inspector for the United Tourist Agencies Recommended Hotels. One star — fair. Two stars — good. Three stars — very good. Four stars!!! My job is to get this place marked four stars. 'Do him well now, Tom,' says Mr Partridge. And I'm doing him. *(Crosses to* SCOTT.) Excuse me sir. Little more soda, sir?

SCOTT: Um. Yes. Um. Small lil' drop. (TOM *pours it out.*) Thanks. Nice here. Comf'ble.

TOM: Yes sir. Shall I put this cushion round a little, sir?

SCOTT: Um. No, no. Quite all ri'. Comf'ble.

TOM: Yes sir. Hope you liked your lunch, sir?

SCOTT: Um. Lunch! Um. Very nice. Comf'ble. Nice.

TOM: Thank you, sir.

(*A little buttons enters with programme cards which he proceeds to distribute. He attempts to give one to* SCOTT.)

TOM: (*Interposing*) Keep away from the gentleman. (*Seizes card.*) What's this?

BUTTONS: New programme. Tonight. Special, with Mr Partridge's compliments. (*He hands one to* MCCLEERY *who, irritated at this interruption, glances at it and throws it away. The* BUTTONS *gives one to* MRS MCCLEERY.) 'Blue Room Girls — first appearance tonight. Special.' With Mr Partridge's compliments. (*Exit.*)

MRS MCC: (*Reading the programme*) Oh! Dear! This is nice. John — John dear! The new programme, dear.

MR MCC: The what?

MRS MCC: Last night, Mr Partridge announced he had got something very special arranged for this evening.

MR MCC: (*Annoyed*) Sh! Sh! Just getting it.

MRS MCC: Are you darling? I'm so glad.

(*She puts the programme aside after a glance at it, and resumes her knitting.* SCOTT *relapses into sleep.* TOM *seeing no need for further attention to* SCOTT, *puts programme on table in front of* SCOTT, *and comes over to* MR MCCLEERY.)

TOM: (*Sotto voce and motioning towards* SCOTT) Nice gentleman that, ma'am.

MRS McC: Yes, he seems very contented.

TOM: Yes ma'am. Mr Partridge's orders — 'Keep him full and contented. The best in the house.' (*Coming closer*) The best room in the house — No. 3. A grand room ma'am. Canopy bed, tapestry curtains, cost two hundred guineas. (*Pause.*) When he wakes first thing in the morning, double gin and ginger and dash of lemon. Half an hour later, China tea and crisp toast. Quarter of an hour after, grape fruit and slice of melon. Breakfast — prunes, porridge, Finnan haddock — he must have the stomach of an ostrich. But he has brains too. He's got more brains for guzzling, eating and drinking than the old Roman Emperors down in the catacombs.

(*The noise of guests arriving outside suddenly puts him on the alert. He goes towards the entrance. There is a loud burst of laughter.* TOM *hurriedly goes out.*)

VOICE: (*Off*) Let's go in here for tea.

TOM: (*Off*) Excuse me, gentlemen. Excuse me, ladies. The other lounge, sir. Round the corner. (*Another party of guests suddenly appears at opposite entrance.*) No sir, not here. Round the corner. Thank you sir. Thank you ladies. (*He reappears looking at* MRS McCLEERY *for sympathy.*) Awful life, this, ma'am.

MRS McC: (*Who has again taken up the programme*) John. John, dear.

MR McC: Sh! Don't interrupt.

MRS McC: But this is interesting. Did you see this?

MR McC: What?

MRS McC: They're actually going to have a cabaret show here this evening. (*She reads.*) 'No. 1: Rumba: Halfway to Cuba.'

MR McC: (*Irritated*) Don't — don't interrupt please, Annie.

MRS McC: (*Unheeding*) 'No. 2: Slow Valse: Missouri No. 3: Special' — Peter. (*Repeats.*) Peter.

SCOTT: (*Drowsily*) He's — a funny fellow — is Peter. Um — yes. Um — Very — Um — funny.

MRS McC: Tom!

TOM: Yes, ma'am.

MRS McC: Who's Peter?

TOM: Peter, ma'am? D'ye not know Mr Peter, ma'am?

MRS McC: No. Where is he?

TOM: Mr. Peter's out playing golf with Colonel Blake, ma'am.

MRS McC: Oh, Peter plays golf too, does he.

TOM: Oh yes. Plus four man, ma'am.

MRS McC: Dear me. (*She continues to read.*) 'Last item. The Blue Room Girls, who have now arrived, will appear in a special cabaret scene with Peter this evening.'

TOM: Yes, ma'am. Ballet cabaret and tap dancing, croquet, tennis, golf, badminton, all one to Mr Peter.

MRS McC: John! John dear!

MR McC: (*Testily*) Yes. (*He goes on writing.*)

MRS McC: John darling!

MR McC: (*Exasperated*) Yes. Yes. What is it?

MRS McC: Do you know anything about this young man they call Peter?

MR McC: I don't know anything about him and I don't want to.

MRS McC: I saw him last night. He's terribly like your sister-in-law's first cousin.

MR McC: (*Irritably*) What's that?

MRS McC: They always were a bit inclined, your sister-in-law's family, for dancing and capers. It's in the blood.

MR McC: What is?

MRS McC: Ach, nothing darling. I'm sorry to interrupt you. Are you getting on all right?

PETER: (*Without*) Tom. Tom. (*He enters hurriedly with a golfbag and almost stumbles over* SCOTT'S *outstretched feet.*) Damn! Oh. I beg your pardon. I'm so sorry. Oh Tom. Tom. Lend me a couple, quick. Pay you back when I've seen Partridge.

TOM: Easy, sir. (*He indicates* SCOTT *with a warning gesture.*) Be quiet. Boss's orders. No account to be disturbed. (*Fumbling in his pockets and producing notes*) There's two. Wait. One second sir. Note of your engagements —

MRS McC: (*Excitedly to her husband*) John. John dear. John. It's him.

MR McC: (*Angrily*) Who? What's the matter?

MRS McC: Nothing darling. Nothing.

TOM: (*Handing* PETER *the note of engagements given by* PARTRIDGE) From Mr Partridge. Your engagements for today. And he said to pay particular attention to No. 45 sir.

PETER: (*Studying the note*) No. 45? No. 3 and all following dances with Miss Van de Meizer. (*Anxiously.*) What's she like, Tom?

TOM: Number eleven. Outsize. American. And rehearsal again tonight at 6.30 in the annexe.

SCOTT: (*Drowsily*) Yessm. Partridge'll keep um busy.

PETER: What's this in pencil opposite No. 3. Is it 'M. J.'?

TOM: Yes sir. Excuse me sir. Little note of mine. (*Whispers*) Boss seemed a little upset today, sir.

PETER: At what?

TOM: Wants more jizz, sir.

PETER: More what?

TOM: More jizz, sir. Tell Mr Peter, says he, that he wasn't up to the mark last night at the singing. Tell him to put more —

PETER: I quite understand. 'M. J.' means more jizz.

TOM: Yes sir. (*The sound of an angry altercation outside.* COLONEL BLAKE *appears.*)

COLONEL: Gordon? Where the devil are you?

PETER: Come on in here, Colonel.

TOM: *(Simultaneously)* Ah, Mr Peter, keep that old gentleman out.

COLONEL: So here you are. (*Sees* SCOTT.) Who's this?

TOM: (*Despairingly*) Oh, James's Gate. Here's Typhoon now. No more siesting for you, Mr Scott. (*To* PETER) Afternoon teas in the other lounge sir.

COLONEL: No. None of your wishy-washy teas for me. Whiskey soda. For two. And here. We stop here. Must sit down.

TOM: Over here, sir. (*He guides them to a table as far away from* SCOTT *as possible.*)

COLONEL: (*Looking at* SCOTT) Sleepy sot. Hate that sort of life. Guzzling food all day and no exercise. Snoozing in armchairs all day. (*Suddenly addressing* SCOTT) Fresh air. That's the tonic you want. Wake up, sir.

TOM: (*To* PETER) Careful sir. Don't disturb him sir. You're having tea, gentlemen?

PETER: Yes.

TOM: The other lounge, please, gentlemen.

COL: No. No tea. And I stay *here*. Bring two whiskeys and sodas, here. (*Exit* TOM.)

PETER: I say, that reminds me. Sorry Colonel. (*He hands over notes.*) I owe you two over the last game.

COL: Oh. Right! Yes. Two. (*Counting*) Right.

SCOTT: Hm. How do, Colonel. Um? Nice game golf. Um.

TOM: (*Hurriedly entering with the drinks*) Pardon me, Colonel. Excuse me, gentlemen. (*He places drinks on a table still more distant from* SCOTT.) More comfortable over here, gentlemen. (*To* PETER) Pardon, sir. Star man you know Mr Peter. Inspector. Hotel Vet, sir. Keep off the grass. Excuse me. Keep the man of war off the rocks, Mr Peter.

COL: Look here, what about another 18 holes tomorrow first thing? Nine o'clock?

PETER: Right.

COL: And the usual guinea? Right. (SCOTT *snores.*) Damn that fellow. Stop that, sir! I hate snoozers. Drum them out of the service. (*A piano sounds faintly.*) What's that?

TOM: It's Mrs Blake and your niece, sir. The young lady's in the drawing-room playing the piano.

COL: My wife down from her room, then?

TOM: Yes sir. Came down after lunch, sir.

COL: Good. Your very good health young man. Glad to have met you. (*Drinks.*) Saw you dancing last night. You sing also?

PETER: I try to, sometimes.

COL: Sing? Why?

PETER: Well — Partridge thinks I can sing.

COL: Oh! Well pardon me. I don't. And I hate singing. Never could sing. Don't like it. Like sport, horses, fresh air. None of your singing business for me. Wouldn't object so much but I served 25 years in the 5th Mahrattas, Bungapore. We sang 'Old Lang Syne' once a year. Christmas. Rotten tune. Rotten head next morning. Take my advice, stop singing. Leads nowhere.

PETER: I have to. Sometimes. And tonight I must. With more jizz.

COL: Must! Bosh! My wife said to me — 'We'll try the Excelsior again this year. I believe it's really fine now.' So I said, 'Right. One condition. No more singing doleful things in the evening. Can't stand songs like 'Mona' or 'In the Gloaming'. Too much like cattle lowing.' (*He looks hard at* PETER.) You remind me very much of somebody, Gordon.

PETER: That so?

COL: Yes. Funny. Ever meet you before anywhere else, did I?

PETER: Not to my knowledge.

COL: No? Must be wrong then. Damned funny though. Was sure I had.

PETER: Why?

COL: Ah! (*After another sharp scrutiny*) Now I know who you remind me of! Jordan! That's it.

PETER: Jordan?

COL: Yes. Bungapore. Devil called Jordan from the sappers came out there to fix up a waterworks or something. Never did it. Too much this. (*He motions to the whiskey.*) What about a walk after dinner, before our bridge? Go and see the new harbour works, what?

PETER: Sorry. I couldn't possibly. Do you take an interest in harbours?

COL: Well, I'm Chairman of Company building that new harbour out there. Didn't want the d—d post — refused it last time. Funny thing, my niece Joan takes an interest in it. Most extraordinary girl! Actually found her once reading some book about Docks, Harbours and Canals or something. (PETER *smiles.*) I said to my wife, 'Joan's gone potty.' What the devil does a woman want knowing anything about Docks or Harbours? Bosh! Ridiculous! Waste of time. All right for someone like you or Jordan. (*Suddenly*) What do you do?

PETER: I — you mean what's my profession?

COL: Yes. What the devil do you do for a living?

PETER: Oh, at present — nothing. Just on a loose end at present. Sorry. I suppose — I'm somewhat vague.

COL: Hm. Vague. Vagueness. Vacuity. Hm. Don't like that in young people. (*Suddenly*) Stop being vague. Do what Joan *shouldn't* be doing. Read up Harbours and Docks and go and dig something — Suez Canal or something.

(PARTRIDGE *enters.*)

PART: Tom! Tom!

TOM: Yes sir.

PART: (*Suddenly seeing* SCOTT.) It's all right. Still here I see. You did him all right, did you?

TOM: Yes sir. (SCOTT *looks up.*) You're all right, aren't you?

SCOTT: Um. How do, Partridge? Um. Very nice here. Most comfortable.

PART: Good. Right. Maybe he'd have a couple of coronas.

TOM: Yes sir. I'll get them sir. (*Exit.*)

PART: Brave day, Colonel. How's the golf?

COL: Fair, fair. Do better tomorrow. Getting the stiffness off. (*Looking at* PETER) Made another couple of guineas off this rascal today.

PART: Good. (*He takes out a newspaper.*) And my heartiest congratulations. There's today's *Times*. You might want to see it, Colonel. There's a reference to your election as Chairman of the New Harbour and Port Co., here.

COL: Yes; didn't want it. Refused election last time.

PART: (*Handing over paper*) I marked it for you — page three. One moment. Peter. Excuse me, Colonel. (*He beckons.*) Come here, Peter.

PETER: (*Rising*) Yes? (PARTRIDGE *draws him aside.*)

PART: So he won off you again at golf did he?

PETER: Yes. One up on the last green.

PART: Aye. I seen the last of the match from the office. You missed that last putt on the 18th nicely. Did you pay him yet?

PETER: Well — yes I did. But you told me on Monday that — (*He hesitates.*)

PART: I told you what?

PETER: That you'd stand the racket and not to worry —

PART: I know. Aye. Well, that's all right, I'll leave it for you in the office. But Peter, here — I'll be wanting a little more return for all this cash invested you know. Six quid in three days — a bit thick you know, Peter. I don't just hand out money for nothing. It's due to me to get some credit for it too, you know.

PETER: But I can't very well tell him it's your money, can I?

PART: No. (*A pause.*) But you needn't just pay him for staying on here by missing putts. (*He looks meaningly at* PETER.) The aunt — she's come down.

PETER: Who?

PART: The aunt. (PETER *looks at him somewhat puzzled.*) You've been paying a little too much attention to a particular young lady, Peter.

PETER: Have I?

PART: Yes. Do you not remember I told you of a particular young lady?

PETER: Yes.

PART: Aye. Well, I haven't mentioned it to you yet, but — well, that's her now. Playing the piano. She's the old warrior's niece. So mind what I told you and nose off. Look after him and the aunt.

(*Piano ceases.*)

PETER: (*Aghast*) So then Miss Blake —

PART: Aye. Miss Blake —

PETER: She's the — she's the —

PART: Aye. She's the one.

PETER: She's the nice girl that —

PART: Aye. The nice-class girl that Sammy Partridge told you about. That's her. D'ye understand? (PETER *makes no reply.*) And the aunt has come down now. Do you see?

PETER: Her aunt —

PART: You seem to be a long time taking it in Peter. You were just paying a little too much attention to the niece. D'ye follow, Peter? Well, just you transfer that attention to the auntie. And give me that bit of scope that we arranged. D'ye see, Peter? The gooseberry season now commences. D'ye follow?

PETER: You never told me this before.

PART: No. But it struck me after last night when I saw you dancing with her, the sooner I told you the better. The auntie's been laid up since they came, but she's up today, I understand. So keep her and the Colonel in good humour. I don't mind investing a couple a quid a day in the old warrior, but I'm the preference shareholder in this business, Peter. You follow.

PETER: (*Grimly*) I do.

PART: Right. Now, just a word more. You weren't quite up to the mark last night in the singing. Course I understand you being a bit — well — I know the crowd was a bit stiff, but — put a bit more jizz into it. Have a ball or two of malt. Just enough like. Sure you needn't mind if you do make a bit of an idiot of yourself. No-one will mind you.

(MRS BLAKE *enters.*)

MRS B: Why, here you are, Tiger. And you never came to inquire how I was. But you needn't bother now. I'm quite fit again, thank you.

COL: Oh, sorry. Bit tired. Just done 36 holes. No lunch.

MRS B: No lunch! Gracious! Have you had your tea?

COL: Wait for dinner now. Far better. Um. Must introduce my partner. Um. This is — what's this they call you, young man?

PETER: Grahame. I mean Gordon.

COL: Oh yes, yes. Gordon — something — Grahame. Gordon Grahame of Claverhouse. My wife, Mrs Blake, Claverhouse. Wife's been laid up since she came here. Just down first time today.

PETER: I'm sorry to hear that.

MRS B: Oh, I'm quite recovered now. And I'm very grateful to you. It's been such a rest having Tiger off my hands for the last couple of days.

COL: Now, now, eh? (JOAN BLAKE *enters. She is a handsome young girl in her early twenties.*) This is my niece Joan. Joan — Claverhouse.

JOAN: (*Smiling*) We met before.

COL: (*Sharply*) When? Oh yes, yes, of course. I saw you dancing with him last night. Hm.

PART: I hope you like your room, Miss Blake.

JOAN: (*Delighted*) I think my room's a charm, Mr Partridge. There's a most exquisite view from the western window. And there's another — (*She laughs*) — do you know, it looks right down on this lounge, uncle! (*She takes* PETER *up the lounge.*) That's it up there. On the first floor!

MRS B: Sorry I can't say there's a view from mine. What on earth made you choose that awful room, Tiger?

COL: Air. I want air. Give me big windows. Don't give a hang for scenery. Windows. That's what I want.

MRS B: Well, you certainly got them all right. It seems all windows. No view, though. I just got so tired of the wallpaper, I got up and came down after lunch. (*Crossing to* PARTRIDGE) Oh, I say, Mr Partridge, I do want to see your new grounds. I've been hearing so much about them.

PART: Certainly. And with the greatest of pleasure, Mrs Blake. Right now if you like.

MRS B: I hear you have a wonderful new rockery garden.

PART: (*Proudly*) Spent six hundred on it last year. Great. A mass of blooms at present. You could almost smell them from here. I'll be delighted to show you round.

MRS B: Come and see it with us, Tiger.

COL: Excuse me, Mary, but I'm too stiff at the moment. You go along with them, Claverhouse.

JOAN: Come along then, Peter. (*Exit with* PETER.)

MRS B: What did she call him?

PART: Everybody here calls him Peter. If we go down to the right and follow them, Mrs Blake, you'll see the new walk I made last year. Full of rhododendrums. The scent of them on a balmy night in June — ach — I couldn't describe it to you. You'd never forget it as long as you lived. (TOM *enters with cigar box.*) Don't forget the Colonel, Tom, with them Coronas. Have a couple, I can guarantee them, Colonel.

COL: Not now. After dinner I will. Prefer pipe at present.

(MRS BLAKE *and* PARTRIDGE *go out.*)

TOM: (*Bringing box to* SCOTT) Cigar, sir, and Mr Partridge's compliments.

SCOTT: Um. No. Not now. After dinner. (*He examines them, however.*) 'Corona de Corona'! Um. Nice. Um. (*He extracts a handful of cigars and puts them in his pocket.*)

COL: Here, waiter!

TOM: Yes, sir.

COL: I'll have one if that clown leaves any —

TOM: (*Hurriedly*) Yes yes. Certainly sir. (*Bringing the box*) They're the real thing sir. We only keep the best here, sir.

COL: Remains to be seen. (*Takes and lights one, then looks hard at* SCOTT.) Is that fellow awake yet?

TOM: Oh yes. Yes sir. (*Suggestively*) Little walk would do you good, sir. What do you think ? (COLONEL *shakes his head.*) Excuse me sir. (*Sotto voce*) Would you mind, sir, if I asked you a request, sir — just a little favour sir. (*Motioning to* SCOTT) The gentleman's an invalid, sir.

COL: Devil of an appetite for an invalid.

TOM: Yes sir. He's got what you call it, the eating diabetes, sir.

COL: Um. More like sleepy sickness. (*He scrutinises* SCOTT *disapprovingly.*) Lazy devil.

TOM: (*Soothingly*) Perhaps you'd like the other gentleman, sir. (*Nodding to* McCLEERY) Very nice gentleman and his wife over there, sir. No. 18.

COL: What?

TOM: No. 18, sir. Poetry.

COL: What?

TOM: Poetry, sir. Ulster poet, sir.

COL: Ulster what?

TOM: Ulster poet, sir.

COL: Bosh! Never heard of such a thing, did you?

TOM: No sir.

COL: Not at all. (*He rises and walks up and down, occasionally stopping to eye* SCOTT *disgustedly. The ball of wool slips from* MRS. McCLEERY'S *lap and attracts his attention. He picks it up.*) What's this?

MRS McC: Oh, I beg your pardon. It's mine. I'm so sorry. I'm afraid —

COL: (*Amiably*) Don't apologise. Don't apologise. Useful work, knitting. (*He hands her the ball.*) When it's well done. If it's not — awful. (*He looks at* McCLEERY.)

MRS MCC: (*Nudging her husband*) This is my husband, Colonel —

COL: How do, No. 18? Must have a name of some sort, eh?

MR MCC: Oh, I'm just plain John McCleery.

COL: Um. Good old Ulster name. Mine's Blake. 5th Mahrattas. Bungapore. 25 years out there. (*Testily*) Hell.

MRS MCC: Indeed life in India must be a very trying thing indeed. I believe the heat —

COL: Quite. Heat. Mosquitoes. (*Looks at* SCOTT.) No snoozing in India. 130 degrees in the shade, Bungapore. Hottest Station in India. (*He looks hard at* MCCLEERY.) Ulster poet?

MR MCC: Well, I'm not exactly a poet. I'm just in my old age indulging in a little versifying.

COL: Um. Ever publish anything?

MR MCC: Well, the *Whig* took one or two little things I made out last winter.

MRS MCC: Oh indeed he's just a little too modest, Colonel Blake. They took one in *The Bell* the other day.

COL: Um. Did they?

MRS MCC: And now he's thinking of getting out a little book of verse.

COL: Um. Read me one of them. Short one.

MRS MCC: Go ahead, John. It's no harm to see what a man like the Colonel would think.

MR MCC: (*Diffidently*) Well, I was just working out a wee one here. It's a wee bit like what you know Mr Yeats would be trying. I think it's something in his style like:

'Away where the curlews cry on the bog,
There sounds the faint wild bark of the dog,
And oh! to be there
When the caravan fair
Billows and sways in the evening air.'

COL: (*Delightedly*) Right! I say, jolly good! Bog — dog. Damn fine! Love bogs and dogs. On you go. Another verse.

MR McC: I'm just working at the next one. I — well — I — I haven't quite got the idea for the next one.

COL: (*Enthusiastically*) Well. Extraordinary. Yes. Jolly good idea. Now let me see. We're out in the bog. Yes. I have it! Next verse. Grouse. Drive. Butts. Grouse coming over you with a following wind. 90 miles an hour. Grand! Next verse. Get into the butts. Describe the grouse coming over with the wind. H'up! Over they go! Bang! Bang! Right and left barrel. Got 'em! Good dog! Fetch 'em!

MRS McC: (*Hastily*) Of course, it's very difficult work you'll understand Colonel.

COL: Oh quite, quite. (*The ball of wool slips again, he retrieves it.*) Your ball, madam.

MRS McC: Oh, thank you. I'm afraid this ball of wool of mine is a bit of a nuisance.

COL: Yes yes, quite. Husband here should invent something. Pocket or something to keep it in. Cartridge bag or pocket.

MRS McC: That's a nice young man you had out golfing.

COL: Oh, yes yes. Quite.

MRS McC: I suppose you know him very well, Colonel?

COL: Don't know the rascal from Adam. Got here on Monday. Told Partridge I wanted a game. He put up this Claverhouse chap. Ha, ha! Took a couple of guineas off him so far. Must have another rattle at him tomorrow. (*Suddenly — going towards entrance.*) Must have a little stroll before dinner. Must see what's become of my womenfolk. (*Looks at* SCOTT.) Lazy devil! Get up, sir.

TOM: (*Hurriedly*) Excuse me sir I think I see your party out there, sir. (*The* COLONEL *looks, nods and goes out.*) Thanks be to God! He puts me in a tremble every time he looks at you, Mr Scott.

SCOTT: (*Sleepily*) Um.

TOM: Yes sir. Drat them flies. (*He flicks serviette.*) It's all right he's gone out, sir. (SCOTT *opens an eye and nods sleepily.*) Never mind him, Mr Scott. A dasint ould gentleman but he can't stand still for two seconds. Not like you, Mr Scott.

SCOTT: (*Drowsily*) Um. Yes. Um.

TOM: Yes sir. Them Indian soldiers has all their livers gone wrong. Eating nothing but curried chicken and Bombay duck. Not like you, sir. (*He busies himself attending to the screen and cushions, and talks soothingly to* SCOTT.) Not like you sir. You know what's what. None of them made-up dishes for us connoisseurs, Mr Scott. You and me, we knows better than that. No shepherd's pie for us, Mister. Not likely. (SCOTT *grunts.*) Another little snooze sir. Right. (TOM *retires to watch him from a distance, then catches* MRS. McCLEERY'S *eye.*) The boss getting on well, ma'am?

MRS McC: (*Warningly*) Shush! Yes, Tom, very well.

TOM: That's good. (*He looks hard at* McCLEERY *who has all the appearance of distraction.*) D'ye know, ma'am, he should get Mr Peter to help him.

MRS McC: Peter?

TOM: Sure, isn't that what Mr Peter is here for? Helping people.

MRS McC: I wonder who he is!

TOM: He just landed out of the sky like, one day with Mr Partridge. And I suppose he'll go off again the same way.

MRS McC: I wonder where he comes from.

TOM: The divil a one of us knows, ma'am. But Mary, the housemaid up on No. 5 floor tells me he has some old label on his bag with an address on it. Something like — Bally — Bally-Something, Co. Leitrim.

MRS McC: I wonder by any chance could it be Ballywilder?

TOM: That's it. That's it! Ballywilder!

VOICE: (*Off*) Waiter.

TOM: Yes, sir. (*He goes out.*)

MRS McC: (*Excitedly*) There, there. I just knew it was him! John! John! Darling!

MR McC: (*Angrily*) What?

MRS McC: Wasn't it at Ballywilder in Leitrim that John Grahame, the wild young man lived, who made the runaway match with your sister-in-law's first cousin?

MR McC: Yes, yes. Why? These people are all dead long ago, thank goodness.

MRS McC: Indeed, nothing of the kind. There was a young boy and girl left, anyway. And your sister-in-law's first cousin died and then he died, and the place was sold afterwards to Joseph Halliday, their uncle. And they were all living there two years ago.

MR McC: Don't interrupt me any more. *(Heatedly)* The old Colonel has the whole thing destroyed on me.

MRS McC: Ah, don't say that, darling.

MR McC: He has, he's got my imagination into them butts and I can't get out of them. (*Maddened*) Damn him with his right and left and bang! — bang! That sort of thing is all right for epic poets but I'm a lyric poet —

MRS McC: (*Soothingly*) Indeed, you're a lyric, darling.

MR McC: And the last thing you want in a lyric is guns and shots and bangs!

MRS McC: Yes, yes, I know that, darling. But it's interesting, isn't it, to get the outlook of that class of people on your work? After all, it's him and his class that really reads anything worthwhile. Isn't it, love?

MR McC: I wonder!

MRS McC: (*Musingly and to herself*) The same name too. I just did right, I know I did, to write Joe Halliday that letter yesterday.

MR McC: Write? What were you writing to Joe Halliday yesterday? If there's one man I detest it's that Joe Halliday. What did you write to him about?

MRS McC: It's all right, darling. Don't worry. (*A pause.*) Do you not think we should go and dress for dinner, darling? You didn't do it last night, but tonight's a bit special. And a wee rest would do you good. You've been a long time now composing.

MR MCC: Ach! Damn that man and his right and left and bang! — bang!

MRS MCC: There there, darling. Let's go upstairs for a change. Come along.

(MCCLEERY, *grumbling, obeys, and they both go out. There is no one left in the lounge but* SCOTT, *who snores contentedly. A gong sounds, booming through the lounge.* SCOTT *wakes suddenly, yawns and stretches himself.*)

SCOTT: Um. Where's everybody? Um. Company seems to have gone. Um. Must dress — Better have a little walk before dinner. Um. (*He picks up the programme, feels for his glasses and puts them on.*) Um. Not menu. (*He throws it down.*)

COLONEL: (*Off*) Um. Must have little stroll. Um. (SCOTT*exits hurriedly.*)

PART: (*Off*) Off for a little walk, Mr Scott! Good. (*Enters with the* COLONEL *and* MRS BLAKE.)

MRS B: I must say, Mr Partridge, the view from the little walk was certainly exquisite.

PART: Aye. Your niece seems to be taking a long interest in it.

MRS B: Well, certainly no one could keep from admiring it. I couldn't blame her. (*A pause*) Didn't we hear a gong going?

PART: Aye. We sound one three quarters of an hour before dinner as a warning to dress, like.

COL: I see — Snoozer's wakened up and gone out. Only thing wakes him up!

MRS B: Joan had better hurry. You'll tell her, Mr Partridge? We'd better dress now, Tiger.

COL: Poet's gone too, I see. Bog. Dog. Hm. Funny. (*The* COLONEL *and* MRS. BLAKE *go out.*)

PART: (*Looking out L*) What's keeping that young pup! After me warning him, too.

(*He watches moodily.* JOAN *and* PETER *suddenly enter.*)

JOAN: We stayed to see the sunset. It was really wonderful. Do you know, Mr Partridge, I've seen very few views to compare with that from the old cromlech. The picture you get there of the little village in the sandhills at the foot of Slieve Aughlish across the bay is most remarkable.

PART: (*Somewhat mollified*) Maybe you'd do a little picture of it sometime. (*He picks up a hotel guide.*) There's a photograph of it here, of course, on this, but I would prefer something a bit more arty, like.

JOAN: You certainly chose a beauty spot for your hotel.

PART: Sammy Partridge o' Ballymena isn't backward when it comes to recognising the beautiful. (*Looking at her*) Beauty always appealed to Sammy Partridge.

JOAN: (*Laughing*) I believe you.

PART: (*Emboldened*) In old days, Popes and noblemen and the like encouraged the Arts. They're not able to afford the like now. So it's up to us, to them that has it, to take their places, like. (*Looking at his watch*) It's getting close on dinner time, and you Peter, you have a rehearsal —

JOAN: What?

PART: It's all right, Miss Blake. I just want a word with Peter.

JOAN: Oh. I really must thank you Mr Partridge for that lovely room. Last night it was wonderful to see the new harbour away in the darkness, all lit up with flares — I must be off. See you later, shall I, Peter?

PETER: Yes. (*Exit* JOAN.)

PART: Aye. Sit down here, Peter. (*The latter does so.*) You seem to be forgetting something.

PETER: What?

PART: Aye. I suppose — (*Suddenly*) She's a nice girl, isn't she, Peter?

PETER: Yes.

PART: Aye. (*A pause*) You managed that very nicely.

PETER: Managed what?

PART: Oh aye. Oh, you're very simple, oh yes. You done it very well. (*Sarcastically*) Peter the Great! Peter Simple, the Midshipman! But don't try it on again, Peter.

PETER: I don't understand what you're driving at.

PART: Didn't you agree to do something for me?

PETER: Yes I did. I'm doing all you asked me.

PART: Aye. And a bit more. Didn't I tell you that was the girl?

PETER: Yes.

PART: Aye. Well, that girl's for Sammy Partridge, not for broken Peter Grahame, the botch student. I'm one that likes a bargain to be a bargain. Your job is gooseberrying. None of your love-making. You can do that with them Blue Room Girls if you want to. (*Suddenly and furiously*) What d'ye give me the slip for?

PETER: I didn't, I never thought of you, not for one second. She wanted to see the view from the cromlech so I took her there. Why shouldn't I?

PART: Aye. View from the cromlech! You leave me, young man, to show her the views of the place. D'ye understand? Them views is mine. I've paid for them. And I've paid for you to mind your business. (*Angrily*) D'ye hear me? Keep that old fellow going with his golf. I'll pay the damages. And if the old lady wants a bit of a walk, go and show *her* the views if you wish. But stand aside when it comes to the young one. That's your contract — keep it.

PETER: I want to tell you something, Partridge. When I entered into this contract, I — I had no idea that it was — well, that it was Miss Blake — was the particular girl you mentioned to me.

PART: (*Sarcastically*) Did you not, Peter.

PETER: No.

PART: And what are you going to do, then? (*A pause*) You going to fight me for her? All right. Go on then. But if you do — clear out of the hotel. And hand me back what you owe me before you go. There's a tidy little sum owing me as you know. Can you square it up?

PETER: You know well I can't.

PART: Right. What are you going to do then?

PETER: I — I —

PART: Aye. What can you do? Don't be a fool. What hope is there for you, man? Honest? Is there any? I suppose you think because you're young that you'll win her some day! Twenty years hence? Don't be a fool, Peter. Leave her alone. Leave her alone to them that has a right to claim her. Have you any? Have you any money? Have you any brains?

PETER: (*With a movement of anger*) I — I have a right to —

PART: Have you anything at all that gives you a right to even ask for her? Have you? (PETER *does not answer.*) You haven't! Then keep your word to me. Stand clear of the course. That's all.

PETER: (*Despairingly*) Very well.

PART: (*Delightedly*) That's the way. Besides it's not fair to her, you know, Peter. You're a kind of half-baked student with nothing but cabarets and capers to live on. Leave her for them that suits her. (*Suddenly*) Here, we'll have a nip in my room before the rehearsal. Where's Tom? Tom! Are you there, Tom?

TOM: (*Entering*) Yes, sir.

PART: Tom! Send a couple of cocktails to my room, quick.

TOM: Yes sir. (*He looks round excitedly.*) Where is he?

PART: Who?

TOM: The *Star* man, sir. Mr Scott. He's given me the slip.

PART: He's all right, Tom. I saw him out there, having a breath of air, I suppose.

(TOM *goes to one entrance.* PETER *is leaving by the other when he catches sight of someone at a window above. Forgetful of* PARTRIDGE, *who is watching, he smiles and waves as if in answer to a signal.)*

PART: Humph!

(PETER, *suddenly conscious of* PARTRIDGE, *exits hurriedly.)*

PART: Tom! Here Tom!

TOM: Yes, sir.

PART: D'ye see that window up there?

TOM: Yes, sir.

PART: Isn't that in No. 6?

TOM: Yes sir.

PART: Miss Blake's?

TOM: Yes sir. (*He looks at* PARTRIDGE *enquiringly. Then it dawns on his consciousness that there is something afoot which he cannot quite grasp.*) Yes, sir. Anything I can do for you sir?

PART: No.

(TOM *looks at him, then up at the window, and goes out silently.* PARTRIDGE *remains as if awaiting further developments. Moves towards the entrance as if to look up at the window, then changes his mind. He sits down.*)

PART: Right. Aye. Right, Mr Peter, right. We'll see.

(CURTAIN)

ACT THREE

TIME: *Some hours later in the evening of the same day.*

SCENE: *Another lounge of the Excelsior Hotel. There is a large archway at the back closed off by curtains. A similar archway at the side, with looped curtains, gives access to the ballroom which is visible from the lounge. A dance band is playing and an occasional glimpse of the dancers can be seen through the archway. The only occupant of the lounge is* MRS BLAKE *who is seated at a table sipping some coffee and listening to the music. It suddenly ceases; there is the usual applause and the guests who have been dancing come into the lounge. With them is* PETER *accompanied by* MISS VAN DE MEIZER, *a large imposing figure of a woman. They sit down at a corner of the lounge. Following them after a short interval, enter* COLONEL BLAKE *and* JOAN *who go over and sit beside* MRS BLAKE.

(PARTRIDGE *suddenly appears through the curtains from the back.*)

PART: Pardon, ladies and gentlemen. Just before you go off for some refreshment, I want to say that there'll be a longer interval than usual before the last item. I think some of you already know what it is, so I needn't say very much beyond hoping that you'll all appreciate it. I think it only right to mention that most unexpectedly, Viscount and Lady Merton and their party have just arrived and are honouring us with their presence this evening. It is a great pleasure to welcome them, both as regards the management and, I am sure, all the guests who are here tonight, and all I can say is that I hope they and all the other guests assembled here tonight will enjoy their stay in the Excelsior Hotel. Supper now ready. (*Exit.*)

(Faint applause. All the dancers disperse except PETER *and his partner,* COLONEL BLAKE, JOAN *and* MRS BLAKE *who remain behind.* BUTTONS *enters from Ballroom.)*

BUTTONS: No. 18 wanted. No. 18 wanted. Phone telegram, No. 18. No. 18 wanted.

COL: What's that?

BUTTONS: No. 18. Phone telegram.

COL: What name, boy?

BUTTONS: McCleery. No. 18.

COL: Oh yes. Hm. The poet. Go on!

(TOM *the waiter enters from back. He pounces on* BUTTONS.)

TOM: Here. Didn't I tell you to watch Mr Scott? What d'ye mean going off like this, shouting?

BUTTONS: The head boots told me to.

TOM: The head boots has no business to do anything of the kind. Go back at once and look after Mr Scott, and don't let him attempt to go up to his room without letting me know. Off with you at once.

(*Exit* BUTTONS. TOM *goes slowly round the room examining the seats.*)

MRS B: 'Poet' did you say, Tiger? (*Laughing*) Are you actually getting interested in poetry?

COL: This fellow's quite good. Good sport. Something like that Australian bushranger chap who wrote about horses. Forget the name. Entree reminded me of him.

JOAN: The what?

COL: Entree. Snipe we had at dinner. Bog. Hm. Just took a note before dinner in case I saw him again, all the game you find on a bog. Grouse, hare, duck, teal, widgeon — forgot snipe.

VAN: Gee, I say kid, you suits me just cruel.

PETER: Beg pardon, Miss Van de Meizer?

VAN: I say I guess you just suit me A1. You didn't tramp on my Paris footwear or anything. Say, do I book you again in the office or do you carry a slate?

PETER: Why?

VAN: Cause I'm just going to have a cinch on you, kid, for a few lessons. Do you know what I want most particular before I goes back to Sunflower Country and Chico City? Can't you teach jigs and reels?

PETER: It all depends on the pupils.

MRS B: Gee, ain't you modest. (*Laughs.*) Well, I gotta book you for to-morrow and next evening, so just put me on your slate right away.

PETER: Very well.

COL: What about supper?

MRS B: (*Rising*) No, I'm going to the drawing-room to finish that Edgar Wallace.

COL: Joan?

JOAN: No. No supper for me, thanks, Uncle. I'll stay on here. Shall I keep your seats?

COL: Not for me. Can't stand this dancing business. What about a game of bridge?

MRS B: Couldn't you rest yourself, Tiger! You had a very strenuous day. Give your brains a rest.

COL: Oh — game of bridge wouldn't hurt anybody's brains. My mind — quite active now — must do something. Compose poetry or bid five no trump or something. (*He sees* TOM.) Waiter!

TOM: Yes, sir.

COL: Any party looking for a fourth for a game of bridge? Gentlemen preferably.

TOM: Sixpence, shilling, half-crown or pound a point, gentlemen, sir?

COL: Oh, half-crown.

MRS B: Shilling's quite enough, Tiger. Be careful.

COL: Half-crown. Not going to spend my brains on shillings. Half-crown, waiter.

TOM: Yes, sir, I'll see. You won't be occupying this seat, then, sir?

COL: No.

TOM: Thank you. Excuse me, sir. (*He slips a card on to back of chair behind the* COLONEL.) For another gentleman, sir. Whenever you leave, sir; no hurry. (*Exit.*)

MRS B: What on earth has he put behind you, Tiger?

JOAN: (*Reaching over for the card*) 'Reserved.' Oh, I suppose the Viscount wants this particular seat.

MRS B: Well, keep mine for me, darling if you're not coming. Don't be too long at the bridge, Tiger. (*Exit.*)

VAN: When I see Mr Sam Partridge again I'll sure give you some boost, kid. How many dollars a week you getting here?

PETER: Oh, I'm all right that way. Please don't worry.

VAN: (*Persistently*) What you getting? Fifty dollars?

PETER: Thereabouts.

VAN: (*Refectively*) Um. Fifty? 'Taint much. Yep. Guess I can be of some help here all right. Say, did you ever hear of the Helpers' League, over here in Ireland?

PETER: Can't say I did.

VAN: Well, Fire Chief Mulligan of Chico City, he started it. Help someone, somewhere, every day. That's our motto. And I was just wondering who I'd help here, and I guess it's you, kid.

PETER: Thanks very much, but really — I don't need help.

VAN: Now, don't say so. Everybody needs help. You sure need some more dollars and a boost up. I'll speak to your friend Sam, and you bet Sam'll listen to Van de Meizer. You know why?

PETER: I don't.

VAN: There's a party, twenty-five of us from Chico City, doing Europe, and they always send me on in front for enquiry. They're all waiting up in Eustonville Hotel, waiting on Van to send 'em word — cut out or come along.

PETER: I see. Twenty-five.

VAN: Yep. You guess I let our friend Sam know size of our party pretty quick when I came along here. That's how I got room 45 and you for dancing partner. (*Suddenly*) Guess I'll phone them tonight and confirm all O.K., when you and me we've seen Partridge.

PETER: I don't want to see Partridge.

VAN: Well, I gotta see him. *(Rises.)* Say kid, I want to tell you, and you believe it. There ain't no hotel where Van de Meizer of the Helpers' League has stayed at in this whole country, where there ain't someone special on the hotel staff — bell-hop or chef or waiter, that ain't got a rise in wages 'cause of me and my Helpers' League. Ain't that what you call helping people?

PETER: It certainly is. (*They go off.*)

COL: (*Rising*) Any money, Joan?

JOAN: I'll stand in with you for a five. (*She gives it to him.*) Is that enough?

COL: Oh, quite, quite. Sight's getting very bad. Wasn't that Claverhouse?

JOAN: Yes, it was.

COL: Oh. What the devil does he dance with all the old dowagers for, all night?

JOAN: Why does he play golf with cross old Tigers all day?

COL: Oh that's different. Totally different. Can't compare golf with dancing. Bosh!

TOM: (*Entering*) I've got three gentlemen for you, Colonel. On the main landing. Five-shilling gentlemen, sir.

COL: Right. Mum's the word, Joan. (*Exit.*)

TOM: (*Arranging chairs*) Excuse me miss. For Mr Scott.

JOAN: Who?

TOM: Mr Scott, miss. A very quiet gentleman, miss. But how long he'll stay that way this evening, I don't know. Terrible commotion this evening, miss. (*Confidentially*) Had to change him out of No. 3. We're putting the Viscount into it. 'Keep Mr.

Scott well dosed, Tom,' says the boss, 'and he won't be a bit the wiser. And keep him downstairs at all costs out of the way.' But I tell you, Mr Scott isn't just as stupid as he looks. You don't hold a job like that without brains stowed away somewhere. (*Suddenly stopping and looking at* JOAN) Are you fond of dancing, miss?

JOAN: Yes.

TOM: Aye. Why wouldn't you be? Excuse me, miss, but do you know what I think is the loveliest thing in the world? A young girl dancing! Rosebuds in the springtime. Be me soul, but it is too short a time that they are that way too. Aye. The Lord be with them. Here he is! (SCOTT *escorted by* BUTTONS *appears chewing an unlit cigar.*) Here's Mr Scott now. Excuse me miss. Now sir. Your seat. (SCOTT *nods vaguely but pays little attention. He insists on examining the texture of the curtains.*)

TOM: (*To* BUTTONS) Were you with him all the time since?

BUTTONS: Yes.

TOM: You're sure he didn't go upstairs?

BUTTONS: No.

TOM: (*With sigh of relief*) That's all right. Did they get all the Viscount's stuff into No. 3 yet?

BUTTONS: Not yet. I never seen as much baggage to get in. And — (*pointing to* SCOTT) his was just as bad to get out.

TOM: Tell them to hurry. I can't keep the gentleman downstairs all night. (*Exit* BUTTONS.) Now, Mr SCOTT. Your seat, sir. How does it suit you?

SCOTT: (*Settling down*) Excellent. V' good. (*He sees* JOAN.) Excuse me. Hope you don't object to cigar, um?

TOM: Ach, the young lady won't mind. Sure you don't miss? Smoke away sir. (*He lights a match.*) Now sir. A good long strong pull and all together. That's it. Going strong now, sir?

SCOTT: Um. Thank you. V' good cigar. Um. Nice room. Um. Programme please.

TOM: Programme? Here you are sir. (*Hands him one.*) All over now but the last item, sir. The ballet, sir.

SCOTT: Um. Yes. Ballet. Um. Waiter! If you see that boy Peter, tell him I want him. Um. Most important.

TOM: Certainly sir. I'll get him for you. Like a little curacoa and brandy sir? Go very well with the cigar, sir.

SCOTT: Um. Quite so. Um. (*Looking at* JOAN) Young lady like something too?

JOAN: Oh no thank you. I have some coffee here.

SCOTT: (*To* TOM) Um. V' good. And about so much brandy — Courvoisier.

TOM: Yes sir.

SCOTT: Can't read this programme without glasses. Must go up to No. 3 and get them. (*He attempts to get up but is restrained by* TOM.)

TOM: Don't attempt to be running up and down them stairs. sir. Bad for you. Where are the spectacles, sir?

SCOTT: Room No. 3. Um. On the dressing table.

TOM: Yes sir. And don't stir sir, whatever you do till I come back. Curacoa, glasses, Curvoisier. Right. (*Exit.*)

SCOTT: V'obliging fellow that waiter. Um. Splendid hotel this. Um. My room No. 3 couldn't be beaten for comfort in the Hotel Cecil. *(Looks at programme.)* Orchestra keep very good tempo. Um. Don't you think?

JOAN: Yes.

SCOTT: Partridge very clever. Does it well, you know. Um. *(Laughs knowingly.)* Um. Oh clever! Picks up talent all r'. Good sense. Um. Good staff. Um. Chefs and waiters. Um. But — Peter! I like that boy! Um.

JOAN: (*Beginning to take new interest in his talk.*) Do you? Really?

SCOTT: Yes (*Confidentially*) V'funny last night. Partridge gave lil' party in his room. Peter there. V'funny. Clown. Um. Partridge sort of ringmaster. Um. Made me laugh. Um. But Peter — extrar — extraor — ekstrtaor — Life very ex — ex — extra — must get away from that word. Life very — much up and down — round and round, v'difficult — constant movement

— river flowing along — um — carry you along — um. (PETER *enters.*) Hm! V'man I wanta see. 'Scuse me. Goo' boy. Goo' boy. (*Fumbling in vest pocket.*) Pardon me, my card. (*Producing it.*) S. Nelson Scott. S. for Seosamh. Irish part. In Eire — Seosamh N. Scott. In Northern Ireland — S. Nelson Scott. (*He stares hard at* PETER.) I want most particularly speak to you, Peter. (*Turns suddenly to* JOAN.) This young lady — interested in you in any way? Um? (JOAN *looks at* PETER *and smiles.*) No? V'well. You and me, Peter, we talk. You stand there. Just a moment. Now. (*He pauses.*) What's the most important thing in life? Um? Peter?

PETER: (*Smiling at* JOAN) Hard to say.

SCOTT: Well, I don't consider it hard to say; it's being absolutely thorough. (*Emphatically*) Whatever you do — do it — thoroughly. (*He sips his drink.*) Yes, thoroughly. For instance, I thoroughly vet and examine this hotel. Don't I? Yes, I do. Thoroughly. And I have to see what it's like to sleep in, and eat in, and drink in. And I do it — thoroughly. And that's why I'm Chief Inspector of the — um — the — doesn't matter. Understand?

PETER: I do. Thoroughly.

SCOTT: Right. (*He turns to* JOAN.) Colonel thinks I snooze all day on sofas. Quite entitled to his opinion. But I do more'n snooze all the time. Quite wide awake is S. Nelson Scott. Quite. Quite. If you want to be — engineer — be an engineer. If you want to be cabaret artist — be one — but be thorough. Very well, now. I help you. I go — other hotels. Much finer — bigger than Excelsior. And I'm interested in you Peter. Sufficiently to write to big hotel man at Llandadero — inth — and I got letter back. Letter I want most particularly show you. (*Fumbling in pocket*) Must have left it in my lounge suit. (*Suddenly*) Wait. Wait. Just you stay here. Most important. Secret. Um. Get it from my room. No. 3. Important letter. Um. Keep my seat. (*He rises.*)

JOAN: (*Laughing*) Oh please, Mr Scott —

SCOTT: Won't laugh when Peter sees letter. Must get it. Um. (*Exit.*)

JOAN: Forgive me, Peter, for laughing. I can't help it. Tom was asked to keep him back while they were changing his room. (*She grows serious. A pause.*) Peter!

PETER: Yes.

JOAN: You seem afraid of something.

PETER: (*Breezily*) No. I'm not. I don't care. (*Sits by her.*) There. He can do what he likes.

JOAN: Who?

PETER: I'm near you again, so it doesn't matter. That's all I care about.

JOAN: What are you doing in this place, Peter?

PETER: I thought you might have guessed by this time.

JOAN: Partridge has bought you?

PETER: Yes.

JOAN: For how long?

PETER: As long as he likes to keep me, I suppose.

JOAN: Peter, last night when I looked out and saw away across the bay the big flare lights and shadows of men, and gantries, and the great blocks of stone moving into place — I —

PETER: Yes?

JOAN: I was sure you'd be out there among them, somewhere, and instead — Oh Peter! It's hard to say what I think, down here — in this place. There was once upon a time a Peter who told me he couldn't build harbours or docks or canals until he got a certain book — (*She pauses.*) But when he got it —

PETER: Joan!

JOAN: — he forgot all about it and went off to play. You won't need that book, any more now Peter, so would you please give it back to me?

PETER: Give back — your book?

JOAN: Yes. It won't be any use now — any more to you, Peter. But I would like to keep it — just as a memory of a boy who once — passed by.

PETER: (*Desperately*) No, I won't. You don't understand — it's no use trying to explain to you, I suppose, but I'm not going to give up that book — that's something of you I'll never give up. Never.

(TOM *comes in with tray and glasses, puts it on table beside* PETER, *then looks up with a gasp of dismay.*)

TOM: Oh! James's Gate! Where is he?

PETER: Who?

TOM: Mr Scott.

PETER: Gone to his room to get a letter.

TOM: Heavenly Father! I'm ruined! (*Hastens out, muttering.*) Them four stars will remain in the heavens, now and forever, amen! All the Holy Apostles Peter and Paul — (*Exit.*)

PETER: Joan. I — I want to tell you something. You believed in me once — I know you did — That's true. Isn't it?

JOAN: Yes.

PETER: I didn't tell you before Joan, that I — I failed. Went down in the final. That seemed to end everything. Then Partridge came and offered this — this chance of an escape. I took it — that's why I'm here. And I tried down here to forget all that happened until I suddenly met you last night. When you spoke to me, I knew that you hadn't guessed the truth. (*Despairingly*) That big wonder work out there — that great new harbour that you saw — it has been calling to me ever since you came — calling out at night to me with its sirens and its gantries — 'tell her the truth, Peter Grahame, so that she might forgive — and say goodbye.'

PART: (*Without, loudly*) Peter!

PETER: That thing shouting — it owns me!

JOAN: No no — I —

PART: (*Loudly*) Peter! (*Enters.*) Ah, this is where you are! Time you was changing for the ballet. Go and put on your clown's clothes, man. You're late.

PETER: Good-bye then, Joan.

JOAN: Until I see you again, Peter, good-bye.

(*Exit* PETER.)

PART: I'd like to see you after the show is over, Miss Blake. There's something I'd like to talk to you about. It —

(MCCLEERY *enters. He peers anxiously round room.*)

PART: Looking for something, Mr McCleery?

MR MCC: Yes, my wife and I have been looking for Mr Gordon or Grahame, or Peter, I think you call him. We have important news for him. (*Sits down wearily.*) Oh, dear; Oh dear! It's very hard to get anything done in this life. He's not here?

PART: He won't be available until the ballet's over.

MR MCC: How soon would that be?

PART: Very soon now. A word with you afterwards, Miss Blake. (*Exit.*)

MR MCC: A most extraordinary thing. This young Peter man turns out to be a relative of mine that's been missing from home for some time.

MRS MCC: (*Entering hurriedly*) Did you find him yet, John darling?

MR MCC: No, he's dressing for the ballet.

MRS MCC: And here's his Uncle Joe coming tonight — expected any time now — and if he finds him in the middle of all this goings-on sure we'll only have made things worse than ever.

MR MCC: Worse! I should say so. And what about me? Oh dear! It's been the same for forty years as far as I'm concerned. Just when you get the inspiration coming and just when you're on the tick of getting exactly what you want and believe is right — there's a knock at the door, or the dinner gong goes, or that military gentleman butts in or some child borrows your pencil or your pen, or you — you with your putting your nose into things you've no business to put them into — sending off messages to Ballywilder and bringing that fellow

Joe Halliday down here. A man I have the utmost abhorence for. An old Jansenist heretic that never saw beauty in anything but the Bank of Ireland on a pound note. You bring the horror of my life down here on me, and for what? What's this young fellow to you or to me? Or what matter does he make to either of us one way or the other? (*Excitedly*) If he wants to to go to hell his own way, let him!

MRS McC: (*Soothingly*) Well, sure I did it for the best darling. And there now, there, now that there's quiet here, perhaps you could just try that wee last line again? Wouldn't you darling? Do!

MR McC: (*Grumbling, taking out pencil and notebook*) Some of these days I'll just go ahead and finish what I'm at, and everybody else can go to Beelzebub.

(A gong sounds the warning for the ballet. SCOTT *appears accompanied by the* BUTTONS *and* TOM, *carrying a glass.)*

TOM: (*Luring* SCOTT *with the glass*) Here you are, Mr Scott. (*Mops his brow.*) And here's your whiskey and soda, sir. (*Arranges chair and speaks excitedly to* JOAN.) Thanks be to God, miss, he seen the Colonel on the landing and that delayed him till I caught up on him. (SCOTT *puts on his glasses, and wanders slowly over to* McCLEERY.) It took three of the best green chartreuse in the house, and the head waiter himself, to keep him downstairs while I went up and found the letter he wanted, and the spectacles he wanted, and stuck them in his pocket. Bad luck to him! (*Suddenly finding* SCOTT *has wandered off*) Come on, Mr Scott, here's your seat. Over here, sir. (*To* BUTTONS) If he attempts to leave that seat, or this room, and you don't tell me, I'll have you drummed out of the service. Don't dare leave him. *(Exit.)*

SCOTT: (*Sitting down*) Oh. Um. (*Bowing to* JOAN) How do? Oh. Yes. Um. We were interrupted that time. Um. I — most interesting man — head waiter — I've met for a long time — mos' interesting. Um. Now. (*Fumbles in pocket.*) Letter here from Llandanderointh — head waiter knew — hotel there well —

(*A second gong sounds, and the orchestra is heard playing a lively air.* PARTRIDGE *enters from back followed by* PETER *dressed as a Pierrot and both cross to ballroom off-stage. The lights in the lounge grow dim, but the ballroom lights throw a beam on* PETER *as he moves towards it.*)

SCOTT: Goo' boy Peter — I — (*There are cries of 'Hush' and he is silent. Exit* PETER *and* PARTRIDGE. *The lights dim slowly then blackout, to indicate the passing of a few minutes, as the music swells. Suddenly they grow bright again, the music ceases, and there is a loud burst of applause from the Ballroom.* PETER *enters, exhausted, and makes for exit at back.*)

SCOTT: (*Endeavouring to catch* PETER, *but restrained by* BUTTONS.) Peter! Just take this letter and read it. Offering you engagement — winter season — Llandanderointh. Ten a week — don't stay — hic — here, Partridge — hic — no good, not big — go to Llandanderointh. (BUTTONS *brings the letter to* PETER.) Read letter and come up and see me later in my room. No. 3. Talk it over. Going there now to wait for you. Ta ta! (PETER *takes the letter hurriedly, motions at* JOAN *to stay, and goes out followed by* SCOTT *and the* BUTTONS.)

MRS BLAKE: (*Entering*) Time you were going to bed dear.

JOAN: Yes Auntie. I — I'd like to stay just for one minute or so. I'd like to speak to Peter.

MRS B: Peter? Oh. The boy who was dancing?

JOAN: Yes. I want to say something to him.

MRS B: Say it tomorrow, darling. Come along with me. Come. (*She and* JOAN *go out.*)

MRS MCC: We'll wait and see Peter, John. We must see him. We must save him if we can. I don't know if you agree, but it's a kind of squandering of youth, this sort of life. I'd like to get him back to earth — to realities, I mean. (PETER *enters centre.*) Oh Peter, Peter! (*Rushing to him.*) Peter, do you not know me?

PETER: No.

MRS MCC: And your cousin John, John McCleery?

PETER: (*Dazed*) McCleery? Yes, I do now, faintly. You were at Ballywilder once — long ago.

MRS McC: Ah, he remembers! How well he remembered! The poor, poor boy. Peter dear. Peter. Joe — your Uncle Joe, he's coming tonight to take you home.

PETER: I haven't any home.

MRS McC: Yes yes, you have. You poor wandering boy. Your Uncle Joe — he'll take you back again. He wired us today. (*Producing telegram.*) 'Am certain it is he. Tell him be ready return with me tonight. Have situation ready for him here.'

PETER: I — I thank you, Mrs McCleery, for all your kind thought but — (*Bracing himself*) — I'm never going back to Uncle Joe — Never, never!

MRS McC: When he comes and you see him, you poor wandering boy, you'll think better of it. Indeed you will. Won't you now?

PETER: Never! I'll say goodnight — and thank you. (MCCLEERY *looks at him and then shakes his head.*)

MRS McC: Maybe tomorrow! You'll —

PETER: Never. Goodnight.

(*The* MCCLEERYS *go out sadly. There is a pause. The lights dim.* PETER *sits down dejectedly.* JOAN *appears suddenly. She tiptoes over and puts her hands over his eyes.*)

JOAN: Guess!

PETER: It's you, Joan.

JOAN: (*Laughing*) Yes. I couldn't go to bed until I came to see you, first. And then — to kiss you goodnight. (PETER *rises, they embrace.* PARTRIDGE *enters and stands looking at them.*)

PART: Peter! (*They fall apart.*) Come on. I have a wee party. The Viscount and Lady Merton and some friends in their private drawing-room.

PETER: Again? Tonight?

PART: Yes.

PETER: I just wanted to tell you —

PART: Now go on and none of your fool talk. Go and get changed and smarten yourself up. And do what you're paid for and what you promised to do. You're a man — you're supposed to be one anyway. You made a man's promise. If Sam Partridge said to a man 'I'll do it' — Sam Partridge does it.

PETER: I've tried to.

PART: Tried, have you? Do you want to know the truth about him, Miss Blake?

PETER: She knows the truth.

PART: Oh, does she. Does she know you got ploughed in the exam? Does she know you got thrown overboard by your people? That you daren't go back to face them? An idle, useless, floating straw; no money, no means, not even enough to pay his lodgings. Does she know all that? Did you tell her how I found you down and out? Yes, I found him like that Miss Blake. And what does I do? Pays his debts for him, feeds him, keeps him, gives him a fiver a week. Tell Miss Blake the truth! Aren't you just a botched student without one farthing — that's only fit for the job he's at? (JOAN *moves.*) I'm sorry, Miss Blake — I lost my temper. And I'm sorry, Peter. I — I want you to show these big people what you are — an artist, man. Show them if you can't build harbours, you can do a few fancy leps.

PETER: (*Grimly*) I didn't tell Miss Blake quite all that you have said to her, but Joan — he has told you the truth. (*He goes off through the curtains at the back.*)

PART: Right. (*A pause*) He's gone. (*To* JOAN, *suddenly*) Forgive me, Miss Blake. I — I hope you'll excuse me. I only want to tell you that at the back of me — inside of me — I'm not really so rough, uncouth. (*Overcome with genuine passion.*) Pardon my keeping you, but — I've seen you coming here, off and on — and would you remember — perhaps you'd hardly — all the little things you've said to me, the little hints you dropped about making some difference here and there in this place. (JOAN *moves*) I beg of you — don't go. Listen. Last year you said you thought a rockery garden would look wonderful down at the south foreland. It's there now. It is wonderful, isn't it? But it's only for you it was made, only for you. Your room up there — that blue room — you said once you liked a soft blue shaded room. I got it done! Special from France it come, that wallpapering — 20 shillings a yard! If it had cost 50 shillings a yard, do you think I'd grudge it if I knew you cared for it? And there's hundreds, aye, thousands of little things I'd do for you. Say the word and all I have is yours — yours for all time if Sam Partridge can make it so. (*The lights in the room begin to wane still further. He continues madly.*) Let that little dancing Pierrot go; he's not a man. I'm one, I tell you. Fighting Sam Partridge o' Ballymena! I'm yours, do you hear? I'm yours, ever always — Now the truth is out — and I don't care no more. (*The figure of* PETER, *still dressed in the Pierrot costume, reappears through the curtains at the back, dimly seen in the fading light.*) What is he? Cut him out. Only fit for the job he's at. A dancing jig-penny. A lounge lizard. Something to cod the hours away with — not to use them!

(*The light fades still more.*)

VOICE OF PETER: Listen to him, Joan, for he speaks the truth.

PART: All he's got is youth! That's all — youth! Bah! But oh, believe me — I couldn't keep it back no longer — even though I'm not fit to kiss the hem of your garment — I'm not, I know I'm not — but I've money, money; and if money can make you happy, all that Sam Partridge has, ever will have, ever can hope to have, all that is yours, yours to throw, spin, gamble, buy, bind, lose, bury, toss to the sky — every penny, every sovereign, all of it, all of it — d'ye hear me? Hear me?

VOICE OF PETER: Do you hear him, Joan?

JOAN: I have heard him. (*The room is now almost in darkness.*)

VOICE OF PETER: And what is your answer?

JOAN: (*To* PETER) That you are my true love, Peter, ever and always; and all that he has offered to me, I also offer to you. My love (*Her voice becomes a faint far-off echo.*) My love.

(*The siren of the harbour works begins to blow softly.*)

(*Blackout.*)

(CURTAIN)

EPILOGUE

(The siren continues to blow softly. The darkness gives way to a dim glow of light. As it grows clearer, PETER *is discovered lying asleep in bed in his shabby lodgings. It gradually becomes full daylight. On either side of the bed are* STEPHENS *and* CHARLEY PRENDERGAST. STEPHENS *is blowing into* PETER'S *ear with a small siren whistle.)*

PETER: (*Mumbling in his sleep*) Do you hear him Joan?

STEPHENS: (*Stopping his blowing*) What was the name, Charley?

CHARLEY: Sounded like 'Joan'. Here, wake up! (*He shakes* PETER *vigorously.*) Wake up, Peter!

(*They both shake him.* PETER *wakens, stares at them dazedly. They laugh.*)

STEPHENS: Joan heard you darling.

PETER: (*Bewildered, rubbing his eyes, hoists himself up in the bed.*) Yes, yes. (*A pause.*) This is the queerest — Where is she?

CHARLEY: Who?

PETER: I — I don't quite understand what's happened. (*He laughs joyously, then begins to grasp the fact that he is in bed in his dingy lodgings. He gives a gasp of dismay, and buries his face in his hands.*)

CHARLEY: What's the matter Peter? (PETER *makes no reply.*)

STEPHENS: Poor devil, he's had a nightmare! Usual thing after exams. Hi there Peter! Cheer up, man! What you crying for on a morning like this? The bright and glorious morning of your deliverance, man!

PETER: The morning — of my deliverance.

STEPHENS: Sure is. Poor old Peter! Were you dreaming, son? (*Thumping him on the back.*) You're through, man, through!

CHARLEY: Can't you take it in, Peter? Look here. (*He pulls a newspaper out of his pocket.*) There you are, you old stupid — I marked it for you. Final Engineering Examinations. B.E. Peter Grahame. No. 3 on the list! Distinguished answering in Docks, Harbours and Canals!

PETER: Docks, Harbours and Canals! Her book — and she wanted it back again!

STEPHENS: Who did?

CHARLEY: Wanted what?

PETER: Nothing. It was — only a dream I had. And you tell me I'm through — honest?

CHARLEY: Read the paper, idiot. (PETER *reads, puts it down in silence.*)

STEPHENS: Do you believe us now?

PETER: Yes.

CHARLEY: We met your Uncle Joe this morning.

PETER: Uncle Joe?

CHARLEY: Yes.

STEPHENS: Just in from Ballywilder.

PETER: Ballywilder?

CHARLEY: Yes, he'll be round to see you in an hour or so, after the cattle market's over.

STEPHENS: Peter! He's in great form, Peter. Heard it yesterday, he says.

CHARLEY: And he has that job for you.

PETER: Job? What job?

CHARLEY: Clerk of works on a new reservoir near Ballygilder.

PETER: Reservoir near Ballygilder.

CHARLEY: Yes, said you'd get it easy now and certain, with the degree in your favour. That's all he was waiting on. Said he had the crowd all squared up in the County Leitrim —

PETER: County Leitrim —

CHARLEY: Yes, County Leitrim. Two guineas a week and you can get digs there. Five bob a day and all found.

PETER: Five — five bob a day and all found.

CHARLEY: Yes. You'll be able to save a bit on it. He says so.

PETER: Yes. Two guineas a week and five bob a day. Seven shillings a week in County Leitrim — the land of mud and rushes. What a life! (*A pause.*)

STEPHENS: Here. Your socks, Peter. (*He throws over a pair.*) Rosie found them in the sitting room. One of them had a hole in it and she put a stitch in it. Darned it, I mean.

CHARLEY: And by Jove! I nearly forgot. Sorry Peter. Letter I picked up for you in the hall below. (*Handing the letter to* PETER) Hurry up and get dressed. We'll wait for you outside. (*Exit with* STEPHENS.)

PETER: (*Glancing at envelope, then opening it excitedly.*) It's from Joan! (*He is dismayed on finding only an illustrated circular.*) 'The Excelsior Hotel, Portahoy — Dining-Room — Drawing-Room — the South Foreland Rockery — the Lovers' Walk —' (*A pause*) This is surely the queerest — the funniest thing — Ah! Here's something she has written. 'Old Tiger consented when he saw your name on the lists. Says you're to come here and start work at once on the big new harbour they're making here at Portahoy. We are staying at this hotel. It's owned by a man called Sam Partridge of Ballymena. I wish you heard him talking about it last night — and the wonderful new wallpaper he put specially in my room. He also talked about some young student he is bringing down to entertain the guests, who it appears is an absolute genius at 'singing, dancing and capers.' (PETER *pauses for a moment, then resumes reading.*) 'Some boy called Jordan. He showed me Jordan's photo. I couldn't help laughing and then crying because he is so like you, and because you often told me you were better at that sort of thing than at Docks, Harbours and Canals. Are you, I wonder? What matter if you are. You are my own love, ever and always.' (PETER *folds the letter.*) And she said that to me in the dream. (*He repeats joyously.*) And she said that to me in the dream —

(CURTAIN)

BRIDGE HEAD

A Play in Three Acts

Bridge Head *was first performed in the Abbey Theatre, Dublin, on June 18th,* 1934, *with the following cast:*

STEPHEN MOORE	E. J. McCormick
MARTIN	Arthur Shields
HUGH O'NEILL	Denis O'Dea
MRS MARCUS MORRISEY	Maureen Delany
INARI GOSUKI	Michael J. Dolan
DERMOT BARRINGTON	Tom Purefoy
CECILY BARRINGTON	Eileen Crowe
JOHN KEARNEY	Eric Gorman
DAN DOLAN	Barry Fitzgerald
MAURICE MOCKLER	P. J. Carolan
MICHAEL MORRISEY	W. O'Gorman
PHILIP WATERSLEY	Joseph Linnane

The play was directed and produced by Lennox Robinson.

It was subsequently produced under the direction of Michael MacOwan at the Westminster Theatre, London, for the London Mask Theatre on May 9th, 1939, with the following cast:

STEPHEN MOORE	Wilfrid Lawson
MARTIN	John C. Bland
HUGH O'NEILL	Stephen Murray
MRS MARCUS MORRISEY	Christine Hayden
INARI GOSUKI	J. Hwfa Pryse
DERMOT BARRINGTON	Edward Lexy
CECILY BARRINGTON	Ruth Lodge
JOHN KEARNEY	Adrian Byrne
DAN DOLAN	Charles Victor
MAURICE MOCKLER	Tony Quinn
MICHAEL MORRISEY	Jackson Gillis
PHILIP WATERSLEY	John Brooking

AUTHOR'S NOTE

In the West of Ireland are those areas of overcrowded little tenant farms known as the Congested Districts. They are the rural slums of Ireland.

The tragic history of the Plantations is explicit from the character and situation of the land on which these small-holders earn their livelihood. These congested areas are to be found fringing the western seaboard, the bog and moorland plains of Mayo and Galway, and the lower slopes of the mountains of Connemara, Kerry and Donegal.

Sometimes adjoining, but more often at a distance are the larger holdings — an odd still-existing demesne of one of the former landed gentry, or the wide pasture fields of the grazier tenant.

Successive efforts of legislation since 1891 have been directed towards obtaining this external land for allotment to the people of the congested areas either as enlargements of their little holdings or as new holdings for migrants, whose surrendered lands are used to ameliorate the lot of their neighbours remaining at home.

But the clan feeling of territory still exists, often in a narrow parochial form, and the advent of the congested migrant into a new holding in a strange district is rarely welcome to the local people.

To deal justly with those who have to give up their land so necessary for relief of the congests, to allot this land equitably to the numberless applicants and to install the migrants in the teeth of what is often determined and strenuous opposition, is not an easy task.

The brunt of this work falls upon the local officers of the Irish Land Commission. On the manner in which they deal with all these varying elements of the local population depends the success or failure of land settlement in these remote districts.

It is in memory of those officers who, like Stephen Moore, have given their life and vision to this work, that *Bridge Head* has been written.

RUTHERFORD MAYNE

ACT ONE

SCENE: *The sitting-room of* STEPHEN MOORE *in Mooney's Hotel in Western Ireland. One door opens on to a landing outside. Another door leads into* MOORE'S *bedroom. An old-fashioned fireplace and mantel at the back. A large window on the right looks out on the Market Square. The room is furnished with side-table, chest of drawers, a large table, four or five chairs and a couple of old armchairs. There is a litter of maps, ordnance sheets, files, etc., in all sorts of nooks and corners of the room.*

It is late afternoon of a day in autumn, and MOORE, *who is seated at the table, has just finished writing. His correspondence has been thrown over into one of the armchairs, which serves as a receptacle for his outgoing mail.*

MOORE'S *appearance is that of a hardy, grizzled, weather-beaten official of middle age, with a brusque, alert manner, used to command of men and to working amongst them.*

The chimes of the village clock strike the hour. MOORE *rises, stretches himself, and then quickly goes over and rings. There is no response. He rings again impatiently and then resumes his seat, takes up a sheet of paper and starts in an abstracted way to write on it. The door suddenly opens, and* MARTIN, *the boots, enters.*

MARTIN *is elderly, clean-shaven except for a large drooping white moustache, and his connection with the hotel is indicated by an old braided cap which he seldom or ever discards.*

MARTIN: Did you ring, sir?

MOORE: Yes. I tried to. Bring those letters there to the post. Are the bells out of order again?

MARTIN: Gone to hell, sir. I'm sick telling the boss about them.

MOORE: Where is he?

MARTIN: Ballyhaunis Races. The only bell he gives a damn about is the starting bell on a racecourse. (*He goes over to the letters.*)

MOORE: Hm! (*He goes over to the chest of drawers, extracts a map and sits down to study it.*) Is Mr O'Neill back yet?

MARTIN: No, sir. That reminds me, I was given this picture card to give him. (*He produces a photo-card and reads the writing on it.*) 'The Rose Garden, Mount Nevin.' If he knew as much as I did, he'd have been back in Kilrea a couple of hours sooner. (*He replaces the card in his pocket and starts collecting* MOORE'S *correspondence.*)

MOORE: (*With a sharp glance at him*) Why?

MARTIN: Ach! He's not like you, sir. Sure, you're a kind of a monk. But Mr O'Neill is young yet, and so is she.

MOORE: Oh! So *she* is young, is she?

MARTIN: (*Confidentially*) She is. They always begin with sending picture post-cards, young ones do. (*He sorts over the letters, reading the addresses.*) 'The Secretary' — 'The Secretary' — 'The Secretary.' Aye — That's the gentleman never answers the letters, but never forgets the rent. (*He suddenly peers closely at one of them.*) 'Dermot Barrington, Esq., Mount Nevin House.' (*A pause, then with a look at* MOORE.) That's the father.

MOORE: The what?

MARTIN: The father of the lady. Mr Barrington, he's just come into town and sent word he was calling to see you. I needn't post this, sir.

MOORE: All right. Put it upon the mantelpiece. (MARTIN *obeys.*)

MARTIN: I hear yous are going to give out land up in that country.

MOORE: Who told you?

MARTIN: Sure Mr O'Neill and Mr Kearney went off that way with that little man from Addergoole that was down waiting in the yard this morning.

MOORE: You've a great intelligence, Martin.

MARTIN: Be the same token, Mr Moore, you'd be wise to be putting no migrant up into that country. Begor, the rising that was in 'sixteen' will be nothing to what's coming on yous, if you plant strangers up in that bedlam.

MOORE: I daresay.

MARTIN: It's not blathers I'm talking. Maybe that fellow might refuse to go.

MOORE: He might, if he's fool enough.

MARTIN: If he does, maybe you'd remember Micky Hennessy — my first cousin — that I spoke to you about a Wednesday, that's living up at Sheskin above Gort on the Clare side. Hennessy would take land at the North Pole, if yous would give it to him. And what's more, would pay any rent yous asked him for it.

MOORE: Here, I'll go out for a breath of air to the post office. Give me the letters and I'll post them. Clear up this litter and get those windows opened and a breath of fresh air into the room. (*He folds up the map he has been studying and throws it on the side-table.*)

MARTIN: Right, sir. (MOORE *goes out.* MARTIN *starts to clear up and tidy the room. Goes to the window, opens it and calls out.*) Hi, Jimmy!

VOICE: (*Without*) What?

MARTIN: Any sign of the boss?

VOICE: No.

MARTIN: Right! (*He goes over to the table where* MOORE *has been writing, tidies up the papers, and then picks up the scrap on which* MOORE *has been scribbling.*) Bal — Balnasheeda — The name of God, what's he writing about that back o' beyont about! Something scratched out. O — O'Neill — He's been writing O'Neill and scratched it out again. Kearney, and scratched it out again. (*The door opens and* O'NEILL, *a young man dressed in rough old tweeds, enters. He is flushed and excited looking.*) Oh! Begors, are you back, Mr O'Neill?

O'NEILL: Yes. Where's Mr Moore?

MARTIN: He was expecting yous and Mr Kearney long ago. What kept yous?

O'NEILL: Business. I got a good stroke of business done.

MARTIN: You're a great man, Mr O'Neill. And there's more than yourself thinks it. Now. Here's a picture post-card come for you. (*He hands it to* O'NEILL.)

O'NEILL: Oh! (*Reads.*) 'The Rose Garden, Mount Nevin.' Yes. She said she'd send me this. Beautiful, isn't it? (*He puts it on the mantelpiece.*) Where's Mr Moore?

MARTIN: Gone to post the letters. (*Pointing to the mantelpiece*) Bar that one.

O'NEILL: (*Lifting the letter and looking at it*) Oh!

MARTIN: I told him Mr Barrington was in the town.

O'NEILL: Oh, is he?

MARTIN: Yes. And has the young lady with him!

O'NEILL: Oh! (*Suddenly*) I say, Martin!

MARTIN: Yes?

O'NEILL: You wouldn't notice anything, would you?

MARTIN: About you, sir?

O'NEILL: Yes.

MARTIN: (*After a contemplative examination.*) No sir.

O'NEILL: Well, Kearney told me not to be going near Mr Moore for a couple of hours.

MARTIN: (*Sitting down*) Well now, if I was Mr Moore and was your Commanding Officer, do you know what I'd tell you?

O'NEILL: No.

MARTIN: Go and get Miss Mooney to give you a big double of brandy, and go and brush your hair, and then come and tell me all the great business you've done. And I'd have a great character of you then to give Mr Barrington. (*Maliciously*) Tell me, Mr O'Neill, did you ever hear of a place called Ballnasheeda?

(Knock at the door. It opens and a large buxom woman peeps in. It is MRS MARCUS MORRISEY.)

MRS MORRISEY: Is Mr Moore at home?

MARTIN: No, ma'am, but he'll be in presently.

O'NEILL: Martin! I'll be back in a minute or two. Tell Mr Moore.

MARTIN: Yes, sir.

(O'NEILL *bows to* MRS MORRISEY *and goes out.*)

MRS MORRISEY: Who's that young man?

MARTIN: Mr O'Neill of the Commission.

MRS MORRISEY: Oh! I think I seen him now, somewhere before.

MARTIN: Aye. With somebody, maybe?

MRS MORRISEY: Aye. Just so. Aye. Just so. And a couple of times or more, maybe. (*Suddenly spying the card on the mantelpiece*) What's that up there?

(MOORE *enters suddenly.*)

MARTIN: Mrs Marcus Morrisey, sir.

MRS MORRISEY: And how is yourself, Mr Moore? And I'm glad to see you. And thank you, Martin — you may go. It's just a few words in private I'd like to be saying to Mr Moore before the rest of the beagles get at him.

MARTIN: (*Sententiously*) The land for the people!

MRS MORRISEY: Thank you, Martin, I'd be obliged if you'd attend to them people that's down below waiting this last half hour for news of what Mr Mooney is to bring home from the races. (MARTIN *withdraws.*) And I'd be obliged if you'd shut the door after you. (MARTIN *does so with a bang.*) Now! (*She sits down and smiles genially at* MOORE.)

MOORE: You're Mrs Marcus Morrisey?

MRS MORRISEY: Ah, indeed, and well you know it. And often I've heard of you, Mr Moore, and your kindness to the people. (*A pause.*) Them were terrible nice young men you sent down to our country to work amongst us, Mr Moore. Terrible nice young men, indeed. Ah, but they hadn't the wisdom of Mr

Moore. That's what I said to Marcus. They hadn't it. It wasn't there. Ah, nothing like the real gentlemen for wisdom. Give me Mr Moore every time, Marcus, says I, for he's the gentleman for me!

MOORE: Hm! (*He gives her a hard, sharp look, takes out a notebook and begins writing.*) The land as usual, I suppose!

MRS MORRISEY: Well — we'll come to that presently — I managed to get a lift with Mr Barrington — the gentleman in the big house — Mount Nevin — that you took the land from at Ballyglass. I see a photo of his garden up there. (*She nods towards the mantelpiece.*) Ah! Isn't it nice? A very nice man is Mr Barrington. Ah, there's nothing like the real old gentry, Mr Moore. Nothing like them! The manners of them! Ah, the manners of them! I've often said to Marcus, it's a pity to be taking the land off them, the creatures, but sure it must be done. And Mr Moore will do it, I'm sure, in as nice a way as anyone in the government will do it. Ah, leave that to you, Mr Moore, you'll always do it nicely.

MOORE: Very hard to do everything nicely, Mrs Morrisey.

MRS MORRISEY: Indeed it is. (*A pause.*) Ah, but you — you'll always do it nicely, but them young men of yours — they mean well, Mr Moore, but they don't understand. (*She gives a meaning glance at the card on the mantelpiece.*)

MOORE: Understand what, Mrs Morrisey?

MRS MORRISEY: Well — Just the right way to do things — and then — there's — the — the country people. They just think the land's there to be given to them. And they don't understand all the examination and the selection of them that's selected. It's hard on them, the creatures. They come in and talk in my place in the evening and indeed they have it all planned out. Who is to get and who isn't. But you and I, we know better than that. (*She laughs.*) Heah! Aye! Aha! We — (*She laughs immoderately.*) We know better than that — indeed we do, Mr Moore. The poor creatures! (*Knocking*) Come in.

MARTIN: (*Opening the door and looking in*) Beg pardon. Mr and Miss Barrington's below and wants to see Mr Moore. (*He looks knowingly at* MOORE.) They said they had an appointment and are waiting.

MOORE: Hm! All right — I'll see them presently. (MARTIN *disappears.*)

MRS MORRISEY: I'm glad now Mr Barrington's calling. Pay particular attention to him, Mr Moore. He'll speak the right way of it, and so would Mr Mockler if you happened to know him, the county councillor. He's a splendid man, is Mr Mockler. And I'm so glad you gave that fine holding to Pat Morrisey, the herd. Ah, that was justice — the poor creature! Many's the hour and day that poor creature used to come and tell me his hopes and fears. Ah, but you were the kind gentleman to him. Indeed, I could just kiss you, Mr Moore, for the way you treated that unfortunate man. He's my first cousin by Marcus's side.

MOORE: (*Drily*) I see.

MRS MORRISEY: But Pat's brother Jack — Ah now, Mr Moore, you must do something for poor Jack. The nicest, decentest poor creature that ever walked. Wait till you hear the Barringtons about him.

MOORE: (*Hopelessly*) I'm sure.

MRS MORRISEY: Well now, we heard today, and I could hardly believe it, that Mr Kearney had brought some strange outsider of a man from Addergoole down to show him land. Indeed, I pity Mr Kearney. He doesn't understand, you know, Mr Moore. (*With a sudden change, and vehemently*) They'll never tolerate anyone outside the parish getting land at Ballyglass. Oh, indeed, Mr Kearney may make up his mind to that. (*She rises, goes over to the door, opens it, listens and then determinedly closes it and puts her back to it.*) Is there any chance now, Mr Moore, that I'd get a portion ? You see, the licensed business doesn't pay anything like it used to, and there's my two sons, Michael and James, and I fret about their future. You won't forget about them now, Mr Moore? It would be a great thing now that you have that new house and out-office vacant that you put one of my boys into it.

MOORE: No. I'm sorry, but that's impossible.

MRS MORRISEY: Oho! (*Bridling with fury*) And is it to that little scampeen and cattle-jobber and outsider and stranger from Addergoole that the best land in Ballyglass is going to be given?

MOORE: Yes. It's to be given to Dolan, if he'll take it.

MRS MORRISEY: Oh, indeed! If — if he'll take it! And my two sons that always were foremost in the fight and poor John Morrisey that was the same, they're to be given the go-by, are they, for the stranger, and the outsider? Oh, we'll see more about this, Mr Moore. We'll see more about this, Mr Moore!

(*Knocking at door.*)

MOORE: Come in.

MARTIN: (*Opening the door and speaking to someone behind him*) Come along, sir. (*In a hurried whisper to* MOORE.) Japanese gentleman to see you, sir. (*He ushers in a little dapper Japanese. It is* INARI GOSUKI)

GOSUKI: (*Bowing low, and taking in his breath*) Eh. Go men ma sai. Misterre Moore, I presume —

MOORE: Yes, I'm Moore.

MARTIN: The little Japanese gentleman has just landed by car from Dublin, sir.

GOSUKI: Yes. Dublin! (*He produces card case and hands card to* MOORE.) Card. (*Produces a letter.*) Note of introduce — (*He hands both* to MOORE.) Not — English — good — speak — but — (*Tapping his ear*) Understanding — (*He smiles.*) — good!

MRS MORRISEY: There's a deal in this country very hard to understand. I shall come again, Mr Moore, and I know you'll not say no. Ah! it's not all over yet, please God. It's not all over yet between us. Good-day, gentlemen, good-day. (*She and* MARTIN *go out.*)

MOORE: (*Reading the card*) 'Mr Inari Gosuki. House of Representatives. Diet of Japan.'

GOSUKI: So.

MOORE: I see by your letter, you are studying the land problem in Europe.

GOSUKI: Eh — especial Ireland. Irish peoples land problem — much interest.

MOORE: I see. By the way can I offer you anything? Tea?

GOSUKI: Arignato. No. I thank. No.

MOORE: They didn't send any word from Dublin you were coming.

GOSUKI: No. Excuse. I — to Dublin's people say 'Surprise visit — allow — please.'

MOORE: I see. So you want to know what we're doing here. What our work is.

GOSUKI: Yes. So. Is not all Irish farmer owner of his lands?

MOORE: Yes.

GOSUKI: Den excuse me. Why more want? Do farmer want land and — ze sky also?

MOORE: Mr Gosuki, did you ever look at the sky — at the stars on a clear night?

GOSUKI: Oh. So. Yes.

MOORE: Some parts of the sky, there are thousands of little stars, all close together. Then there's other parts of the sky — almost bare — with very few — but very big stars.

GOSUKI: Eh so.

MOORE: Well, all the places where the little stars cluster together would be like the congested districts of Ireland where the little farmers are huddled together, same as they are around here (*He makes a gesture*) at Kilrea. Thousands of them. If you don't move them out, make the big stars give them room — space — their lights grow dim and are quenched.

(*A low, cheery voice is heard outside, then a loud knock at the door.*

Without further ceremony it is opened, and BARRINGTON *enters, with his daughter* CECILY. BARRINGTON *is elderly and shabby, but unmistakably one of the 'quality'. His daughter* CECILY *is a young, handsome girl in her twenties.*)

BARRINGTON: Aha! We've got the villain in! How are you, Moore? I don't think you've met the daughter before. Cecily, this is Mr Moore. (*With a look at* GOSUKI.) How d'ye do?

MOORE: Oh! May I introduce Mr Inari Gosuki?

(*The introduction is duly made.*)

BARRINGTON: Japanese or Chinese, sir?

GOSUKI: Please — not — Chinese. No. Japans belong.

BARRINGTON: You're a long way from home, sir!

GOSUKI. Eh! Yes. (*Rising*) Perhaps this meeting of family — and — not — official.

BARRINGTON: Stay where you are. We don't care a hoot, if it's all one to Moore. I only want to see him about the land.

GOSUKI: (*Delighted*) Ah! So! (*He extracts a notebook and waits eagerly, pencil in hand, to take notes of the conversation.*)

BARRINGTON: You sent down two of your staff to our place today, Moore, with some rascal from the Addergoole country.

MOORE: Yes.

BARRINGTON: And do you mean to tell me that you're in earnest, planting a stranger like that up there? Bad enough stripping the land off me, but to go and put tinkers from Addergoole on it under my very nose — well, you're asking for trouble!

MOORE: From whom?

BARRINGTON: From the locals.

CECILY: It is quite true, Mr Moore. There will be trouble. I've already told Mr O'Neill.

BARRINGTON: Who's O'Neill?

CECILY: He's one of Mr Moore's inspectors.

BARRINGTON: With all respect to you, Moore, that's no recommendation in his favour. (*To* CECILY) Bless me if I know the half of these people you run about with. Was it that long thin fellow I saw, when we were shooting at Muckanagh Bog?

CECILY: Yes. He's in charge of all that new drainage and roads you admired so much. (*She smiles mischievously at* MOORE.)

BARRINGTON: Admired, did you say! The best duck shoot in Ireland ruined. Absolutely ruined.

GOSUKI: Excuse. Zis gentlemans — is — landlord class?

MOORE: He is.

GOSUKI: And — enemy of — peoples?

BARRINGTON: No, sir. I never was — nor any Barrington that lived! That blackguard there (*He points to* MOORE) — at least, that blackguard department he belongs to, they're the real enemies of the people. Taking land off people that knew how to use and work it, and giving it away to a lot of useless tinkers and tailors that let it or set it or sell it the minute they get hold of it. Confiscation. That's what I call it.

GOSUKI: You — in Japans — same as — daimio. In Japans also confiscations of daimio.

BARRINGTON: The whole damned world's gone upside down.

GOSUKI: Eh! So. Not nice for daimio. For young ladies — (*He looks and bows to* CECILY) troubles also?

BARRINGTON: Yes. She probably won't have a fluke.

GOSUKI: Please what mean fluke?

BARRINGTON: Pounds — pennies — money.

GOSUKI: (*Writing solemnly in his notebook*) Irish daimio angry — lands confiscations — childrens not money much.

BARRINGTON: (*Impatiently*) Moore. What about our own tenants up there. Are they going to get any of that land left over?

MOORE: Any of your tenants who were entitled to land got it.

BARRINGTON: Oh yes. I know all that old official rigamarole. I know that you gave land to Paddy Moran and Johnny Smith, and Mary and Kitty Walsh, and some dozens of other smallholders, and that Pat Morrisey, the herd, got a holding. But they didn't get as much as they should have, and you've kept back forty acres of the best of the land. And now the latest is that you're giving it to some outsider from Addergoole. There'll be hell to pay if you do, Moore. Listen. There's a string of hungry greedy devils, sons of the larger tenants and others that you left out, and they'll raise Cain. And what about John Morrisey, the herd's brother? You've done nothing for John.

MOORE: No.

BARRINGTON: Something must be done for John Morrisey.

CECILY: What has Mr Moore got to do for him?

BARRINGTON: Provide the rascal with land. When the land is there, why shouldn't he get it? He's the head bottle-washer of all that crowd up there, and if he doesn't get it now from Moore, they'll turn round on to me, and that means good-night to Mount Nevin for me. Something must be done for John Morrisey. He's entitled to that land, and a deuced sight better than any outsider.

CECILY: Is he, Mr Moore?

MOORE: No. Our orders were to put in a migrant and we're doing so.

GOSUKI: Please! What migrant?

MOORE: A migrant, Mr Gosuki, is a person who surrenders land for the benefit of others, and migrates to a new holding.

BARRINGTON: Yes. Well, put your migrant somewhere else than Mount Nevin.

CECILY: There always seems to be a lot of bother over land down here. Will it ever come to an end?

BARRINGTON: There'll be miaow over the land till Kingdom Come.

GOSUKI: Excuse, please. What miaow?

BARRINGTON: Cat calls. Pussy calls. (*Mewing*) Miaow!

GOSUKI: Arignato. (*Smiles*) Understand. Cry of cat — nako — milk want. Irish peoples land wants no miaow.

BARRINGTON: Exactly.

GOSUKI: Arignato.

BARRINGTON: Look here, Moore, if you don't give something to those local rascals, life won't be worth living at Mount Nevin. I might as well pack up and get out. So be a sport and a friend of mine and get it done, or else — (*He makes a gesture of despair.*)

(*Knocking at door.*)

MOORE: Come in.

(KEARNEY, *a middle-aged, nervous individual, dressed in old tweeds, wearing glasses, enters.*)

KEARNEY: Oh, I'm sorry, Moore. I didn't know you had company.

BARRINGTON: (*Looking hard at him*) Oh, it's you Kearney! Come in. You're mixed up in this business too.

KEARNEY: In what?

BARRINGTON: Putting some tinker into land up at my place. You and that long thin fellow. And I'm doing my best to tell Moore I object, and in the strongest way I can put it.

KEARNEY: Oh! (*He looks at* MOORE.) The tinker, as you call him, wouldn't take it. How d'ye do, Miss Barrington? (*He nods to* GOSUKI *who bows.*) You're the Japanese gentleman that's arrived? How d'ye do? (*To* MOORE.) Yes, Dolan's refused. And sorry to be so late, but O'Neill had to come home by O'Flaherty's at Killasolan.

BARRINGTON: I know the chap. He has a pub there, hasn't he?

KEARNEY: Yes.

BARRINGTON: Well, I'm very glad to hear you didn't succeed with your business. And don't try any more of that game up there if you value your skins.

O'NEILL: (*Entering, after knocking*) Oh, sorry! (*He makes to retire.*)

MOORE: Don't go, O'Neill. Come in. (O'NEILL *comes in.*) This is O'Neill, Barrington.

BARRINGTON: How d'ye do? You know my daughter, I believe.

O'NEILL: Yes. (*He smiles at* CECILY.)

BARRINGTON: Well, young man, if you want to continue on friendly terms with her father, don't be out on any more jobs bringing small fry from Addergoole up there.

MOORE: By the way, I was almost forgetting, Barrington, there's an official note for you on the mantelpiece.

(O'NEILL *hands it over to* BARRINGTON.)

BARRINGTON: Excuse me. (*He opens it and reads it, then turns and looks hard at* MOORE.) Moore! What's the meaning of this?

CECILY: What is it, Daddy?

BARRINGTON: It's a notice of inspection of our old home. (*With an effort to hide his feelings*) On Monday 8th inst. at 11 a.m. (*He bows his head.*) So it's come to this at last, has it? (*With a sudden bravado*) Here, Moore, you can kill two birds with one stone. Come up and see the old place as my guest on Sunday. Come up, the whole crowd of you, and have a few sets of tennis and a bite of lunch.

MOORE: I'm sorry, I can't.

BARRINGTON: Oh, come on, Moore, and share pot luck, and bring Mr What's-his-name — we might raise a couple of racquets somewhere.

MOORE: I'm sorry. It's impossible.

BARRINGTON: (*Turning to* O'NEILL) You'll come, then? The day after that I'll meet Moore — officially. Goodbye, everybody. Coming, Cecily.

CECILY: Yes. (*With a quick smile, to* O'NEILL.) Be sure to come.

(BARRINGTON *and* CECILY *go out. There is a pause.* KEARNEY *looks at* O'NEILL *and laughs sarcastically.*)

MOORE: So Dolan refused! That's bad news! I want that man put in. (*Moodily*) Refused! (*Sharply to* KEARNEY) Why?

KEARNEY: Said it was the worst bit of land he's ever seen.

MOORE: Did you tell him the annuity on it?

KEARNEY: No.

MOORE: Where is he?

KEARNEY: Below waiting to see you, in the hope of getting land somewhere else, I suppose.

MOORE: We haven't any other holding. He refused me twice before. It's my last chance to get him sanctioned for exchange.

O'NEILL: It's hard on the Barringtons if he accepts.

MOORE: Why?

O'NEILL: If that forty acres were left to Morrisey and the other people up there, they'd leave Mount Nevin alone.

KEARNEY: Aye. For another three or four years.

O'NEILL: Cecily hoped — (*He stops suddenly, a little abashed.*)

KEARNEY: Who?

O'NEILL: Miss Barrington told me her father hoped that in another four or five years, he would be able to stock and work it again, himself.

(MOORE *rises and goes over to the chest of drawers, unlocks it, and extracts a map. It is evident from the way he handles it that it is of importance. He looks over at his two juniors as if slightly hesitant. Meanwhile they continue talking.*)

KEARNEY: Same old yarn her father told Moore and myself ten years ago. The cruel fact is, O'Neill, that the flood of life around this Kilrea countryside can't afford to let people like the Barringtons stay on the land. So some day (*He nods his head to indicate* MOORE) he'll have to do the butcher.

O'NEILL: I hope he never will.

KEARNEY: (*With a slight remorse for the youngster*) I say, Moore. Could you possibly drop that idea of using that forty acres at Ballyglass for a migrant — for Dolan? Make some sort of special plea that it would be in the interests of peace, and law and order — all that stuff — to use discretion and give it to the locals, what?

MOORE: I can't. (*He brings over the map and spreads it on the table.*) And here's my reason. There's Addergoole. Where Dolan lives. Sixty to seventy wretched holdings all in miserable patches of rundale. Look at them. Like a mosaic pavement. But that's not all. (*Impressively*) Look where Dolan's holding runs from the main road down to the River Shivna.

KEARNEY: (*Somewhat indifferently*) Yes. I've seen it often enough.

O'NEILL: (*Who has certainly taken a keen interest in the map.*) I see what Moore's driving at. Fitzgormanstown Ranch and its three thousand acres of prairie over the River Shivna!

KEARNEY: (*Derisively*) Fitzgormanstown over the river! Good Lord, Moore! Talk of the River Jordan? A bridge would cost thousands. And we'll never get Fitzgormanstown. You can't. Not under the present Acts.

MOORE: No. But it will come in some day. Nothing can stop it.

O'NEILL: (*Excitedly*) I say — Kearney — look at this! Why, it's actually a scheme map of Fitzgormanstown with new roads, new holdings, plantations and fences and sites for new houses all planned. Hundreds of new holdings! (*He looks at* MOORE *with wonder.*) Hundreds of new holdings! (*Sadly*) But on a place we may never get.

MOORE: Yes. Hundreds of new holdings on a place we may never get. To struggle to get forty acres today, for just one migrant, and then to look across the Shivna and see that three thousand acres of magnificent kindly land stretching out to the sun. No shivering little gossoons on that side of the Shivna on a winter day herding the cow on a rundale patch! We must — we must get Dolan's land and drive a road right through it right up to the river there.

KEARNEY: And then?

MOORE: And then wait.

O'NEILL: Reserve a bridge head?

MOORE: Yes. Dolan's holding is the one point, the only one point on the Shivna where we can fling a bridge across. No ash-plant on a cattle drive ever struck a beast on the three thousand acres of Fitzgormanstown. Why? Because the Shivna saved it. But some day we'll capture it — and get the money for that bridge. So Dolan must come out. (*He replaces the map in the drawer.*) Where's his agreement?

KEARNEY: O'Neill has it. (*There is a pause. They both turn to look at* O'NEILL *who sits lost in thought.* KEARNEY, *loudly*) O'Neill!

O'NEILL: (*With a start*) Yes!

KEARNEY: O'Neill, I used to sit that way thinking about Ellen, now I do it over the accounts for boots and shoes. Where's Dan Dolan's agreement?

O'NEILL: (*Producing it from his coat pocket*) There you are.

MARTIN: (*Knocking, and entering hurriedly*) Beg pardon, sir, but Mr Cossacks is wanted below.

GOSUKI: Eh, me?

MARTIN: Yes, you, sir. (*To* MOORE) It's the boss, sir. Just back from the races. He's in the greatest form I ever seen — has all the bookies broke. Someone from Dublin at Ballyhaunis told him the little Japanese gentleman was coming down, so he went and backed The Chink at fifty-to-one in the Trader's Plate and it galloped home. He says it's all due to Mr Cossacks. (*Turning to* GOSUKI) If you don't come down, sir, he'll be sure up and you'll get no more business done today. I'll engage to get you free in half-an-hour.

GOSUKI: (*With a smile.*) All ri'.

MARTIN: Follow me, sir.

(MARTIN *and* GOSUKI *go out.*)

KEARNEY: Good-night! No more study land problem for Japan tonight!

MOORE: (*Rapidly scanning the agreement*) Forty acres. Twenty pounds. No use telling that to Dolan. He'll want it at ten! Bring him up, Kearney.

KEARNEY: Right-o! (*Exit.*)

O'NEILL: Who's the little man?

MOORE: Jap taking notes on the land question.

O'NEILL: Oh!

MOORE: Like to go out there?

O'NEILL: If they paid me.

MOORE: Hm! Is the pay all the interest you have in work?

O'NEILL: Why shouldn't it interest me?

MOORE: If you want to move, why not go? (O'NEILL *does not answer.* MOORE *eyes him keenly.*) You came home by Killasolan?

O'NEILL: Yes.

MOORE: By O'Flaherty's pub?

O'NEILL: Yes.

MOORE: I see.

O'NEILL: Anything wrong?

(*Conversation is interrupted by* DAN DOLAN *and* KEARNEY'S *entrance.* DAN DOLAN *is a shrewd-looking old peasant farmer of small stature and strong physique. He carries an ashplant.*)

KEARNEY: Dan Dolan of Addergoole, Mr Moore.

MOORE: Nice day, Dan.

DAN: Yes.

MOORE: Sit down. (DAN *does so.*) Well, you saw the new holding?

DAN: Yes.

MOORE: And walked all the land?

DAN: Yes.

MOORE: And were told the acreage?

DAN: Yes.

MOORE: Forty statute or twenty-five Irish.

DAN: Yes.

MOORE: And saw the new house and out-office on it?

DAN: Yes.

MOORE: And refused?

DAN: Yes.

MOORE: Why? (*A pause.*) Well, Dan?

DAN: I want a pig-house.

MOORE: What?

DAN: I want a pig-house.

KEARNEY: As well as the new house and the forty-foot out-office?

DAN: I want a pig-house.

KEARNEY: We don't include pig-houses.

DAN: I must have a pig-house.

MOORE: All right. Note that, O'Neill.

O'NEILL: Pig-house granted?

MOORE: Yes.

DAN: With a cement floor in it?

MOORE: With a cement floor in it.

(*A pause.* DAN DOLAN *looks meditatively at the ceiling.*)

DAN: Aye. A bad farm. The worst I ever seen. No meadow in it.

KEARNEY: There's fifteen Irish of arable.

DAN: I want them two fields next to the herd's house.

KEARNEY: You can't get them.

DAN: Is that true, Mr Moore?

MOORE: Yes.

DAN: Aye. The worst land I ever seen. Have yous no land elsewhere to show me? What about Fitzgormanstown over the river fornenst me?

MOORE: No. We won't get that until a new Land Act is passed and a new bridge built.

DOLAN: I'll wait for that so.

MOORE: And when that comes, no-one will get land but the landless.

DAN: Aye. No land. How is it Mr Beckett of Taylor's Cross was transposed by yous to that grand new place he got at Navan — in the county of Meath?

MOORE: He surrendered three hundred acres.

DAN: Aye. Oh, aye. There's always an explanation for everything yous does. Is it only the black Protestants that yous are going to take out of Connaught? Answer me that? Wasn't there a cry in Maynooth again the way yous were tricking the true church and its following? Nothing but atheists and freemasons getting the fat of the land and the likes of us that suffered seven hundred and fifty years of fruitless fighting gets nothing. I tell you things will come to an end some of these days. Why can't I get a holding in County Meath?

MOORE: We're not here to discuss any exchange to County Meath. We were ordered to show you a new holding in Ballyglass and we've done so.

DAN: And why should you be so set on me to come out? There's a dozen others could come as ready as me.

MOORE: Because your holding is the key to our work.

DAN: Would yous give any other key man that come out the same sort of a house?

MOORE: Depends on the man and his family. What family have you?

DAN: Eight boys and two girls.

KEARNEY: You've only three boys.

DAN: Yes — three at home.

MOORE: Where are the others?

DAN: There's one in America, one in Kilkelly in the County Mayo and one at the Curragh in the Free State Army.

MOORE: That's six accounted for. Where are the other two? (*The old man does not answer.*) Where are the other two?

DAN: There's one went wrong in the head in the troubles and is in Ballinasloe, and the other's in France, God rest him!

MOORE: In France?

DAN: Yes, your honour. He went out with Tom Kettle that's beyond in Stephen's Green. (*A pause.*) What's the rent on the holding, if you please, gentlemen?

MOORE: (*With a glance at* KEARNEY) Twenty-six pounds.

DAN: (*With a gasp*) Ah, Glory be to God! Twenty-six pounds! Where's my hat? I'll be going, gentlemen! Twenty-five acres — fifteen to twenty of it old, sour callows and cut away bog for twenty-six pounds! Are yous humbugging me, Mr Moore?

MOORE: No. Twenty-six. Remember we build your fences and dwelling-house and out-offices.

DAN: And a pig-house?

MOORE: And a pig-house with a cement floor in it.

DOLAN: Aye. And the meadow fields next the herd's house?

MOORE: No.

DAN: Well, yous may keep the holding, gentlemen. Leave my own little snug house, is it, with the best of arable and the spring water and the callows and the bog? — Aye — be damned but I was forgetting the bog. Where's the bog?

KEARNEY: You saw it over in the distance at Muckanagh to the west.

DAN: Muckanagh? Sure there's no way into it!

O'NEILL: The gangers are working at a new road to it.

DAN: Aye. Is the bog included in the rent?

MOORE: Yes.

DAN: Aye. So yous won't give me the meadow field?

KEARNEY: We can't, I tell you. Pat Morrisey, the herd, has already signed for it.

DAN: Aye. Twenty-six pounds and the worst land I ever saw. And full of disease, red water, fluke and murrain.

KEARNEY: No such thing. Don't mind what that blackguard of a herd told you. He wants the land for his brother.

DAN: Aye. That's the proper lad would answer for a neighbour. Aye. And them was two nice sour-looking gentlemen that wouldn't give you the time of day when we come out and found them talking to the shover. Begorras, good neighbours is worth a fortune to any man and between them people that we saw to-day and that rogue elephant of a herd and his brother, it's *Cead Mile Failte* to Dan Dolan of Addergoole down there, I'm thinking. (*Suddenly*) Begor, I won't face it, Mr Kearney.

KEARNEY: It's hopeless, Moore. He has no courage.

DAN: (*Angrily*) Courage, is it? There never was a Dolan yet that wouldn't face a regiment of Satans —

(*The door opens noiselessly and the little Japanese looks in, smiling.*)

GOSUKI: Excuse, please — (*He smiles.*) I have escape — on parole — from horse talk. *(He looks at* DOLAN.) Please to meet —

MOORE: Mr Dan Dolan of Addergoole. This is a Japanese TD, Dan.

DAN: 'Morrow to your honour.

(*There is a knock at the door, then* MRS MORRISEY *opens it and enters.*)

MRS MORRISEY: Oh, excuse me. I think I left my umbrella here. I'm so sorry to disturb you. I think I was sitting over here and I might have left it beside me. (*She makes a futile search, in which everybody but* DOLAN *joins.*)

GOSUKI: Please description give.

MRS MORRISEY: It had a nice silver-mounted horn handle with a red silk tassel. (*To* DOLAN) Excuse me. (*She gives him a hard look.*) I think I know this gentleman. From Addergoole he comes, if I'm not mistaken.

DAN: Yes. I'm Dan Dolan of Addergoole. And who might you be, ma'am, when you're at home?

MRS MORRISEY: Oh, Mr Moore there will tell you. From Ballyglass I come, where the land is that we're all expecting a share of soon, thanks to Mr Moore. Now, where could I have left it? Isn't that strange now? I'm always losing things when I get full of anxiety. Ah, dear! It's an anxious time for us all in Ballyglass. A great misfortune to be running about and leaving your home. I'd never leave my home, Mr Moore — never. (*Looking hard at* DOLAN) There's always sorrow on them that leaves their homes. (*The* JAPANESE *chuckles.*) Ah well, it's well the little Chinese gentleman knows it. But I was tempted to come and see you, Mr Moore, and see what comes of it. My good silk and silver umbrella. (*With another look at* DOLAN) There's never any luck comes to them that can't abide at home!

MARTIN: (*Opening the door*) I've searched the whole house for that umbrella of yours, Mrs Morrisey, and Kate is after telling me you had none when you came in.

MRS MORRISEY: Well, I declare! I must have left it down in Owen Kelly's. I did! I did! I'm so sorry, gentlemen, indeed I am, to disturb you. Goodbye and thank you, Mr Moore. And don't forget it'll take all the land up there and twice over to satisfy the just claims of the Ballyglasses. Well, good-day, gentlemen, and thank you. (*Exit, followed by* MARTIN.)

DAN: (*With a movement of his ashplant after them*) Is that one to be a neighbour of mine?

KEARNEY: Yes.

DAN: Aye. A nice, friendly-spoken woman!

KEARNEY: She's all that.

DAN: And more if she took the notion.

KEARNEY: She might take a notion to you, Dan.

DAN: Ah, God forbid! I've troubles enough as it is. She's strong on the home life, maurya! Begor, I never was in Kilrea yet I didn't see that one somewhere. She must spend a power of time looking for umbrellas. Aye. A champion for a neighbour. Aye. (*Meditatively*) Aye. Twenty-five acres.

MOORE: Yes.

DAN: And a house and a forty-foot out-office?

MOORE: Yes.

DAN: And a pig-house?

MOORE: Yes.

DAN: And twenty-six pounds rent?

MOORE: Yes. Twenty-six.

DAN: (*Rising*) Well, yous can keep it.

KEARNEY: And a bog plot in Muckanagh.

DAN: (*Going toward the door*) And a bog plot in Muckanagh. And the best of neighbours. All nice friendly-spoken people. (*He suddenly turns.*) Here! (*He spits on his hands.*) Sixteen pound rent and the meadow field in it!

MOORE: (*Ignoring him*) O'Neill!

O'NEILL: Yes?

MOORE: Make out a note there to Jennings of Esker to come in tomorrow and show him that holding. (*To* DOLAN) Well, good-day, Dan. Sorry we couldn't come to any agreement.

DAN: Here! (*Holding out his hand*) Seventeen, and leave out the meadow!

MOORE: Can't be. (*To* O'NEILL) And put in the note we agree to his terms.

O'NEILL: (*Writing*) Yes.

DAN: Here! Mr Moore! (*Then addressing the* JAPANESE) What do you say, Mr Cossacks? Damn it, we'll split the differ. Now that's a fair offer. What d'ye say?

GOSUKI: (*Entering into the spirit of the affair*) Ah! Good! (*To* MOORE) Yes? No?

O'NEILL: I'll take this note out. It would just about catch the post.

KEARNEY: Hold on! Make it twenty for him, Moore.

GOSUKI: Ah! (*To* DOLAN) Yes? (*To* MOORE) No?

MOORE: No.

GOSUKI: Ah!

DAN: Here! Be damned but I'll take it at the twenty. Now, Mr Moore!

MOORE: All right. Where's the agreement?

KEARNEY: Here. (*Hands it to* MOORE.)

MOORE: There you are, Dan. Take it to your solicitor and get it signed.

DAN: Ah, begor, I won't pay six-and-eightpence to any solicitor. I'm tight enough in money as it is. Give me the pen, Mr

O'Neill, if you please, and I'll sign. (*He sits down, fumbles for his glasses, puts them on, and starts to read the agreement.*)

KEARNEY: I read it all out to you before, except the rent. Sign here.

DAN: There's nothing here about a house or out-offices or a pig-house.

MOORE: No. But aren't they all there on the holding bar the pig-house? (DAN *laboriously signs the agreement, watched with interest by the* JAPANESE.) Well, you've a long way to go to Addergoole, Dan. Will you have a drop of whiskey?

DAN: Troth and it's a very odd time now I touch whiskey, your honour —

MOORE: Well — (*He looks at* O'NEILL.) No — Kearney!

KEARNEY: Yes?

MOORE: Take Dan down with you and get him what he wants, to drink luck to the new holding, and take Mr Gosuki down with you and explain the procedure to him. I want to talk to O'Neill.

GOSUKI: Eh, so. Much interest new farm making —

(KEARNEY, DOLAN, *and* GOSUKI *go out talking.*)

(A pause.)

O'NEILL: What do you want to talk to me about?

MOORE: How long are you down here now?

O'NEILL: About three years.

MOORE: Would you like to be over twenty at it?

O'NEILL: I don't know.

MOORE: You'll have to make up your mind soon.

O'NEILL: Why?

MOORE: (*Suddenly*) Because, like Dolan, you'll have to say either yes or no. Stick it or quit and get out. If you want to quit, quit now. What's your answer?

O'NEILL: What else could I do but stick on?

MOORE: You're young yet.

O'NEILL: Yes. I mightn't — I mightn't be stuck here all the time. I might get back up east some time.

MOORE: Do you know the old saying, O'Neill? 'Once west of the Shannon, you never go back.' Do you think Dan Dolan goes in to work his new holding with the same ideas as you? There's a transfer of staff to be carried out in this area, but I'm not going to touch it before I know that you're prepared to stay the course. If you're not inclined to stay the course, get out and go somewhere else. But I want your answer tonight.

O'NEILL: I'm staying.

MOORE: Very well. Come back here, then, at nine tonight.

O'NEILL: Tonight?

MOORE: Yes. See what you can do re-arranging Addergoole. And let me give you a tip. Don't get messed up with people like — like — Barrington.

O'NEILL: Why?

MOORE: Some time or other we'll be in tangles about land with him. So keep clear.

O'NEILL: Keep clear?

MOORE: Yes. You know what I'm driving at. Keep clear of them all. The top and the bottom. And there's only one way. Work!

O'NEILL: And what about — about —

MOORE: Next Sunday?

O'NEILL: Yes.

MOORE: I've given you my advice.

O'NEILL: (*Fiercely*) I won't! It's not fair! It's not just — out all day — walking, arguing, fighting, wrangling, and then coming in at night to start putting it all down again and sweating here with you to midnight! (*With a flash of defiance*) I won't!

MOORE: Ease up! You called at O'Flaherty's coming home?

O'NEILL: Yes, I did.

MOORE: The public house at Killasolan Cross?

O'NEILL: Yes.

MOORE: What did you want with O'Flaherty?

O'NEILL: To swap that ten-acre plot of his for a bit on the Blake estate. I went into the whole thing with you before.

MOORE: I didn't think it was the publican.

O'NEILL: Yes. He's the owner now.

MOORE: I see. Were you in his back parlour?

O'NEILL: I don't know what you call the room.

MOORE: And had a drink or two?

O'NEILL: Yes. (*A silence.*) What else could do?

MOORE: No. You wouldn't see any alternative.

O'NEILL: No. Not to get what you wanted. He wouldn't agree.

MOORE: Just so.

O'NEILL: It's all right to plan out things here in this room with you, but it's different when you get hearing his side of it.

MOORE: Yes.

O'NEILL: I know well what you're thinking, Moore. That I drank his whiskey and let him talk me round. Think it if you like. And if you want to know what I was doing with him — (*He pulls a document out of his pocket.*) There — there's his old Za. agreement. Agreed to the swap. It took me two solid hours to get him. But I've got him! Yes. And I had to stop and drink his rotten two-year-old poteen — ugh! — but I got him. It's bizzing my head a bit, but it gives me courage enough to say to you what I'd like to say to those fellows up in Dublin. Go to hell!

MOORE: Go home to bed, you silly young ass!

O'NEILL: No. I'm not going home, and I'm not going to bed either. I've fixed up the Blake estate that you and Kearney have been tangling at for the last twenty years, and I'm going down below to the bar, and I'm going to hit up this rookery tonight! (*He blunders out angrily to the door, and barely avoids a collision as it opens suddenly and* MARTIN *appears.*)

MARTIN: Did you ring, gentlemen?

O'NEILL: No. But I'll wring your neck if you don't stand aside. (*He pushes* MARTIN *angrily aside on to the sofa, and blunders down the stairs.*)

MARTIN: (*Looking after him, and then turning with a slow smile to* MOORE) He's powerful like yourself used to be in the old days, Mr Moore.

(CURTAIN)

ACT TWO

(*The same* SCENE *as* ACT ONE. *A few days later.* MOORE *and* KEARNEY *are engaged comparing a map and the relating schedule. It is late in the evening.*)

MOORE: Plot 29? (*He pores over the map.*)

KEARNEY: Yes. Do you see it?

MOORE: Right! I see it.

KEARNEY: Sixteen acres, one rood. It goes to John Hennessy, who surrenders (*He pauses to emphasise the numbers and also to allow* MOORE *to follow him on the map*) 16A — 16B — I6C — 16H — I6L — and the undivided three-sixteenths of No 18B.

MOORE: (*Laboriously following him*) 16C — 16H — 16L. (*The town clock strikes nine.* MOORE *is still intent on his map, but* KEARNEY *yawns and gets up.*)

KEARNEY: I say, Moore!

MOORE: (*Without much heed*) Yes?

KEARNEY: If you don't mind I'm chucking. It's gone nine.

MOORE: Yes. (*He continues examining the map.*)

KEARNEY: (*Loudly*) Moore!

MOORE: Yes?

KEARNEY: I want to get home, if you don't mind.

MOORE: All right! All right!

KEARNEY: Sorry to stop, but — it's Ellen — She's got a bit fidgety lately. Always gets that way when the long nights begin.

MOORE: She should have got used to it by this time.

KEARNEY: No, she hasn't. It's a bit lonesome down there at Tubber Knockmore in the winter. Nothing but the kids and herself there, you know, the live-long day. I wonder what it'll be like when they grow up and go away!

MOORE: H'm! (*Looking at the map*) Yes. It's not a bad bit of work. All right. We can have another go at this on Friday.

KEARNEY: Very well. (*A gust of wind and rain.*) Rotten night for the drive back. (*A pause.*) Any chance of a move up for me, Moore?

MOORE: Not yet.

KEARNEY: I say, Moore! Do you never want yourself, sometime, to move out of this?

MOORE: Not now.

KEARNEY: H'm! Content to spend your life dividing land — devising bridge heads to places you find you can't get, like Fitzgormanstown. I'd certainly like a change now and again if it was only to be taking the missus — if ever you have one — for a spin on the Bray Road of a summer's day out to Killiney or Greystones.

MOORE: No.

KEARNEY: Or a night like this going in to see the latest at the pictures or the theatres?

MOORE: No.

KEARNEY: (*Disgustedly*) Ach! I suppose I'm younger than you, but it's a rotten life. All right for some, maybe, but out there at Tubber — all hours of the day — and often at night — knock — knock — knock — someone at the door. 'If yous don't repair the kish that was put down for the right of way at Ballindine Bog, we'll have a question asked in the floor of the Dail — the drain between O'Flaherty Pat and Mick Hennigan is choked and Jack Dempsey Red has the water stopped on them below — the big wind of Friday last week has stripped the slates off Mick Dolan's new house — Tim Casey has put on a jennet for grass where he had only the right of a donkey —' I wonder do they ever think up in Dublin of all that we ever go through down here?

MOORE: (*Smiling*) Do you ever think of all that they go through up in Dublin?

KEARNEY: (*Pointing at the schedule*) Sure that stuff there only represents one-tenth of what we go through. Even if you said no — no — no — you can't stop it. You haven't the heart to curse and damn them off your doorstep like the old agents did in the seventies. And agents had offices. I've nothing but my miserable little home and the only decent room in it is given up to this Moloch. (*A pause.*) Sorry, Moore, to be grousing.

MOORE: Grouse away, old man. It does no harm even if it doesn't do any good. (*Pause.*) There's a lot more work come down.

KEARNEY: What side? Fitzgormanstown?

MOORE: No. That waits a new Land Act. Down Ballinasheeda way.

KEARNEY: Where McCartan used to be?

MOORE: Yes.

KEARNEY: Well, there are worse places than Tubber! And Ballinasheeda's one of them.

MOORE: You're not inclined to face it?

KEARNEY: Not me, thank you! (*With a sudden note of alarm in his voice*) For God's sake, don't send me down there, Moore. It would kill her — Ellen, I mean. It drove McCartan mad. Those people down there, they all go over the water to work in the summer and come back to sleep in the winter, and they don't come back the better for what they learned across the water, I tell you.

MOORE: Well, someone's got to go there. Read this. (*He extracts a memorandum from an envelope on the table and hands it to* KEARNEY.)

KEARNEY: (*Reading*) 'Estates of O'Mara — Fitzgibbon — estimates — now required — 700 tenantry — re-arrangement — of holdings — provision — of — new roads — housing.' (*He hands it back to* MOORE.) Thanks. Pie for somebody!

MOORE: I suppose you wondered why I'd been giving you additional work lately?

KEARNEY: To tell you the truth, I thought it was about time you were handing a bit over to O'Neill.

MOORE: I've been deliberately easing off O'Neill.

KEARNEY: Why?

MOORE: You have the reason in your hand.

KEARNEY: This?

MOORE: Yes.

KEARNEY: You're sending O'Neill to Ballinasheeda! (*He laughs.*) He'll only go phut like McCartan.

MOORE: Well, we'll see.

KEARNEY: A bit tough on him, Moore!

MOORE: It's come up to the time when he's got to be flung into the water to see if he can swim.

KEARNEY: Or drown!

MOORE: Maybe.

KEARNEY: Does he know?

MOORE: Not yet.

KEARNEY: Where is he?

MOORE: Out with the little Jap somewhere.

KEARNEY: Hm! I suppose somehow or other they'll manage to get Mount Nevin way!

MOORE: I don't quite follow that remark.

KEARNEY: You didn't hear anything lately?

MOORE: About O'Neill?

KEARNEY: Yes — and that Barrington girl.

MOORE: No.

KEARNEY: I met our Mrs Marcus Morrisey yesterday.

MOORE: Well?

KEARNEY: And she dropped a few remarks about the pair.

MOORE: Hm! (*Knocking at the door*) Come in. (O'NEILL *enters.*) Hello! Back safe?

O'NEILL: Yes.

KEARNEY: So our Japanese friend turned up again on his way back from Mayo?

MOORE: Yes — full of notes and notebooks on his way home to Dublin tomorrow.

KEARNEY: Where is he now?

O'NEILL: Talking below with Mooney.

KEARNEY: (*With a glance at* MOORE) Was he out with you today?

O'NEILL: Yes. On Muckanagh Bog.

KEARNEY: Anywhere else?

O'NEILL: No.

KEARNEY: Thought you might have gone Mount Nevin way and seen Dan Dolan.

O'NEILL: I didn't.

KEARNEY: How's Dolan getting on out there? Didn't he move there this week?

O'NEILL: Yes.

KEARNEY: No opposition?

O'NEILL: No.

KEARNEY: You weren't talking much to anybody out there then?

O'NEILL: No, I wasn't.

(*A gentle knock, then* GOSUKI *appears.*)

GOSUKI: Excuse. Just now — man — not know — say — give this — (*He shows a letter*) Mr Moore — and — pouf! — he run — not wait — reply. (*He hands the letter to* MOORE.)

MOORE: (*Opening it and reading*) Hm! (*He smiles grimly.*) Interest you perhaps, O'Neill. (*He hands it to the latter.*)

O'NEILL: (*Reading*) 'If Dolan the grabber does not leave Ballyglass by Sunday, himself and you will have the following ready for ye and O'Neill. Captain Moonlight.'

KEARNEY: (*To* O'NEILL) Show. (O'NEILL *hands it to him.*) Hm! Three coffins, labelled Moore, O'Neill and Dolan.

GOSUKI: Excuse. May I please? (*He stretches out for the letter which* KEARNEY *hands to him.*)

MOORE: Kearney!

GOSUKI: (*Studying the letter*) Eh! Much interest. Captain Moonlight — is — name — for — not real name?

MOORE: Yes. It's only a joke.

GOSUKI: Eh! So. Irish peoples much fun and laughings make all times, and merry! Ha! Ha! May I keep, please? Example — curio — humour of Irish peoples — for Japans to see!

MOORE: (*Aside to* KEARNEY) Damn you! (*To* GOSUKI) All right. I'd prefer you burned it.

GOSUKI: I thank. (*Looking critically at the letter*) Irish peoples not artist good. Japans peoples all artist good.

(*There is a sudden knock on the door. Then* BARRINGTON, *flushed and excited-looking, enters.*)

BARRINGTON: Hello! Got you all in, Moore!

MOORE: You're late abroad tonight!

BARRINGTON: I am, and thanks to you. I've come to warn you. There may be some trouble tonight. Some blackguards came in last night when I was out and pinched my two guns.

MOORE: Nothing new about that, is there?

BARRINGTON: No. But as far as I can gather there was no official raid about it. Damn the whole silly crowd of you! Have you no sense, Moore?

MOORE: Depends on the point of view you take.

BARRINGTON: You know mine, anyway. You went and took up all that home farm of mine and put outsiders on it. You've given the last bit of it now to that little rascal of a Dolan, and he can thank his stars if he doesn't get about fifty pickle of shot into him if he doesn't slip out by Sunday. If he lives through it all, and you do, I suppose the demesne will have to go next to satisfy them. (*A pause.*) It's damned unfair, Moore, the way you people deal with us. Go and take up the only bit of land we could make a profit on to keep up the demesne. Then when we can't stock and work what you've left us, and have to set it in conacre and grazing, you say we're not working it properly, and then seize what's left. Damn you! Damn the whole lot of you! *(A pause.)* Sorry! I'm a bit on edge, but if you had known what that old place was like when I was a boy — a hive of industry, and see it now — grass growing in the yards, and the roofs of the stables caving in, because I've got no capital to work it with — the mortgagees took every penny you paid us. (*Suddenly*) Are you going to take Mount Nevin?

MOORE: You'd be the first to get that information.

BARRINGTON: Oh, yes! But a lot depends on what you wrote about it.

MOORE: Barrington, I wonder could you ever detach yourself from the personal point of view and look at Mount Nevin, and the way the place is used, as a cold examiner bound to report the truth without prejudice or favour?

BARRINGTON: And that's the way you've done it?

MOORE: I have tried to tell the truth.

BARRINGTON: I see. (*A pause.*) I had no post for two or three days, so I sent in Morrisey today to get my letters. He called and got them all right, but went off east to see his cousin and left word he'd call this way coming back. More devilment, I suppose! And they tell me one letter was from the Land Commission. Did you write me, Moore?

MOORE: No.

BARRINGTON: Hm! Then it's from Dublin direct.

(*Knocking.* MOCKLER, *a big heavy man, enters. He is flustered and excited.*)

MOCKLER: And how are you, Mr Moore? And it surprises me nothing to find you here, Mr Barrington. It only confirms my suspicions that there's more behind this business at Mount Nevin than the people think. We had a mass meeting out at Ballyglass today and it is my duty to convey to you, Mr Moore, the unanimous declaration of the people there protesting against the despicable methods adopted in the recent division of land in our parish.

GOSUKI: Excuse, please. You — policy of official — condemn as bad?

BARRINGTON: Damned bad! Couldn't be worse.

MOCKLER: (*Looking hard at him*) Eh? Are those your true opinions or are they assumed for the moment? We've had experience of your tactics before, Mr Barrington. You were quite willing to surrender the land in 1920, but when different times came you reneged and fought the case through every court of appeal you could take it into.

BARRINGTON: And why shouldn't I? My people were sent to Hell or Connaught, and out of Connaught I'm not going till I get my rights. Stick that in your pipe and smoke it, Mockler.

MOORE: You are under a misconception, Mockler. Barrington came here to object to our proceedings.

MOCKLER: I'd like to have some more proof of that. (*He turns to* O'NEILL.) Wasn't it you put Dolan in yesterday?

O'NEILL: Yes.

MOCKLER: Aye. And you were out at Mount Nevin the Sunday before. (*A silence.*) Hm! Aye. And company keeping since with Miss Barrington.

BARRINGTON: Keep my daughter's name out of this matter, please.

MOCKLER: Very well. But keep your back-door influence to yourself. The land at Ballyglass has always been regarded as the rightful and lawful property of the people of Ballyglass from time immemorial. —You're out of it at last and I advise you keep out of it.

BARRINGTON: Here! Enough of that.

MOORE: Ease up, Barrington!

MOCKLER: A man named Dolan, a complete outsider, and stranger, without the knowledge or consent of the people of Ballyglass, has been put into possession of land in that parish.

BARRINGTON: I agree.

MOCKLER: And I want to warn you all that any attempt on the part of any official here or in Dublin to override and trample on the just claims of the people to land in their own locality will be met with all the fighting opposition that an united and determined people can offer.

GOSUKI: Excuse, please. You and artist of this — (*He produces the Moonlight letter*) — same?

MOCKLER: (*Waving it aside*) No, sir. I repudiate any connection with that sort of method. If I have anything to say, I say it openly and without resort to cowardice and threats. But it is an indication of the feelings of the people and if disregarded, the end can only be disorder and bloodshed. You have had your warning, Mr Moore.

MOORE: Am I to be told that as a threat?

MOCKLER: It follows your action as night the day.

BARRINGTON: I agree.

MOCKLER: You — I don't want your approval of what I say — I feel too strongly that any representations of the people have been and are overruled by the Junkers and Mussolini at Headquarters.

GOSUKI: Ah! Mussolini — and — Italy — much interest! (*To* MOCKLER) Have you study make of Italians people and — reclamations — please?

MOCKLER: (*With a gesture of disgust*) Ach! (*To* MOORE) What message am I to take back to the people of Ballyglass tonight? Is it peace or war?

(*A loud knock at the door. It opens suddenly and* DAN DOLAN *appears in the doorway. Regardless of the rest of the company, he makes his way at once towards* MOORE.)

DOLAN: (*With a wild lash of his ashplant on the table nearest to*

MOORE) Damn ye, when are you going to put the cement floor in my pig-house?

MOORE: Is it not in yet?

DOLAN: The divil an in! It's there to this day the same as when this gentleman here — (*Pointing at* O'NEILL) — seen it last Friday and promised me in front of the ganger and John Morrisey, would be put in that night. And the damn the shovel or spade was ever laid on it since.

MOCKLER: Ach! We're talking here about something more serious than pig-houses and cement floors.

DOLAN: Are ye? Well, yous can talk away till yous are all blue in the face about anything yous like, but short of getting fair play and justice done me, I'll — (*He makes another lash at the table but* O'NEILL *intercepts and prevents him.*)

MOCKLER: That's enough, you little omadhaun! You aren't in Fogarty's public house.

DOLAN: And travelling I am since seven this morning to get a hoult of you, Mr Moore — for that ganger you have down there is nothing short of a common cheat and deceiver. Mark my words, says I to him, I'm off to Mooney's of Kilrea to the Commissioners, and I'll expose you, you big omadhaun of a gobhaun carpenter and a mason, that you're only a three-card-trick man and a thimble rigging trick of the loop scut ye, cheating honest men out of what was promised them.

MOCKLER: That's the proper talk. Nothing but bribery and corruption from the highest to the lowest. You done well to come away from the place you should never have ventured into.

DOLAN: And I've come where I can get justice! (*With a resounding blow on the table*) Damn ye! When are ye going to put the cement floor in my pig-house?

MOORE: *(Suddenly rising)* Here — a minute before you destroy that table altogether! Sit down. (DOLAN *does so.*) Put that stick on the table. And take off your hat. (DOLAN *sullenly obeys.*) Aren't you married?

DOLAN: Yes.

MOORE: And did you get your breakfast this morning?

DOLAN: Yes.

MOORE: Tell me! Is this the way you asked your wife for it? (*Suddenly seizing the ashplant and welting the table with it*) Damn ye! When will ye give me my breakfast?

MOCKLER: That's right, Mr Moore! Learn the little omadhaun some manners that he can go back where he comes from, and teach it to them in Addergoole!

DOLAN: I will — and if yous don't put that floor in my pig-house, I'll resign all to yous — house and lands and pig-house, and go back where I come from.

KEARNEY: Back to Addergoole?

DOLAN: Yes. Back to Addergoole, and it's black sorrow is on me since ever I left it.

MOORE: Back to the bog-garden and the dobey-house and the one room?

DOLAN: Yes. I'll resign all to yous and go back. Isn't it a laughing-stock yous have made of me for the whole countryside?

MOCKLER: That settles the matter. I'm glad to see there's some glimmerings of sense in you yet, Dolan.

GOSUKI: Excuse please — (*To* DOLAN) Not land or breakfast annoy but house for pig, not cement of floor?

DOLAN: Yes. And all the arable I have is eight acres of cold blue stiff clay, full of sleeping water, and double that of old, sour, wet callows and cut away bog that's full of red water and murrain.

BARRINGTON: Hold on there! It's the best land in Connaught if it was properly worked.

DOLAN: Oh, glory be! The best land in — ! Drains in it the size of the Suez Canal that lost me two ewes and their lambs, and a yearling heifer, and a cut-out strip of a brown bog that hasn't two spits of turf in it, and what I have to be dragging home on the ass's back a mile to the county road, and has all my childer perished — I'll resign all to yous gentlemen. I'm going back.

MOCKLER: (*Putting out his hand*) Lay it there, Dolan! I'm proud to meet you and to know you're vacating and surrendering land yous never should have got.

DOLAN: (*Ignoring him*) The divil a surrender till I get justice! No surrender, and damn the penny rent I'll pay yous!

MOCKLER: What kind of a crooked little gnat are you? Are you refusing now to go out of it and back to Addergoole?

DOLAN: There's no man living will put me back to Addergoole till it's failed me to get justice.

MOCKLER: (*Maddened*) Ach! You're only a contrary little, sucking little, pigeen of a man! A little twisted gnat of an adder from Addergoole that would bite the hand of any decent man that ever handled ye! (DOLAN *makes to strike him, but is restrained by* O'NEILL.) And I tell you, it won't be many days or weeks either that you'll be worrying about cement on the floor of your pig-house, but the heat of the floor of the place you'll be standing in alongside of the boneens of Judas Iscariot! (*He goes to the door.*) Goodnight to ye, gentlemen, and be sure you pack him off, and all his little boneens with him, back to Addergoole this night, and no need to be wasting good powder and shot. *Bannach leat.* (*Exit.*)

GOSUKI: Excuse — please — parish — name of place — where — only — Christian peoples is?

BARRINGTON: Yes. We're all Christians, I hope, in the parish of Ballyglass.

GOSUKI: Most difficult — understandings — for Japanese. Christian doctrines and peoples — not same. (*Pointing to* DOLAN) Ah! Small man's not Christian?

DOLAN: I'd like to see anyone calling me a heathen!

GOSUKI: So! But why angry because of house for pig? Pig in Ireland object of respects?

KEARNEY: Oh, the pig is a most important animal!

GOSUKI: Ah! So! In Japans — Inarisama — Fox — animal — symbol — cunning! Much venerations — all peoples — give and small temple — shrine — small — nice — house build. Also Nakosama — Cat — animal — symbol — wisdoms — venerations give. What symbo — venerations — please — pig?

BARRINGTON: You don't know what a pig stands for?

GOSUKI: No. Please?

BARRINGTON: It's supposed to be the greediest animal alive.

GOSUKI: Ah! Now understand. (*He takes notes.*)

MOORE: Better get home, Kearney.

KEARNEY: You're right. Goodnight, everybody. (*Exit.*)

DOLAN: Are yous Christian gentlemen going to do nothing for me?

MOORE: Look here, Dolan. The cement floor will be put in your pig-house. Get it put in tomorrow, O'Neill.

O'NEILL: Yes, sir.

DOLAN: A slip of a note now, Mr Moore, to Pat Burke that has the caretaking of the woods up at Muckanagh.

MOORE: For what?

DOLAN: For a few deal trees to be making half a score of rafters for a bit of a lean-to shed I'd be wanting next to the pig-house.

MOORE: We can't.

DOLAN: Aye. No orders. No timber. No cement floor. Would yous write me an order, if yous please, for a couple of larch poles then, for the makings of an ass cart?

MOORE: No.

DOLAN: An order then for a larch tree for a sheepcock pole? Ah, bad cess to it, Mr Moore. Ah, damn it, Mr Moore, you wouldn't be refusing me that?

BARRINGTON: Don't be so hard on the little beggar, Moore, if he is going to be idiot enough to stick to his holding. Ask him for plenty, Dolan. Ask him for plenty.

DOLAN: It's well I've a friend in one of the old gentry. And maybe the new kind of gentry we have now will listen to me when you're in it, your honour. The old landlords, God rest them! were some of them blackguards, but there's none of them ever treated us like some of the upstarts we have now on top of us.

MOORE: That's done it! (*He sits down and writes.*) Here, take this note for the half-score of deal.

DOLAN: Long life to you, Mr Moore! (*Hesitatingly*) There's a nearing between myself and that thief of a Morrisey would want a couple of stakes, and a few strands of wire.

BARRINGTON: (*With a sudden burst of anger*) What! Wire! Wire, did you say? If I see as much as an inch of wire up in my country I'll shoot you at sight!

DOLAN: Shoot me, is it? Mind what you're saying now! Maybe it's yourself, and Mockler, and that old soupladler of a Morrisey is at the back of this divilment, Mr Moore. (*He fumbles in his pocket and produces a note.*) That's the second of its kind that Norah found stuck on the door of the pig-house. (*He hands it to* MOORE.) And it's well I know who put the fist to it.

MOORE: (*Critically examining it*) Hm! Same paper, same rotten drawing.

DOLAN: And I can tell you, Mr Barrington, as I told the Morriseys yesterday, and that ganger of yours, Mr O'Neill, that's in the swim, that I posted up a notice on Morrisey's new poultry-house that he got by swindling the department, that's none of your 'nonymous ones, but that's signed by me in full — Dan Dolan. That'll put the fear of God into that mean, yellow rent-warner and grabber.

BARRINGTON: Here! Keep a civil tongue in your head about the Morriseys. The best gamekeepers and faithfullest retainers the Barringtons and the old stock ever had.

DOLAN: (*Angrily*) Faithful to the Barringtons and the old stock, maurya! For every pheasant yous got, he sold two and ate one, and it's well everybody but yourself knows it. Presarving game, maurya! Presarving foxes for a covert that ates all the laying ducks, for no pay but the delight they has in annoying decent neighbours. Only that he got some job from yourself, Mr Barrington, to come in for letters this morning, I tell you I'd make that Morrisey sorrow for the day he ever put a fist to them papers. (*With a resounding whack of his ashplant on the table*) That's the way I'll sign my signature on him when I sees him! Long life to you, Mr Moore! And no harm to Mr Barrington, but it was the great day for this country when Parnell, God rest him! swept away the whole of yous in '81! (*Exit.*)

BARRINGTON: There you are, Moore! What sort of an infliction is that you've blistered me up with at Mount Nevin? Well, there's not much use, I suppose, in discussing the matter further. Yourself and O'Neill and that little blackguard can face all the consequences.

MOORE: Yes.

BARRINGTON: (*Turning to* O'NEILL.) I think you'll understand the situation, O'Neill, but for fear you didn't, I stayed to express it. I have no desire for further observations from Mr Mockler about my daughter's association with you. So let that end now, please. Is that clear enough?

O'NEILL: (*Bowing.*) Yes.

BARRINGTON: Thank you. Goodnight to you both. (*Goes out.*)

GOSUKI: Mr Moore! Excuse, please — may I — small mans of pig-house letter see? Please.

MOORE: (*Producing note* DOLAN *has left behind*) This?

GOSUKI: Yes, please. (*He takes it and then compares it critically with the previous one in his possession.*) One joke — but — two — not nice — not fun. (*He hands them both back to* MOORE.) Much interest — but — not — clean. (*He makes the gesture of washing his hands.*) Much interest but not keep. Much troubles all nations — land — (*Turning to* O'NEILL *and smiling*) But most troubles young peoples is — (*He smiles.*) Love! Pardon — and excuse. Go men ma sai — Good-nights.

MOORE: Good-night. (*Exit* GOSUKI.) I suppose you understand what Barrington meant?

O'NEILL: Yes.

MOORE: I'm very glad. I thought —

(He stops short.)

O'NEILL: Yes. What did you think?

(MOORE *makes no reply, but sits down quietly and takes up the map he had been working at with* KEARNEY.)

MOORE: That's not a bad scheme of Kearney's by any means.

O'NEILL: (*After an uneasy silence*) What did you think?

MOORE: Oh! (*He does not look up, but continues to examine the map.*) I thought — (*He suddenly lifts his head and looks straight over at* O'NEILL) — that you were fond of the girl.

O'NEILL: (*With an effort*) No. (*His voice trembles slightly.*) Not a bit.

MOORE: Well, that will make things easier then. Take Kearney's schedule there, and call out the numbers of those plots till I have a view of this. We stopped at the sixteens. John Hennessy.

O'NEILL: (*Sitting down.*) John Hennessy!

MOORE: Yes. See it? 16L. Next.

O'NEILL: 16M — 16N.

MOORE: Yes. Next.

(A long pause.)

O'NEILL: (*Trying to restrain himself and then losing control.*) 16 — 16 — 16 — I'm lying to you, Moore! I'm mad — about her — I can't eat — I can't sleep — I can't — I can't — (*He suddenly pulls himself together.*) Forget it. 16N — 16N — 16N (*Despairingly*) I'm sorry.

MOORE: Better have a drink. (*He goes over and rings.*)

O'NEILL: No, thanks.

MOORE: Oh! When did you go on the wagon?

O'NEILL: Since that night you spoke to me.

MOORE: Excuse me, O'Neill, if I don't believe you — I mean, that it was due to anything I said. I'm only judging by the way you took it that evening.

O'NEILL: I'm sorry. I apologise. But I didn't hit up the rookery that night. (*A pause.*) I met her.

MOORE: Miss Barrington?

O'NEILL: Yes.

(*Knocking.*)

MOORE: Come in.

MARTIN: (*Opening the door*) You rang, sir?

MOORE: Sorry, Martin. I meant to order a drink, but changed my mind.

MARTIN: Yes, sir. Great gas below, sir.

MOORE: Eh?

MARTIN: Mr Mockler and the little Addergoole fellow is after having a hell of a set in the yard, and only for the little Japanese gentleman there might have been some bloody business done. He jeejoojed Mr Mockler. Will yous want anything before the bar closes, sir?

MOORE: No, thanks.

(MARTIN *goes out.*)

O'NEILL: I pity that poor little devil going his way home all alone to that country.

MOORE: Yes. Enough to make all of us feel ashamed. If we have to put up with a lot of things we don't like — abuse, misrepresentations — criticisms — what's that compared to all that little warrior's got to go through? Hell for a couple or three years, maybe.

O'NEILL: I'll make him a happier man tomorrow.

MOORE: How?

O'NEILL: Putting in the cement floor of the temple of the pig, as our Japanese friend would call it.

MOORE: Leave that to the ganger — I want you for something

else tomorrow. It'll be your turn to play the migrant, O'Neill.

O'NEILL: I don't quite follow —

MOORE: Did you know McCartan?

O'NEILL: Yes. I was with him once stripping bog, years ago.

MOORE: At Ballinasheeda?

O'NEILL: Yes.

MOORE: You know Ballinasheeda, then?

O'NEILL: Yes. A God-forsaken hole!

MOORE: It is.

O'NEILL: I heard he went wrong afterwards.

MOORE: Yes. He was dismissed.

O'NEILL: What happened?

MOORE: If you want to know the real reason — he was a damned bad migrant.

O'NEILL: It would take some courage to stick out life in that place.

MOORE: (*Grimly*) It would. It was a mistake to put McCartan there. I don't like making mistakes, and I may be making another one, but I've no option. (*Suddenly*) O'Neill, you said you weren't a quitter!

O'NEILL: I'm not.

MOORE: Well — You're going tomorrow to Ballinasheeda.

O'NEILL: To — to Ballinasheeda!

MOORE: Yes.

O'NEILL: To — to Ballinasheeda! Moore! you don't — you can't mean it! Did you ever see McCartan's digs?

MOORE: Yes. I lived in them before McCartan.

O'NEILL: But — Moore — I can't understand — what have I done?

MOORE: Nothing. It's not a punishment.

O'NEILL: What other way could I see it?

MOORE: Do you want to know what it is?

O'NEILL: (*Without heeding him, and despairingly*) It's miles and miles away.

MOORE: Yes. Miles and miles away in one sense. But it's not miles and miles away from the one big thing —

O'NEILL: What's that?

MOORE: The work.

O'NEILL: The work! There's any amount of work — you know there is — round here. Why would you do this on me — why? Why? (*He stops suddenly and looks in a queer way at* MOORE.) It's surely not because of —

MOORE: Some time later you'll ask that question of yourself and you'll be able to answer it.

(*The door opens gently, and* DOLAN *puts his head in.*)

DOLAN: Would you give me an order for a sheepcock pole, if you please, sir?

MOORE: Write one out for him there, O'Neill. How are you getting home, Dolan?

DOLAN: Walking, sir.

MOORE: Walking! This night!

DOLAN: Yes, sir.

MOORE: It's fifteen miles and more!

DOLAN: Yes, sir.

(MOORE, *without further remark, leaves the room abruptly.*)

DOLAN: (*Going over slowly to* O'NEILL) Could you be pleased to make it the double when you're at it, Mr O'Neill? Sure, one more or less would make no matter. (*Confidentially*) She's in the town!

O'NEILL: Who?

DOLAN: Her!

O'NEILL: Who's her?

DOLAN: That one.

O'NEILL: Which one?

DOLAN: Your one.

(MOORE *enters. He is dressed in his waterproof coat and sou'wester hat.*)

MOORE: Dolan!

DOLAN: Yes, sir?

MOORE: I'll give you a lift home.

DOLAN: To Ballyglass?

MOORE: Yes.

DOLAN: God spare your honour the health, but I wouldn't be putting that labour on yourself.

MOORE: Anybody else come in with you?

DOLAN: No, sir.

MOORE: Come on then. You come, O'Neill?

DOLAN: He can't. He has some business that I made for him.

MOORE: Eh? (*He looks very sharply at* O'NEILL.) Very well, O'Neill!

O'NEILL: Yes?

MOORE: (*Going to a bundle of large bulky envelopes and bringing them over to the table beside* O'NEILL) Have a look over some of this stuff. It's the work you'll be taking charge of, out there. (*He goes out, followed by* DOLAN. O'NEILL *goes to the window and looks out. A burst of rain and wind lashes at the window. He shrugs his shoulders despondently and puts down, takes up some notepaper and hastily writes, puts it in an envelope, addresses and seals it. The door opens gently and he looks up with astonishment to see* CECILY BARRINGTON.)

O'NEILL: Why, it's you, Cecily!

CECILY: Yes. I met Kearney and he said — said you were going away. Is it true?

O'NEILL: Yes. Tomorrow.

CECILY: Tomorrow! Where are you going?

O'NEILL: A place called Ballinasheeda.

CECILY: Where's that?

O'NEILL: A long way west of this.

CECILY: So that I'll hardly ever see you again?

O'NEILL: I don't suppose you will.

CECILY: How long will you be there?

O'NEILL: A very long time.

CECILY: Years, maybe? (O'NEILL *nods.)* I see. So they have made this arrangement between them! They must have!

O'NEILL: Who?

CECILY: Moore and father. I saw them talking in the lounge as I came past. (*She suddenly catches sight of the letter.*) You were writing to me?

O'NEILL: Yes. (*He picks up the letter.*) I thought I wouldn't have the chance of seeing you again before I left.

CECILY: What have you written in it?

O'NEILL: Nothing of any consequence. Only a — a few lines.

CECILY: To say goodbye?

O'NEILL: Yes.

CECILY: And is that all?

O'NEILL: No. But the rest doesn't matter.

CECILY: Let me read it, please!

O'NEILL: No. (*He suddenly tears the letter in pieces.*) The rest of the letter was — it was only — (*He looks hard at her and trembles.*) There — I can't help telling you — what good it's going to do, I don't know, but it's the truth, Cecily — I love you!

CECILY: And what reply did you expect?

O'NEILL: I didn't ask for any.

CECILY: So this is the end then! I suppose — (*She hesitates and then holds out her hand*) — we'll have to say goodbye?

O'NEILL: Good-bye! (*He takes her hand and then turns away.*)

CECILY: And neither of us really cared? (*She comes closer and looks up into his face.*) Say that you never really cared?

O'NEILL: You never cared.

CECILY: (*With sudden and passionate anguish in her voice*) I do care. (*He takes her in his arms.*) Oh, believe me. I only want — want you!

(*The door opens and* MOORE *stands on the threshold in his oilskins and sou'wester.*)

MOORE: (*Suddenly entering*) I'm sorry, Miss Barrington — your father is below — asking for you. (*He pauses.*) I'm afraid that he's got rather bad news.

CECILY: Did he get the letter he was looking for?

MOORE: Yes. His demesne has been declared.

CECILY: Oh! (*She trembles, and vainly tries to keep back her tears.*) Poor darling old daddy! (*With a despairing cry to* O'NEILL) You — you didn't do it, anyway. You had no part in this.

(*The door swings open and* BARRINGTON *appears. He is trembling with excitement.*)

BARRINGTON: Cecily! What are you doing here?

CECILY: I came to see Hugh.

BARRINGTON: Have they told you what has happened?

CECILY: Yes!

BARRINGTON: I see. So it has come to this end for the Barringtons! My lands gone — my house gone!

(*He looks at her as if she too were lost to him.*)

CECILY: No! No!

BARRINGTON: (*Looking at* O'NEILL) Make your lot with him, if you wish, with these servants in the temple of the pig — for that's the god they serve, and well they know it, both of them. Good-night, Moore. Good-night, young man. I suppose you are both satisfied with your work. (*He goes out slowly like a broken man.*)

CECILY: (*Looking imploringly at* O'NEILL) I can't — I can't — leave him like this.

(*They all stand silent.* CECILY *makes a despairing gesture and walks out. A pause.* O'NEILL *makes a movement to follow.* MOORE *stops him with a commanding gesture.)*

MOORE: Let him get his agony over alone. (*A pause.*) 'Servants in the temple of the pig.' — I don't wonder he feels bitter tonight. (*He moves over, to the window, looks out, and calls.*) Dolan! Is that you?

DOLAN'S VOICE: (*From below*) Yes, sir.

MOORE: Wait there a moment — I'll be down directly. (*He turns round.*) You needn't stay up for me, O'Neill. I'll be calling on the way back with Mockler.

O'NEILL: With Mockler?

MOORE: Yes. To tell him we're standing by that little fighting devil. He's not afraid to face them. A migrant in a thousand! And let you, boy, have the same courage where you're going.

O'NEILL: I?

MOORE: Yes. You're my migrant to Ballinasheeda.

(*The door opens and* GOSUKI *appears.*)

GOSUKI: Excuse, please. I tomorrow — Dublin — Japan go. Galway — Roscommon — Mayo — have seen. Thousands of new house — new farm — migrants. Most impress. Pardon — one mistake — policy. When government — eh — state — land give to people — eh — control and ownership should keep. My view. (*He takes a small parcel from his pocket and presents it to* MOORE.) Little token — present — small fan of remembrance to Moore Sama. I salute and thank. I, inscription on it have made, 'Remembrance gracious to Moore Sama. Officer of great department of state, Ireland.' Sayonara. (*Exit.*)

O'NEILL: (*Cynically*) This great department of the state.

MOORE: (*Roused*) Yes. This great department of the state that is slowly wiping out the wrongs of centuries of oppression. And if an older man's advice can avail you anything, be proud to serve this great department of the state that gives us power for good or evil, reaching beyond the grave of this generation.

O'NEILL: (*With a cold cynicism that gradually works itself at the end to vehemence*) Did you not hear the Japanese with his houses and his temples of the fox and of the cat? I tell you, Moore, Barrington was right. You and I serve in the temple of the pig. And the floors of it, and the walls of it, are the floors and the walls of a shambles.

MOORE: (*Slowly*) A shambles? I used to think like you once. Years ago. But I do know this. That by this work we carry out, what was once a shambles and a house of greed may yet become. (*He pauses, and, as if hesitant to complete his words, moves towards the door.*)

O'NEILL: (*Wonderingly*) Yes?

MOORE: (*Turning towards the door and speaking as if reluctant to confess outwardly*) A temple — of the Living God.

(*There is the sound of a brisk fusillade of revolver shots outside in the Square. The two men stand still in a shocked, motionless silence.*)

O'NEILL: (*Looking over at* MOORE *with a grim smile*) A shambles or a temple of the Living God — which is it, Moore?

(CURTAIN)

ACT THREE

The same SCENE *some twelve years later. There is but little change in the furniture, and it is only by the alterations of the curtains, and perhaps the wallpaper, that any indication of the lapse of time is conveyed. The little Japanese fan still remains like a forgotten relic on the mantelpiece. The room, however, has been tidied up; all the array and litter of documents, maps, etc., have been cleared away. A couple of rucksacks and an old portmanteau lie labelled and ready for removal.*

MOORE, *now an old man, is seated, asleep, in one of the armchairs. Outside can be heard the faint notes of a flute playing the 'Air of the Gentle Maiden.' It is still daylight, though evening is rapidly approaching.*

A knock at the door, then it is opened and MARTIN, *the boots, comes in, carrying a tray with decanter, syphon and glasses.*

MARTIN: Beg pardon, Mr Moore! (*He places the tray on one of the tables.*) Asleep! (*He goes over to examine the baggage and looks at the labels inquisitively and reads.*) 'Stephen Moore. Passenger to — ' (*He looks up.*) Begor, the ould gentleman didn't finish writing them! Where's he going now at the end of his days, I wonder?

(*The flute stops.*)

MOORE: (*Wakening*) Yes, yes! I heard you! Yes, yes! I'm coming! Oh! It's you, Martin! Time to go, is it?

MARTIN: No, sir. You've another three-quarters of an hour before the bus goes to the station.

MOORE: Very good. I was asleep, Martin.

MARTIN: Yes, sir. I see yous are all packed and ready.

(*The music outside recommences.*)

MOORE: Stop that music. Too mournful.

MARTIN: Yes, sir. (*He goes to the window.*) Hi there, Packy!

VOICE: (*Outside*) Yes?

MARTIN: Stop that one!

VOICE: Right!

(*There is the sound of an alteration, and the music abruptly ceases.*)

MOORE: Thanks. (*He suddenly sees the tray.*) What's all this array for?

MARTIN: Boss sent it up with his compliments. He'd like to see you before you go, sir.

MOORE: Of course. I'll see him. Thank him for me, Martin.

MARTIN: Are ye sure you've got everying packed up, sir?

MOORE: Yes.

MARTIN: You have no address on them labels, sir.

MOORE: No. (*A pause.*) Has the down mail come from Dublin yet?

MARTIN: No, sir. Were you expecting somebody?

MOORE: Yes.

MARTIN: Is it a new man from Dublin is coming to take your place, sir?

MOORE: No.

MARTIN: Miss Mooney got a note this morning from somebody called Watersley.

MOORE: Oh yes, yes — Watersley!

MARTIN: Is he the gentleman that's going to be after you here?

MOORE: Not at all. Watersley is one of the new juniors.

MARTIN: I see. Another colt to be broke in. That'll be three now I've seen in my days. Have you all your papers gathered?

MOORE: I think so, Martin.

MARTIN: Will you want the Japanese gentleman's fan, sir? (*He lifts it carelessly from the mantelpiece.*)

MOORE: Leave it there for the present.

MARTIN: Right, sir! (*He replaces the fan and begins to examine the chest of drawers.*) Nothing here — except the top drawer. It's locked, sir.

MOORE: 'Pon my word, now you mention it, Martin, I didn't look in it. (*Fumbling in his pockets and producing a key*) Give the key to Mr Mooney when you've cleared it out. I was nearly going off with it.

MARTIN: Yes, sir. (*He opens the drawer and examines it.*) Here's something! Photy of a new house. (*He turns it over and reads from an inscription on the back.*) 'Plan of migrant's house. Dan Dolan, Ballyglass.'

MOORE: Oh, that be damned! Burn it.

MARTIN: Yes, sir. (*He throws it carelessly aside.*) Here's another.

MOORE: What's it?

MARTIN: (*After a scrutiny.*) 'The Rose Garden, Mount Nevin.'

MOORE: How did that get there? (*After a pause.*) Burn it.

MARTIN: I'll stick it up here. It's nicer nor Danny Dolan's house's photy. (*He puts it on the mantelpiece.*)

MOORE: As you like. (*Musingly*) Poor Barrington! (*With a sudden note of tragic apology*) 'Thou canst not say I did it.'

MARTIN: (*Astonished*) Not at all! No one could blame you. The will of God, sir. A decent old gentleman, Mr Barrington. He done well to clear out of that place. All gone and divided now, sir.

MOORE: Yes. Wiped out. As we all will be some day or another, Martin. What's the rest of that stuff you've got?

MARTIN: (*Extracting, as he talks, from the drawer*) An old map. (*He throws it carelessly on the table.*) Doesn't look much importance whatever. Here's the last. (*He looks casually at an old diary he has pulled out.*) That's all that's in it. An ould diary of yours, sir. Nineteen hundred and — ach! it's years old. (*He hands it over to* MOORE, *who begins to look carelessly through it.*) Beg pardon, sir. Aren't you sixty-five now, sir?

MOORE: Yes — and two more on that.

MARTIN: There! That's what I told Mr Mooney yesterday. Sure, says I, Mr Moore got took on two years longer than the rest of them, in order, says I, to finish up the Kilrea country.

MOORE: (*Smiling*) Finish up the Kilrea country! Do you know, Martin, there were old fools like me here in Kilrea who thought the same thing three hundred years ago. And I suppose they, too, kept official diaries like this, and divided the land, and gave some to the Barringtons, some to the Burkes, and some to the Blakes —

MARTIN: Divil a sod they gave my ancestors, anyway. (*Wth a final look into the drawer; then locking it carefully and pocketing the key.*) I'll call you when it's time, sir.

MOORE: Thanks, Martin. (*Exit* MARTIN.) Hm! (*He continues looking casually through the diary.*) I suppose when I was scribbling this twelve years ago I thought it most important data. (*As he carelessly turns the pages, his attention is suddenly arrested by an entry. He looks carefully at it, and then, intensely interested, begins to read aloud.*) December 14. Went Ballinasheeda. O'Neill absent without leave. No information whereabouts. Work in order. December 15. Ballinasheeda. Found O'Neill at Lisnashee. (*He peers closer at the page.*) Formed impression he was — Hm! Something stroked out — I remember. Poor devil! — admitted offence — signed statement — sent report Dublin — December 30th. Severely reprimanded and reduced. Gave word of honour if allowed remain at work in Ballinasheeda he would — (*Slowly, and then with a sudden vehemence.*) And, by God, O'Neill, you kept it! (*He rises and goes over to the table, and his attention is suddenly drawn to the map which* MARTIN *has discovered. He lays down the diary, takes up the map, and begins to examine it.*) Fitzgormanstown! The Bridge Head! My old draught map of twenty years ago!

(*Knocking.*)

MARTIN: (*Appearing*) Mr Mockler to see you, sir.

(MOORE *folds up the map and puts it into his pocket.*)

MOCKLER: (*Entering smiling*) Mr Moore, and how are you? And I've someone else with me. (*Speaking towards door*) He's here. Come on in, Mrs Morrisey.

MRS MORRISEY: Well, an' I'm glad to see you, Mr Moore. And how are you? *(She looks at the baggage.*) And all your little belongings packed and ready. Well, well, but this is the saddest day we've had in Kilrea this many a year.

MOCKLER: We both just came to pay our last respects, Mr Moore. And to wish you the best of the best, wherever you're going.

MRS MORRISEY: Indeed, we all wish him the best of the best. Yes, indeed. (*To* MARTIN) You can tell my son to come up. He's waiting in the hall below.

MARTIN: (*To* MOORE) Shall I, sir?

MOORE: Yes.

(Exit MARTIN.)

MRS MORRISEY: And it's today you re going, is it?

MOORE: Yes.

MOCKLER: We had some great arguments in the past, Mr Moore, but sure there was bound to be disagreements occasionally, and on the whole you done fair between man and man.

MRS MORRISEY: Indeed he did. And sure if he didn't do what we thought was justice, there'll be great chances now with that big place of Fitzgormanstown coming.

MOCKLER: Yes. Thousands of acres in it. Room for everybody. Launawallia for the landless and twice over.

MRS MORRISEY: (*Looking through the door*) Ah! Here's my son now. Come on in, Michael. This is my youngest, Mr Moore.

(MICHAEL, *a rather surly-looking man of thirty years of age or thereabouts, comes in.)*

MICHAEL: (*Nodding to* MOORE) Brave day!

MOORE: Yes.

MICHAEL: I hear you're leaving, Mr Moore?

MOORE: Yes

MICHAEL: I suppose there'll be a new man coming?

MOORE: Yes.

MRS MORRISEY: I wonder now who it might be!

MOORE: Don't know.

MRS MORRISEY: I thought they'd have had a matter like that settled long ago?

(MOORE *does not answer.*)

MOCKLER: Begor, this life is nothing but changes!

MICHAEL: Well, I'm not sorry for one. I'm not afraid to repeat what I wrote up to your office as secretary of our committee, that we look on the whole of yous as little short of tricksters.

MOORE: Yes. I read that letter.

MICHAEL: I wanted to come in here today and see who your successor was, because from this out we want fair play given. No more hole and corner secret dodging, but square play. And before you divide one perch of Fitzgormanstown we want to have the say to them that's to get land in it. Who's your successor, Mr Moore?

MOORE: I've already told you I don't know.

MICHAEL: Well, I want to see him when he comes. You done my mother and me here out of land in Ballyglass that was ours by right years ago, but things is going to be different now, I can tell you. Well, seeing the new man isn't here, I'll be saying goodbye. (*He moves off.*)

MRS MORRISEY: Michael! Michael! Won't you wish the old gentleman good luck?

MOORE: He needn't waste his time, Mrs Morrisey. I cannot say I'm glad to have met you, young man, on my last day in Kilrea, but I can tell you this to your face, that if you and your mother had got the land that time you were looking for it, it would have been the damnedest scandal in Kilrea. (*With a burst of indignation*) Go out, and be damned to you!

MOCKLER: (*Motioning to* MICHAEL) That'll do now, go on down. (*Exit.*)

MICHAEL: Don't mind the youngster, Mr Moore. Sure we were all like that once. (*To* MRS MORRISEY) He has no right to be writing stuff like that up to them in Dublin.

MRS MORRISEY: Didn't yourself read it over before he sent it, and you told him it was a grand letter!

MOCKLER: *(Somewhat taken aback)* Aye. Well. *(He quickly recovers.)* Ach! Mr Moore knows well the kind of balderdash them young fellows be's at. Balderdash! Nothing in it!

MRS MORRISEY: Ach! Never mind the young people. They're always at that sort of thing. Kicking out the old ones. Now, land apart and away, here's my hand, Mr Moore, and sure you and I haven't long to be going, but there's no bad feeling between us.

MOORE: (*Reluctantly taking her hand*) I will believe you then, if so you say.

(*She shakes it with emotion, and then, apparently overcome, she leaves the room.*)

MOCKLER: She means it, the creature — for the time being! Sure we all means well, sometime or another. It mightn't last, but sure we all mean it while it's on us. Here. (*He goes closer to* MOORE.) Would you like to know the real reason I cam' up to see you? I was sent up by Mooney. Aye. Now not another word about it, but maybe there'll be a little pleasant surprise for you yet Mr Moore. Just a few of us below in the parlour — (*Knocking.*) Come in.

(KEARNEY *enters. He is, of course older and bent, but little changed otherwise.*)

KEARNEY: Ah — hello, Moore!

MOCKLER: Ah! So you've come, Mr Kearney. Did you see the boss?

KEARNEY: Yes. He's waiting on you below.

MOCKLER: Right. I'll see you again, Mr Moore, below. For the present, *slan leat!* (*Exit.*)

KEARNEY: Well, well! So the day's come at last! *Der Tag*! Eh, well, you're the great old soldier. (*Noticing the bags*) Packed and ready?

MOORE: Yes.

KEARNEY: Of course you're waiting for the — well — you know

MOORE: Waiting for the what?

KEARNEY: Oh, well, it's nothing much. Just a little token — I shouldn't have mentioned it, perhaps.

MOORE: Look here, Kearney. I want to leave this place just as I came into it twenty-five years ago. None of your fussing.

KEARNEY: Like the old Scriptures, eh? 'Now lettest thou thy servant depart in peace.'

MOORE: But that's part of a burial service, damn you! I'm not dead yet.

KEARNEY: Where are you going? (MOORE *murmurs an indistinct reply.*) What? Not goin' home to your friends?

MOORE: Friends? Yes. Your own people?

MOORE: My own people! (*With a faint smile and gesture*) They're all — all —

KEARNEY: Any news who your successor is likely to be?

MOORE: No.

KEARNEY: Strange, word hasn't come yet.

MOORE: It is.

KEARNEY: I suppose, Moore, I'd hardly get it, would I?

MOORE: Kearney — I couldn't tell you.

KEARNEY: There's a huge pile of new stuff coming down.

MOORE: Yes. And I used to think — God help me, Kearney! I used to think we were winding up.

KEARNEY: Winding up! We're only just begun. Did O'Neill come up from Ballinasheeda?

MOORE: O'Neill! (*He carefully puts the diary away into one of his pockets.*) Yes, O'Neill — O'Neill — !

KEARNEY: What about O'Neill?

MOORE: Nothing. (*He looks round the room.*) Do you know, Kearney, it gives me a bit of a wrench to part company with this — this old what-you-call-it — sweating chamber. *(He goes over to the decanter.)* Old Mooney sent this up. Decent of the old man. He's down there in his parlour like a great, big, rheumatic spider unable to do anything but send out messages to the bookies. (*He fills up drinks.*) Cheerio, old comrade!

KEARNEY: Cheerio, old commander! (*He turns away to avoid showing any emotion, and suddenly sees the photograph* MARTIN *has left lying carelessly on the mantelpiece.*) Hm! The Rose Garden, Mount Nevin! Do you remember the rows we had long ago at Ballyglass — old Barrington? His Rose Garden! (*He laughs.*) It's growing the finest of early Rose of Arran spuds for the Morriseys now! My God, what fools we mortals be! What? What? Idiots! What?

(*The door opens slightly and* DAN DOLAN *peeps in.*)

DAN: Mr Moore in?

KEARNEY: Who are you?

DAN: Is Mr Moore in?

MOORE: Yes — I'm here. What is it?

(DOLAN *comes slowly in. His left coat sleeve is empty, for he has lost that arm, and he is bent with age and hard work.*)

DOLAN: D'ye not remember me, Mr Moore? Yourself drove me to hospital the wild bad night they shattered my arm outside that window there.

MOORE: (*Slowly*) Dan Dolan from Addergoole!

DOLAN: Yes, your honour. Dan Dolan from Addergoole that yous migrated.

MOORE: Yes, yes. I know you now.

DOLAN: Well, did the lady call with yous yet?

MOORE: What lady?

DOLAN: There was a lady out at Mount Nevin today, and she told me she was coming in to see the Commissioners about a graveyard.

KEARNEY: A graveyard!

DOLAN: Yes, your honour. There's a kind of a wild old small place there, on the last bit that yous give me extra at Mount Nevin was once an ould graveyard, for it has broke tombstones in it. She says it's hers.

KEARNEY: Who — was she?

DOLAN: Begor now, 'twas Miss Barrington, but she didn't stay no time much, and then she walked up to where the hall steps used to be, and looked kind of bewildered and crying like, as if she couldn't make out what would have been the front and the back of it. Hard for her, when all the stones of the big house had been sold and drew off for the county council stone-breaker of seven years ago.

MOORE: It would hardly be Cecily Barrington!

KEARNEY: Twas a ghost you saw, man! You'll never see a Barrington back in this country again.

DOLAN: Oh, bedad, this was no ghost! Heck! it's a quare ghost that puts you into her car and brings you in along with her. She told me to go ahead of her while she went in to see the Canon.

(*Knocking.*)

MOORE: Come in.

MARTIN: (*At door.*) Mr Mooney would like to see you, sir, and Mr Kearney, if you'd be pleased to come. He's waiting below in the parlour.

KEARNEY: Right! You'll have to come down, Moore.

MOORE: All right, Martin. (*Exit* MARTIN.) One moment! (*He thinks hard.*) Graveyard! Mount Nevin! Kearney, there was to have been a reservation to the Barringtons of a graveyard plot. There's a copy of the map somewhere in that pile over there. (*He goes over to it and searches.*) Yes. (*Extracts a map.*) There it is. (KEARNEY *and he examine it.*) That small plot there in the north-east corner. I can't see very well, but there's something written in pencil on it.

KEARNEY: (*Taking up map and scanning it*) Yes. (*Reading*) 'Vendor originally asked for reservation of this plot but took no final steps to have it excluded. Included in parcel 10A. Dan Dolan, allottee.'

DOLAN: That would be right, your honour. She said she would call here about it.

MARTIN: (*Again at door*) Boss is waiting, gentlemen.

MOORE: Here — sit down, Dolan. (*He pours out a drink.*) Take a drink, and wait a minute or two and have a look at this map. We'll be back directly.

DAN: Right, your honour.

(MOORE *and* KEARNEY *go out.* DOLAN *seats himself and sips his drink, while he closely examines the map.* MARTIN *eyes him curiously. There is a short pause.*)

MARTIN: Have you took to maps or to drink, Dolan?

DOLAN: Would you mind, if you please, looking after your own business?

MARTIN: I might as well be telling you the truth. You'll never answer the job you're looking!

DOLAN: What job?

MARTIN: Mr Moore's. There's a new man coming from Dublin, so you can go home and give up this mapping business.

DOLAN: Here, young man! If you had something was nothing much to yourself but was worth a power to someone else was mad to get it, what would you charge them for it?

MARTIN: (*With a grin*) You're not going to get made a commissioner by stealing my brains! (*Exit.*)

(DOLAN *resumes his seat at the table and continues his study of the map, and meditatively sips his drink. A knock at the door. It opens and* O'NEILL *looks in. He is still young, but his face is lined and careworn.*)

O'NEILL: Where's Mr Moore?

DOLAN: (*With a sharp look at him*) He'll be back presently.

O'NEILL: I'll wait for him here then. (*He sits down at the table opposite to* DOLAN.)

DOLAN: (*Taking a long survey of him*) Be the powers, but it's surely the same!

O'NEILL: (*Returning his look*) Well, have you sized me up yet?

DOLAN: Begging your honour's pardon, but you're the great likeness of a young man that had hard battling since I seen him here the time I was moving to Ballyglass.

O'NEILL: Ballyglass!

DOLAN: Yes. It's convenient to a place there that went by the name of Mount Nevin. (O'NEILL *gives him a sharp, startled look, but remains silent. The daylight grows dimmer.*) 'Tis easy enough to remember a place by custom, but begor, they all changes. Faces and places. And I seen another face today — begor, I wonder would you be remembering it? You'd have more reason than myself for the same, I'm thinking.

O'NEILL: (*Angrily*) What are you saying?

DOLAN: I mind it well now. This very room — a wild bad night it was — twelve years ago — and I went over to you and told you she was in the town.

(*He suits the action to the words, and as if in a dream, the scene between the two men unconsciously repeats itself.*)

O'NEILL: Who?

DOLAN: Her.

O'NEILL: Who's her?

DOLAN: That one.

O'NEILL: Which one?

DOLAN: Your one.

(*A silence. It is now dim twilight. A sudden burst of the strains of 'For He's a Jolly Good Fellow' comes up from* MOONEY'S *parlour somewhere below. As it gradually dies down, the door opens and* WATERSLEY *enters, followed by* MARTIN. WATERSLEY, *a young, well dressed youth in tweeds, carries a small portmanteau and despatch bag, and* MARTIN *follows him with a golfbag, luggage, and a bundle of large brown paper official envelopes.* MARTIN *switches on the light after depositing his burden.*)

WATERSLEY: Hello!

O'NEILL: Hello!

WATERSLEY: Is this the room?

MARTIN: Yes, sir. You can leave these things in here for the present till you gets fixed up. (*Placing the baggage, and then looking hard at* O'NEILL) You waiting to see anybody, sir? (*Suddenly recognising him*) Ah, begor, I'm glad to see you again! And how are you, sir?

O'NEILL: I'm well, thank you, Martin. Don't worry anybody. I want to see Mr Moore when he's free.

MARTIN: All right, sir. The boss says you're to have Mr Moore's room, sir — in there. I'll put your bags in it presently. (*Nodding towards* DOLAN) The boss wants him down there as a representative of the migratory gentlemen to say something. Come on, Dolan — you can bring that map with you.

(*He guides* DOLAN *out and shuts the door.*)

(*The strains of 'Auld Lang Syne' are heard, with sundry yells of enthusiasm.*)

WATERSLEY: What's all the racket?

O'NEILL: Farewell going on.

WATERSLEY: Funny! I had mine last night.

O'NEILL: Indeed! (*The singing ceases abruptly.*)

WATERSLEY: Yes. Some of our chaps gave me a bit of a beano last night. (*He points to the golfbag.*) Gave me that presentation golfbag there. Jolly decent, wasn't it?

O'NEILL: Very.

WATERSLEY: I won the captain's prize this year at Milltown; they took me down three strokes. Any links here?

O'NEILL: I don't know.

(*Sound of applause.*)

WATERSLEY: Hm! Who's getting all the laurel wreaths below?

O'NEILL: Old Stephen Moore.

WATERSLEY: Oh yes — the old chap in charge who's leaving?

O'NEILL: Yes.

WATERSLEY: Jolly glad I got here in time to catch him before he went. I've some letters for him. They should have been posted yesterday, but as I was coming down they made me bring them. I gave them to the boots to deliver. Hell of a journey from Dublin! Took damned near five hours on the train!

O'NEILL: It would.

WATERSLEY: I'd no idea this place was such a beastly distance from Dublin. I say, there wouldn't be much chance of getting back for the weekend, would there?

O'NEILL: Not an earthly.

WATERSLEY: That's a bit tough! You're one of Moore's old squad down here, perhaps?

O'NEILL: Yes.

WATERSLEY: Who's taking his place, I wonder? I hope it's some sporty chap. I heard old Moore was a bit of a Tartar, and gave some of you chaps a bit of a gruelling.

O'NEILL: Yes. What did you hear?

WATERSLEY: Not quite sure what it was all about, but there was something about a girl that one of the chaps got a bit potty about — it wasn't you, by the way was it? No? — Well, the girl jilted him, it appears, and the beau went off the deep end.

O'NEILL: Did he?

WATERSLEY: Yes. And old Moore gave him no end of beans — nearly got him sacked. No fear of me getting sappy like that on girls! It's a proper mug's game. Sport's my line of country. Any chance of a bit of dry fly stuff down here? I brought a rod on the off-chance. Do you live here?

O'NEILL: No. I'm at Ballinasheeda.

WATERSLEY: Ballinasheeda! Where's that?

O'NEILL: (*Beginning to take an interest in the unconscious youngster*) About fifty miles further west by car — sixty by rail.

WATERSLEY: Great Scott! Dublin must be a complete washout for you anyway?

O'NEILL: (*Laughing in spite of himself.*) It is, surely.

WATERSLEY: Hope I'm not stuck there. Where's the nearest links?

O'NEILL: At Lahinch.

WATERSLEY: Jove! That's great! I've often heard of it. How far is it from here?

O'NEILL: About sixty.

WATERSLEY: (*Dejectedly*) Gosh! I say, does old Moore golf?

O'NEILL: No.

WATERSLEY: Or fish?

O'NEILL: No.

WATERSLEY: Do you?

O'NEILL: No.

WATERSLEY: (*Alarmed*) And what the hell do you do?

(*The door opens and* MARTIN *enters carrying a further consignment of envelopes and baggage, which he deposits.*)

WATERSLEY: Oh! I must see where my fishing tackle got to. (*Exit.*)

MARTIN: Power of stuff addressed for you here, Mr O'Neill, whatever something to occupy that young gentleman in his spare time! (MOORE *enters.*) I'll be taking your baggage down now, Mr Moore. The bus will be round in a couple of minutes. (*He takes up* MOORE'S *baggage and goes out.*)

MOORE: Hello, O'Neill! Glad to see you again. So you got my wire? (*They shake hands.*)

O'NEILL: Yes. What did you want me for?

MOORE: Because I was anticipating this. (*He hands* O'NEILL *a letter.*) It came by hand today from Dublin. (O'NEILL *reads it slowly.*) Seems to have got delayed somehow. It is quite clear?

O'NEILL: Yes. (*Slowly*) I'm to be — your successor in Kilrea.

MOORE: Yes. They followed an old precedent. Took the man from Ballinasheeda.

O'NEILL: Thanks, Moore.

MOORE: You won't be sorry to leave it?

O'NEILL: (*With a slow smile*) Were you?

MOORE: No. (*A pause.*) There's someone you and I knew long ago is back again in this place today, and you'll have to meet her as my successor and help her.

O'NEILL: Who?

MOORE: Dermot Barrington is dying and has sent — his daughter down about the burial ground at Mount Nevin. I ceased to be an official yesterday — according to that letter you have — so I can't help, but you can — it's not much, only a formal approval.

O'NEILL: Of what?

MOORE: Giving back to the Barringtons their burial ground.

O'NEILL: Burial ground?

MOORE: Yes. Strange world! One time her people had 40,000 acres and 900 tenantry. Now all they hold is barely a rood of burial ground and that by the grace of Dan Dolan — a stranger like ourselves. Dan Dolan — twice that old man has given land to us for the same purpose — for a bridge head.

O'NEILL: I don't follow you, Moore.

MOORE: He gave land years ago as a bridge head for the living. Today he gives land as a bridge head for the dead — for Dermot Barrington, so he can cross over to his own folk!

O'NEILL: Moore — I can't! I — I suppose you know — it was he compelled her to write me — and break it all off between us — twelve years ago — and I buried her at Ballinasheeda. (KEARNEY *enters.*)

MOORE: O'Neill, I've already told Kearney the news.

KEARNEY: (*Shaking hands with* O'NEILL.) And congratulations, O'Neill. I thought it might have come my way, but I'll try not to grouse, though I know Ellen will. You've had a long tarry at Ballinasheeda and done a powerful lot of work.

O'NEILL: (*Looking at* MOORE *appealingly*) Couldn't Kearney?

MOORE: No. It's your responsibility.

(WATERSLEY *enters.*)

KEARNEY: What's this?

WATERSLEY: My name's Watersley. It was I that brought down the good news.

KEARNEY: The what?

WATERSLEY: The good news. They mugged up things a bit in the office, and I was to have come down yesterday, but instead I caught the mail this morning.

MOORE: I see. So you're our new recruit! Have you met O'Neill?

O'NEILL: (*Smiling*) Yes. I know a fair amount about him already.

(DAN DOLAN *and* MOCKLER *enter.* MOCKLER *is expansive and hilarious with drink.*)

MOCKLER: Hurroo! What d'ye think, gentlemen? Look at him! Dan Dolan! — The Duke of Addergoole! — The man that's after agreeing to sign, convey and assign land free, gratis, and for nothing, to oblige the remains of an ancient ould family. More power to you, Daniel! (*He slaps the latter on the back.*) But weren't you the greatest old omadhaun in the world that didn't wait on the great news that's come down by the Deputy — the new Land Act is through and Fitzgormanstown Ranch will be for the people. (*He laughs uproariously.*) And you! (*He thumps* DOLAN.) You left your holding at Addergoole and faced murder and loss of limb, and if you'd only had the sense of a mouse and waited, you'd have had the grandest and the greatest holding for the asking! The Duke of Addergoole! (*As he talks he drifts nearer the decanter and tray.*) The only bit o' land that they can put a bridge across to get into it, and you sold it for what you got in Ballyglass! Begorras! and there's idiots still walking the earth and you're one of them. But a gentleman, Daniel — you were always a gentleman! (*He commences filling out drinks from the decanter.*)

(*The mention of Fitzgormanstown has made* MOORE *suddenly recollect the map in his pocket. He takes it out and shows it to* O'NEILL *as* MOCKLER *ceases talking.*)

MOORE: If it's true about Fitzgormanstown, this old map of mine might be some use to you, O'Neill. Take it, and welcome. (*He hands it over.*)

MOCKLER: And now, gentlemen, I'm only after leaving our good host Mr Mooney below, and says he to me, 'Mockler, will you go up and make sure that the company above take advantage of what I sent up, and drink a dock-an-dorus to Mr Moore.' (*Turning to the decanter and tray*) And he told me to take no refusals.

MARTIN: (*At door*) The bus is waiting Mr Moore.

MOCKLER: Here! (*Catching him*) Make yourself attentive. Give me a hand with this. Give everybody something. (*Approaching* WATERSLEY *with a drink*) So you're the young one that's come down?

WATERSLEY: Yes. *(He makes a gesture of disapproval.)* No, thanks. No, thanks. Don't drink.

MOCKLER: (*Astonished*) You what!

WATERSLEY: Don't touch. Knocks you off form.

MOCKLER: Knocks you off what?

WATERSLEY: Off form. No, thanks. Don't touch.

MOCKLER: And what d'ye do?

WATERSLEY: Well, I hope — I hope it's no harm: I'm fond of a bit of sport.

MOCKLER: (*Effusively and delightedly*) Good boy! The Curragh, maybe — or the Galway Plate?

WATERSLEY: Oh, no, no. Golf!

MOCKLER: (*As if he hadn't heard aright*) Golf!

O'NEILL: Yes — he golfs.

WATERSLEY: Yes. (MOCKLER *suddenly sees the golfbag and inspects it.*) That's my presentation bag.

MOCKLER: (*With a gesture of surprised explanation towards the company present*) He golfs!

WATERSLEY: Yes.

MOCKLER: Anything else?

WATERSLEY: Yes, I — I fish. Dry fly.

MOCKLER: (*To the company*) Fishes! Dry fly!

WATERSLEY: Yes.

DOLAN: (*Waking up suddenly from a contemplative silence, during which he has regarded* MOCKLER *with growing resentment*) So I'm — I'm the Duke of Addergoole today, is it, Mockler?

MOCKLER: (*Delighted at having roused the old man.*) Yes, Daniel. The Duke of Addergoole, and well named.

DOLAN: Aye. And the greatest old omadhaun in the world! Aye! That didn't wait on the great news and the great new Land Act. Aye. A walking idiot with no sense that could have had the greatest and the grandest holding in Fitzgormanstown for the asking! The asking, maurya! And who now would I be asking, Mr Mockler?

MOCKLER: You could —

DOLAN: Whist! Is it golf sticks (*He points to* WATERSLEY) or O'Neill or the commissioners? Or is it yourself and young Morrisey and your committee? Half-a-crown down and register for land! Twopence on the postage, fourpence on the station'ry, a shilling on the secretary, and the rest — on the crown and feathers! Two-and-sixpence for the greatest and the grandest holding in Fitzgormanstown for the asking! Live horse and get registered for grass! (*With passionate anger*) I asked all I'll ever ask, and I got all I'll ever get from one man here (*He points to Moore*) and the damn the committee, commissioners, Morrisey or Mockler will ever get me to surrender one perch of what I got, for the hundred best acres in Connaught. (*He goes over to* MOORE *and takes his hand.*) Long life to you, Mr Moore, and goodbye. You always treated me decent. (*He makes his way towards the door.*) And may the great God be ever wondering at the luck you'd be having — and goodbye. (*Exit.*)

(*A loud motor-horn blows impatiently.*)

MARTIN: (*Suddenly*) Oh, glory be to God — the bus, sir! The bus! Time to be off.

(*Exit* MOCKLER.)

MOORE: Well, I must say goodbye, boys. (*He goes over to* WATERSLEY *and looks quizzically at him.*) Goodbye, my boy. I don't know whether to laugh at you or cry — I think I'll laugh — Fishing! (*He looks over smiling at* O'NEILL *and* KEARNEY. *Then he begins to laugh.*) Golfing! (*The whole company bursts into laughter.*) Good-bye!

(KEARNEY *and* O'NEILL precede MOORE *through the door. As the latter is on the point of going out he catches the little Japanese fan that* GOSUKI *had presented. He takes it, glances at it, and then quietly throws it into the fireplace and passes out.*)

(*A silence. Then the strains of 'Auld Lang Syne' are heard from below.* WATERSLEY *goes over to the window as if to watch the farewell. The sound of the bus departing; the singing stops.* WATERSLEY, *going over towards the baggage, glances carelessly at the photograph of the Rose Garden, then picks up the fan, and reads the inscription on it.*)

WATERSLEY: 'Remembrance gracious to Moore Sama, Officer of the Great Department of State, Ireland.'

(*He drops it carelessly back in the fireplace, goes over to his golfbag, extracts the putter, and begins practising assiduously with an imaginary ball. He is fully occupied doing so when somebody approaches the door, which has been left open, hesitates, and knocks.* WATERSLEY, *too intent on what he is doing, does not hear. The somebody comes in. It is* CECILY BARRINGTON.)

CECILY: I beg your pardon!

WATERSLEY: Oh, not at all! Do you want to see anybody?

CECILY: Yes. I have a document here — a form of some kind of consent. (*She produces it.*) I was to get it signed by the officer in charge.

WATERSLEY: Oh! Are you in a hurry?

CECILY: Yes. I am going on by car immediately I get it completed. It was to have been signed by Mr Moore, but I understand he's gone.

WATERSLEY: Yes — gone for good. Didn't you hear all the hooley that was going on? 'Auld Lang Syne' and all the rest of it?

Have a seat while I go down and see if I can get the new man for you.

(*He hurriedly goes out, having given her a chair.* CECILY *sits nervously fingering the document she has brought. She suddenly rises as her eyes catch sight of the little picture postcard of the Rose Garden, and involuntarily she goes over, takes it in her hand and examines it.*)

CECILY: (*Slowly reading from the card*) 'The Rose Garden, Mount Nevin. From C. B.'

(*She replaces the card and slowly goes back to her seat. Then overcome, gives way to her tears.* WATERSLEY *re-enters. She hurriedly tries to regain her composure.*)

WATERSLEY: They're just gone off on the bus to the station. Be back in a jiffy. (*He begins unconsciously to resume practising his putter.*)

CECILY: Thank you. (*A pause.*) Are you one of the staff here now?

WATERSLEY: Yes. But as a matter of fact, I only came down today to join up.

CECILY: Oh! And what are you going to do down here?

WATERSLEY: Between you and me, I'm going to try and wangle a few games with this (*Waving the putter*) if I can.

CECILY: Will you be doing anything else?

WATERSLEY: Oh Lord, yes! Work, I suppose.

CECILY: What sort of work?

WATERSLEY: Oh — the usual sort of stuff — you know, taking up land from people and giving it out to people.

CECILY: Do you ever take land from people and give it back to them again?

WATERSLEY: No! Never heard of such a case — did you?

CECILY: No. It's rarely done, I suppose.

WATERSLEY: I should say so. Did they take up land from you?

CECILY: Yes. They took all we had.

WATERSLEY: Oh! And you're wanting some back?

CECILY: Yes.

WATERSLEY: I wouldn't ask if I were you. It'll only mean trouble.

CECILY: It's only a very small plot.

WATERSLEY: Doesn't matter — small or large — same thing! I've seen a man murder another over a few perches of street. They might be different down here, but I doubt it.

CECILY: Will this work of yours ever come to an end?

WATERSLEY: Don't know. I suppose we'll go on dividing to Tibbs' Eve!

CECILY: Until Ireland is all one great sea of small holdings?

WATERSLEY: Yes.

CECILY: Nothing but little cottages and little farms?

WATERSLEY: Yes. Millions of them! The old demesne and those places, they'll all go phut!

CECILY: And no-one will ever remember the people who lived in them once?

WATERSLEY: I say — (*He gives her a suspicious stare.*) No! Sorry, but I can't discuss things like that. Against the regulations. You see, we're forbidden to discuss politics.

CECILY: But we might be talking economics?

WATERSLEY: Same thing. No, thanks. One of our chaps got into the — beg pardon! — he got into the devil's own row last week down in Kildare because he was blathering about rates on a bog — So I'm taking no chances. Talk nothing but golf now. Safer! (*He makes a few strokes with his club, then stops and takes a long look at her.*) Do you belong this side of the country?

CECILY: Yes. We once had a place out here.

WATERSLEY: Oh! What did you call it?

CECILY: Mount Nevin. I came down here today to see if I could get — well, just a little bit of it back again.

WATERSLEY: I know, yes. Site for a bungalow or something like that?

CECILY: No. A place where my people are buried.

WATERSLEY: (*Abashed*) Oh! Sorry! I'm really sorry. (*There is a noise outside.*) Here they are now.

(MARTIN *and* O'NEILL *enter.* MARTIN *is carrying baggage.*)

MARTIN: In here, Mr O'Neill. This way to Mr Moore's old room.

(MARTIN *crosses over to the door to left and goes in.* O'NEILL *is following him when he suddenly sees* CECILY *and stops.*)

WATERSLEY: This lady is waiting to see you, sir — about — a — plot — land up at Mount Nevin.

O'NEILL: Oh, yes. *(He bows formally.)* Moore told me. I'm sorry to hear the reason — Have you the form?

CECILY: Yes. (*She produces it.*) Dolan has already signed it and I understand all that's required is formal approval by you, subject to consent in Dublin.

O'NEILL: Yes. (*He looks over the form.*) Would you mind signing here — on that line. (CECILY *does so. He examines her signature.)* 'Cecily Travers!' — married woman?

CECILY: Yes.

O'NEILL: Then add 'wife of' and put your husband's name.

(*She does so.* O'NEILL *witnesses her signature in silence, blots, and then hands over the form.* MARTIN *passes silently through the room and goes out.*)

CECILY: Might I ask a small favour?

O'NEILL: I would be glad to grant it if I can.

CECILY: If I may, I would like to take that photograph there of the Rose Garden.

O'NEILL: I — I think it belongs to Moore.

CECILY: No. I sent it to you. (*He goes over to get it for her.*) It was the only one I had. May I take it with me?

O'NEILL: (*After a glance at it.*) Yes. I've lost all title — to anything of yours long ago.

CECILY: But did you want to keep it?

O'NEILL: I lost it — as I did something — more important years ago. And today's the first time I've seen — either of them again.

(MARTIN *suddenly appears at door.*)

MARTIN: The car is ready, ma'am

CECILY: Thank you. (*Exit* MARTIN.) It's strange to be back in this same room — and to see you — again — after all these years. Where have you been ever since?

O'NEILL: At Ballinasheeda.

CECILY: All those years ? Ever since?

O'NEILL: Yes.

CECILY: Are you going back there?

O'NEILL: No. I'm here as Moore's successor.

CECILY: To carry on his work?

O'NEILL: Yes, if I can.

CECILY: If you can. Do you believe in it?

O'NEILL: He did.

CECILY: Do you?

O'NEILL: Yes. (*He stops.*) Pardon me — (*He rises abruptly.*) It was the only thing at Ballinasheeda — I could believe in —

(*He goes off abruptly to his room and closes the door.*)

(CECILY *stands irresolutely silent. Then she sees* WATERSLEY, *who has remained a silent spectator.*)

CECILY: Will you give him a message from me? That I — I — I shall come back again to thank him — I'm — I'm very grateful to all of you — to him — and to Dan Dolan — and to Moore.

WATERSLEY: Yes. But Moore's gone.

CECILY: I don't think he's gone. Goodbye. (*Exit.*)

(WATERSLEY *looks after her for a second or so. Then, with a sudden gesture of dismay, he hurriedly starts to search in his despatch case and extracts some documents. He looks at them, and then goes over and knocks at* O'NEILL'S *door.*)

WATERSLEY: I say! O'Neill! O'Neill! (O'NEILL *comes out.*) She's gone — never mind — said she'd come back again soon. But look here — I'm damned sorry! They told me to be sure to give you this first thing. Urgent and most important. (*He hands the document over.*) And I put it away so carefully that I lost sight of the damned thing!

O'NEILL: (*Looking through the file, then with a start*) Watersley! What do you think this is?

WATERSLEY: Haven't the foggiest!

O'NEILL: And the old man hardly gone! It's an order to inspect at 10 a.m. tomorrow. (*Reading*) 'Owner has been already notified direct to meet you at Fitzgormanstown.'

WATERSLEY: Where's that?

O'NEILL: I forgot. Of course you wouldn't know. They say here they've sent blank sheets and a schedule from the Valuation Commissioner's records. The schedule is here. Where are the sheets?

WATERSLEY: Over there. That bundle Martin brought up.

O'NEILL: Open them out. Quick! (WATERSLEY *unrolls them on the table.*) Wait! Wait a moment! The old man gave me his map! (*He extracts it.*) Take those sheets and Moore's map, and compare them and edge off the boundaries in pencil and tick off the townlands, while I read out the schedule. (WATERSLEY *arranges the maps, and begins to work as directed.*) Ready?

WATERSLEY: Yes.

O'NEILL: *(Reads)* Fitzgormanstown Eighter. One thousand, two hundred and six acres, no roods, ten perches.

WATERSLEY: (*After a pause*) — Ten perches. Right! Got em!

O'NEILL: Fitzgormanstown Oughter. Two thousand, one hundred and fifteen acres, three roods, six perches.

WATERSLEY: (*After a pause*) Right! Got em!

O'NEILL: Cloonascragh. Five hundred and nine acres, two roods and fifteen perches.

WATERSLEY: Cloonascragh — can't see it. Cloonascragh — now where the hell is Cloonascragh? Ah! that's where my Irish comes in. The cows' meadow — meadow land — that should be near a river. Right — the River Shivna runs all round the place — except to the south, and that's all swamp and bog. How on earth will you ever get into this place? Cloonascragh! (*He studies the map carefully.*) Hallo! There's roads here on this old map and not a sign of them on the new sheets! New holdings and fences and plantations, and sites for houses — and more roads — and not a trace of them on the new sheets. And here's a — a — bridge. (*Reading from map*) 'Old holding of Dan Dolan. Road to be reserved for' — marked in big letters — 'Bridge Head.'

O'NEILL: Dolan's land! 'Bridge Head!' 'He gave land years ago as a bridge head for the living. Today he gives land as a bridge head for the dead — 'And she is dead. I buried her in Ballinasheeda years ago.

WATERSLEY: (*Interested and intent on his map.*) Eh? There's no Ballinasheeda here. Ah! Here I've got Cloonascragh! Right! Sorry. Go on, please. My Scott! but there's whales of land here. And new holdings — ten — fifteen — thirty — thirty-five — by Jove! — one-hundred-and-sixty new holdings. Phew! Go on, O'Neill. Next, please — I've got Cloonascragh. Next, please. Go on. Next. (*He suddenly looks up aghast at* O'NEILL *who is gazing at him with a blank stare.*) I say — what's up? What are you staring at me like that for, O'Neill?

O'NEILL: My God! (*With a sudden spasm of relief*) It is you, Watersley!

WATERSLEY: Yes. Why, who else would I be?

O'NEILL: You could be — and you were — and you might yet be what I saw in your chair a second ago.

WATERSLEY: Who?

O'NEILL: Something that was old Stephen Moore.

(CURTAIN)